The Lost Teachings of Jesus 4
will change forever your understanding
of the life and teachings of Jesus.

As never before, this volume lifts the veil on
planetary history and takes you back to the lost
continents of Lemuria and Atlantis—to the heights
of their spiritual and scientific achievements.
And to their fall.

It contains the mysteries Jesus himself kept
hidden which are only now being revealed:

- The signs, challenges, opportunities and
  karma of the end of an age

- Factors of control, including genetic
  engineering, used since Atlantis to keep
  mankind in bondage

- How to invoke spiritual protection

- Implications of genetic engineering
  experiments today

- Aliens on earth

- The identity of the "generation of vipers,"
  "hypocrites," "sons of Satan," and "the
  wicked" of whom Jesus spoke

- Causes of cataclysm

- Sodom and Gomorrah and nuclear holocaust

- Fallen angels, Watchers, their ancient history
  of manipulation—where this power elite is
  today and what they're up to

- The Final Judgment and the second death explained

- The Age of Aquarius

- How to meet the challenges facing our civilization today

- How to perform miracles

- The secrets of the ancient alchemists

- How to invoke the violet flame—the flame of the Holy Spirit—and use it to change your life

- How to use the alchemical fire to transmute negative energy

- The astral causes of disease and death

- Visualizations for world transmutation

- Step-by-step instruction for Seventh-Ray disciples

- Techniques of the sacred fire and the science of mantra

- Specific initiations you can expect to receive on the path of Christhood—and how to prepare for them

And you'll receive instruction on the path of your ascension—from an Ascended Master

Here are the keys to salvation in the Aquarian Age!

Blessed readers, bear with us as we unfold the mysteries of God. Be patient with our effort as together we walk and talk with Jesus and the servant-sons in heaven whose revelations we bear. For as emissaries of their teaching, we must attempt to make plain according to twentieth-century thinking and theological modality a vast gnosis of the Lord that does and does not necessarily fit the mind-sets and mind-traps of the very ones for whom his Lost Teaching is sent. . . .

This book consists of fourteen lectures delivered by Mark between 1965 and 1973, illuminated by the lessons Jesus has given us in dictations, sermons and letters over the past thirty years. The message that unfolds as the rose of Sharon is compiled from these as well as private conversations with the Master. It is the Lord's gift to your soul, that you might keep his flame and not lose the way when the darkness of personal and planetary karma covers the land and all else fails of human institutions and nations and their armies and armaments. . . .

We are the two witnesses standing now, one on either bank of Life's great river. We preach his Everlasting Gospel and the hidden wisdom: for the Lamb is come—and the mystery of God which was not to be finished till the days of the voice of the seventh angel.

The prophecy is fulfilled. That which was spoken to the disciples in the upper room is being shouted from the housetops. At last the path of discipleship to which Jesus called his chosen does appear for all to see and know and enter in these end times of the Piscean age—for the Light of Aquarius dawns.

SHE WHO LEADS

THE LOST TEACHINGS OF JESUS

BOOK FOUR

THE LOST TEACHINGS OF JESUS

Mark L. Prophet · Elizabeth Clare Prophet

BOOK ONE
Missing Texts/Karma and Reincarnation

BOOK TWO
Mysteries of the Higher Self

BOOK THREE
Masters and Disciples on the Path

BOOK FOUR
Good and Evil: Atlantis Revisited

THE LOST TEACHINGS OF JESUS

BOOK FOUR

Good and Evil: Atlantis Revisited

MARK L. PROPHET
ELIZABETH CLARE PROPHET

SUMMIT UNIVERSITY PRESS®

*To our beloved friends
throughout the world
who have endured with us
through our trials and triumphs
in Jesus Christ.
Without you
his Lost Teachings
could not have been preached
and published in every nation.*

THE LOST TEACHINGS OF JESUS
Book Four
Good and Evil: Atlantis Revisited
Mark L. Prophet • Elizabeth Clare Prophet

Library of Congress Catalog Card Number: 81-52784
International Standard Book Number: 0-916766-93-4

For information on the magnificent art of Nicholas Roerich
reproduced in this volume, write Nicholas Roerich Museum,
319 West 107th St., New York, NY 10025.

This book is set in 11 point Electra with 1.5 points lead.
Printed in the United States of America
This is the fourth book in the four-volume pocketbook series
The Lost Teachings of Jesus, which contains the complete text of
the original two-volume trade paperback edition of the same title.
First Printing: 1988

Front cover taken from *Issa and the Skull of the Giant* and back
cover from *Treasure in the Mountain,* paintings by Nicholas Roerich.

SUMMIT UNIVERSITY 🐦 PRESS®

THE LOST TEACHINGS OF JESUS
BOOK FOUR *Contents*

243   CHAPTER FOURTEEN

YOU WILL BECOME ONE WITH GOD!

Illustrations

What you have come to is Mount Zion and the city of the living God, the heavenly Jerusalem where the millions of angels have gathered for the festival with the whole Church in which everyone is a "first-born son" and a citizen of heaven.

You have come to God himself, the supreme Judge, and been placed with the spirits of the saints who have been made perfect, and to Jesus, the mediator who brings a new covenant. . . .

Make sure that you never refuse to listen when he speaks. The people who refused to listen to the warning from a voice on earth could not escape their punishment, and how shall we escape if we turn away from a voice that warns us from heaven?

That time his voice made the earth shake, but now he has given us this promise: I shall make the earth shake once more and not only the earth but heaven as well. . . .

We have been given possession of an unshakable kingdom. Let us therefore hold on to the grace that we have been given and use it to worship God in the way that he finds acceptable, in reverence and fear:

For our God is a consuming fire!

Hebrews

Chapter Twelve

THE RELATIONSHIP OF MAN AND GOD

The Relationship of Man and God

It is our desire to create in you an awareness of both the external world in which we live and the creative intent that framed it—that loves us, that loved us from the beginning, that will always love us—whose substance, spun out from His own heart, created all things we come in contact with, including the substance of our own soul.

This is the relationship of Man and God.

And this we must realize. We must realize the infinitude of God's love, a moving Love that moves vitally throughout all the forces of nature. The diastole and the systole of the heart are the closest physical contact we have with this mighty movement of Love because we can feel, even hear, the rhythmic pulsation of the love of God within ourselves.

And this breathing nearness, even to the sacred fire breath, ought to create the awareness in ourselves that something highly intelligent, highly sensory, reaching out and reaching to enfold each of us, is concerned for our welfare and concerned that we love one another.

The love of God is not a human love. It transcends all human loves, and it brings all love to the fructification of genuine purpose that endures not just for our lifetime but endures with the pyramids and particularly with the Pyramid of Life.

Genes and Genealogies of the Holy Spirit

As we begin, then, to examine the external chain of events that manifests around us, weaving together the invisible fibres of mind/memory/emotion that sustain our spiritual/material integration with the Universal, let us consider for a moment the RNA and the DNA factors that, generation after generation, direct the quality of life within the genes which produce the differentiation of man's physical nature and even retain some remnant of his character drives from previous lives.

Let us look for a moment at the substance that God has placed in the sperm and in the egg, each one contributing 23 chromosomes to the embryo. They say the 46 chromosomes contain all of those 'chips' that program everything from the color of our eyes and the texture of our hair to our stature, our body build, mentality, dexterity, our thought processes and attitudes.

What is not generally known is that, just as a miniature replica of physical man is contained in his genes, so the spiritual blueprint, the formula of his relationship to his God, is stamped electronically on the etheric counterpart of his genetic code. Moreover, in the spiritual nucleus of the atom of self, sealed in innermost being, the Sons of God also retain the spiritual 'genes' of their Christic seed. Thus we approach the white fire core of Man's relationship to God.

As lifetime succeeds lifetime, the spiritual attainment (gifts and graces accrued through integration with the Holy Spirit) of a lifestream, though dormant for a season, cannot be lost—unless he himself abnegate his Sonship by free will. Nor can this sacred-fire momentum of true being be transmitted alone through the physical, human genes.

Albeit born to the mundane, among the worldly but not of them, the Lightbearers whose souls come from far-off worlds suffer no dilution of their divinity in their members, nor is their enthusiasm for the things of the Spirit dampened by the genus Homo sapiens—that thinks it begot the Son of God but did not: for the son of man, the vessel only, is its lot.

By the Universal Mind, *you*, beloved of the Light, are the begotten of the LORD! The coats of skins you wear are just that...Never the spirit was born, the spirit shall cease to be never—however so mortal, so subject to mortality the house of it seems...[1]

In the case of spiritual offspring born to spiritual parents, these may be strengthened in externalizing their heavenly patterns through the "passing on" of spiritual traits and the transfer of sacred fire in the life-force, parent to child, as well as by the magnetism of the auric spheres of the father and mother. These spheres envelop them from conception on as a spiritual swaddling garment nurturing the soul throughout their life span, providing the optimum conditions for the embodiment of the causal body of the inner man. Nevertheless, the attainment, in order to be retained, self-realized, must be solely their own.

We find reference in the writings of Paul to the passing on of spiritually hereditary qualities, whether through the genes and chromosomes or by some other means: "The unfeigned faith that is in thee dwelt first in thy grandmother Lois and thy mother Eunice."[2] Do you understand?

So we begin to realize that there is a passing on, even in a spiritually genealogical way, of spiritual qualities. This is through consciousness and the causal body, the aura and the etheric blueprint; for after all, we are not mere creatures bearing after our kind as beasts of the field.

You can be the instrument of the Holy Spirit in all that you do, and your creations as well as your children can receive through you a measure of heavenly light. So don't sell short your potential as a progenitor of Good. Even as you daily re-create your self after the Perfect Design, you can pass on to yourself and to the offspring of your mind good qualities and bad. And you can stamp out the latter just as easily as that, through the violet transmuting flame!

And this violet flame transmutation of one's genes and chromosomes is the only lawful genetic engineering there is! Because inherent in the violet flame is the God-control of the Holy Spirit. This is the spiritual science of genetic engineering practiced by the Sons of God. And this is where true science and the mysteries of God converge in the golden man of the heart.

Yes, there are spiritual forces alive within the 'quick', or quickened, who, by definition, have the divine spark. These forces cannot be touched by the 'dead' grown cold, by self-definition, to the things of the Spirit, who procreate after the natural man. And wisely so, for today, in our time, we are finding once again as in the age of Atlantis (for life does recycle) that 'accidents' of de-evolution as well as experiments in recombinant DNA are producing human mutations.

Extraterrestrials Violate Man's Creative Freedom

Scientists who lived thousands of years ago on that lost continent of which Plato wrote were far in advance of our present-day geneticists. Many people do not realize this, but it is true. More than twelve thousand years ago mutations were created in the laboratories of Atlantis that developed into grotesque formations—half human, half animal.

From the akashic records we read the history of mankind's self-ruination through their cooperation with the experiments of the Nephilim gods and their birth goddesses.[3] And there was no end to the vile 'things' they created for their pleasure— animated robots, slaves that did their bidding—and then got out of hand.

(The sorcerer's apprentice may yet be loose on

planet earth! Which species do you think is most out of control—most capable of wanton recklessness on a whimsy, or by the law of the jungle? What animal or creeping thing or microbe when let out of the zoo is most inimical to his own species?)

It must not be forgot that, above all, they wanted control—of Camelot and *more*. But neither it nor the Once and Future King nor his chelas would be horsed or unhorsed against their will. It's true! The genetic engineering of the human race and lower creatures became their modus operandi of controlling God and Man and their relationship on earth. But not for long.

"Thus far and no farther!" The resounding fiat of Solar Logoi quivered the cocoon of the matter cosmos.

"And GOD saw that the wickedness of man was great in the earth, and that every imagination of the thoughts of his heart was only evil continually. And the LORD said, I will destroy man whom I have created from the face of the earth; both man and beast and the creeping THING..."[4]

And this is something out of the mists of planetary records, stored also in the collective unconscious of the race of mankind, that you ought to take time to think about.

This is why GOD (through Elohim) *had to* destroy the products of Nephilim experimentation—for they stole the genes of the Man made by the Divine Us to imprison both God and his creation in monstrous creatures which were not only distortions of God's purposes and intent, but also a defilement of the Divine Image itself:

The head and torso of male or female humans on the bodies of horses (these were the same sort of people we find today who did and still do allow themselves to be both horsed and unhorsed!) and all kinds of abominations, such as the mythological satyr—hideous goat men and other strange types too grotesque to even speak or think about. Such as these did the bidding of laggard scientists of the left-handed path (commonly called the seed of Satan) who had migrated in spacecraft from other planets, bringing with them their know-how, their assistants, and their laboratory specimens.

According to the Edgar Cayce readings, these mutants were the result not only of genetic tampering but also of the union of animals (Homo sapiens?) with the "THINGS." The most renowned psychic reader of the century left us the following record on the Atlantean era:

"There was not a laboring for the sustenance of life (as in the present), but rather individuals who were children of the Law of One—and some who were the children of Belial (in the early experience)—were served by automatons, or THINGS, that were retained by individuals or groups to do the labors of a household, or to cultivate the fields or the like, or to perform the activities of artisans."[5]

Interpreting his father's readings on Atlantis, Edgar Evans Cayce says the term "THINGS" refers to "the life form creations of the spiritual beings [we believe, the Nephilim] who had projected themselves into materiality....The earth was proceeding along an evolutionary pattern...which was interrupted by the projection into materiality of these thought forms. It sounds as if they, in many cases, mixed with animals, the results being sometimes quite bizarre."[6]

Based on his Cayce research, Brad Steiger in his book *Atlantis Rising* concludes that some of these creations carried "physical deformities such as feathered appendages, webbed feet, and other animal-like features....As an extra, insidious feature of Atlantean culture, the sons of Belial soon discovered cybernetic control of the human brain. They cracked the DNA code, enabling them to shape heredity. Such control resting in unethical hands could only result in the creation of more 'THINGS.'"[7]

Well, it was precisely this violation of the RNA and DNA chains that interfered with and severely curtailed Man's relationship to God. "How could this be?" you say. You see, through the control of the brain waves and the neurological system with its delicate balance in the interchange of the life-force from Spiritual Man through the chakras to the organs and cells of generic man, the sons of Belial,[8] to use the Cayce term, altered humanity's genetic capacity for psychic (*soul*, or '*solar*') awareness.

They interfered with the web of light (the antahkarana[9]) that interconnects the etheric, astral and physical/mental vessels through which the intimations of the Godhead are received in the spiritually evolved lifestream. By this genetic 'brainwashing' and then the control of the four lower bodies through the mass media and the programming of the young from earliest years, the sons of Belial reinforced the blunting of the thought receptors in generic man and shortcircuited his receptivity to the higher frequencies of Spiritual Man attuned to the Universal Mind.

In other words, the sons of Belial waged war against the seed of the Ancient of Days by engineering a mortal man, subject to their genetic formulas of built-in limitation—and planned obsolescence. They purposed to stunt the soul faculties of the Lightbearers by tampering with the physical instrument, the earth bodies they would wear, the vehicle through which the soul was intended to recall and re-create not only the divine gnosis from the causal body but also the knowledge gathered in other lifetimes and on other systems of worlds.

And this is the story, in part, of the conspiracy by which God 'died' on Atlantis or, shall we say, was effectively eliminated, by premeditated murder, from generic man's conscious soul-awareness.

You see, where the Spirit of the LORD is not free to be, to move, to evolve and to reveal himself in Man, in Woman, as the twin flames he created out of the white fire core of his Being, then we say God is 'dead' because his reason for being has been aborted—in manifestation.

If God is not free *To Be* himself *in us*, if the I AM THAT I AM cannot establish his essential be-ness *through us*, then he is not alive in us. And if we do not give him his essential freedom to be alive in his children on earth by the free will he first gave to us, then it is not possible for us to be alive in him.

This denial of the spiritual freedom of God to be himself, at home within us, is the means whereby some have violated the only real relationship they have, for all other relationships proceed from it. Truly, we have no greater Friend than God (for he contains all others) in the whole of the universe.

Yet this man did.

Or, we should say, the fallen angels did! And the fact is they're still doing it. And mankind are still their victims—still falling for their fallen ways and their synthetic images flashing to their beat on the screen of the mind and the movies.

People don't consciously know this, because they've blocked it out. So when they hear about it, the shock factor makes them deny it by reflex. In their panic to preserve their sense of reason and sanity, they suppress what they know subconsciously but really don't want to know. Even in our day the conspiracy theory of history is ridiculed. They say there's no evidence of a connection between the historical events of evil and war, population management and planetary takeover.

Well, it's an inner tie, you see—and intergalactic. It's the astral connection. These ties are tied by wavelengths of the mass consciousness and the collective unconscious of the false hierarchy who are very well connected indeed. The higher-ups are aware of their connection, if not in their outer minds, then definitely on the inner through their sympathetic vibrations.

Many who are involved with the forces of Anti-Light in the planetary conspiracy of Darkness don't know it on the outer; nevertheless, they respond on command or to preprogramming, and suddenly you find friends or people in high places you believed in coming out on the wrong side of Right—our Divine Right. And you just can't understand why they suddenly switched and voted for the enemy and not to give *meaningful* aid to the freedom fighters holding up the canopy of world freedom with their bare hands—or to *really* save our children or to wipe out drugs, drug-pushers, pornography and other foul things that debase the human spirit.

Don't look now, but Candid Camera's watching you watching factors of control from the invisible conspiracy!

We're telling you about the "Watchers" so you won't be fooled anymore and so you'll call upon the LORD's angel for protection—so you'll befriend that great prince Archangel Michael and ask him to bind the descendants of the fallen angels he long ago cast out of the heaven world[10]—before they completely destroy this earth.

Let those who don't want to know (or don't

want you to know they know) laugh if they will when you tell them about this conspiracy of the fallen angels working through the ICCC—that's the International Capitalist/Communist Conspiracy—which this seed of the wicked have contrived and propped up in their so-called Order and ordering of 'things' in our universe: Because it's an uneasy laugh and it's a cover-up—whether conscious or unconscious.

People of America, mankind of earth: you cannot forever escape your collective unconscious, which retains every detail of this traumatic race memory. The akashic records are there for all to see, and they do not lie. Jesus wants you to know this.

The Ascended Masters have shown us that the Atlantean records of genetic horror and cataclysm which remain in the subconscious of everyone alive today on planet earth as an indelible race memory are the real cause behind modern-day anxiety, insomnia, hysteria, psychosomatic diseases and mental disorders and so many karmic ailments outcropping in the flesh.

Likewise, mankind's vulnerability to religious and political fanaticism—seeking a saviour or a demagogue for deliverance from impending genetic manipulation, the nuclear nightmare, and ensuing cataclysm—derives from their prior subjugation by the "giants in the earth" and the records of the nuclear annihilation of Sodom and Gomorrah[11] and the Sumerian civilization; as well as those of the sinking of both Lemuria and Atlantis.

These records which constantly crop up in psychic readings and predictions are cast upon the screen of the future by those who do not properly pace the "time-frames" in the perspective of the "then" and the "now." While watching the replays of "the thing greatly feared," of ancient, horrific holocaust and violent geologic change with endless scenarios of the unbelievable evil wreaked upon a naïve and trusting child-humanity—that very "thing feared" becomes their own self-fulfilling prophecy of the present.

It is proverbial: history repeats itself because men do not transmute the records of their fears and transcend by Love those fearsome things which otherwise will be forced upon them by the Law of Karmic Resolution and the Law of Compensation, her twin sister. To paraphrase the oft-quoted Santayana, "Those who refuse to remember or to take corrective action concerning the past are condemned to repeat it."

For the Law of Nature and Nature's God demands resolution in all planes of life, and until the Law is satisfied, there will be no escape: the returning planetary karma will come upon the people, and their untransmuted fears will beget—and they are already begetting—a terrified and terrifying inertia. Thus, just beneath the threshold of the conscious mind in the now superficially sophisticated Homo sapiens, we discern the source of the inescapable torment of twentieth-century man.

Driven to surface levels of experience by the

nonresolution of what lies just beneath, they seek escape in noise, an unceasing nervous agitation (addiction) of rock music, the fictions of TV and the fantasies of the sexual squandering of the life-force. And everywhere they are pounded by synthetic sounds satiating and further dulling their senses, already dulled by sugar, alcohol, drugs and chemical/astral alternatives to *the direct apprehension of Reality*, frightening as it may be—and to conscious contact with the living God, demanding as it is bound to be.

It reminds me of that funny song they used to sing in the 1950s called "The Thing." You'd hear them going down the street, "Oh, get outa here with that _ _ _ and don't come back no more!" And they'd stomp their feet. The words were harmless enough but they had sort of an ominous, or maybe I should say uneasy, feeling about them. Now I know why. See what you think:

> While I was walking down the beach
>   one bright and sunny day,
> I saw a great big wooden box
>   afloatin' in the bay.
> I pulled it in and opened it up
>   and much to my surprise,
> Oh, I discovered a _ _ _ (stomp feet three times)
>   right before my eyes.
> Oh, I discovered a _ _ _ (stomp feet three times)
>   right before my eyes.[12]

Personally, I think the suggestion is clear when you understand the subconscious and just what it knows about the THINGS of Atlantis or such stories as the one about the frightful golem (robot) of the sixteenth-century that rebels against its maker and terrorizes the townspeople.[13] The stories of Frankenstein, the Munsters, and endless science fiction on the subject shows the necessity for a periodic discharge of the "THINGS" lurking in the collective unconscious with which present humanity is unable to deal *because of the power factor.*

People have a desperate need (and Hollywood's Atlantean comebacks generously oblige) to experience films on horror and disaster, murder and the macabre in order to neutralize what is underneath. They watch the movies all together in packed theaters as a group catharsis (like in ancient Atlantis when they huddled and cowered before the gods); they scream, cry, eat popcorn, and it's over: "It was only a film, fascinating food for thought, a release of physical/emotional tension. Such things can't be real." So they tell each other. And they exit in a wave—back to surface thinking and feeling, the "surf-er"/reefer/coke generation, comforted in their mutual head-in-the-sand, ostrich reinforcement.

In the song, the singer is walking down the beach—the place where earth meets water, where the rational concrete mind contacts the deep and the monsters of the subconscious and the unknown, unprobed depths of oneself. A "great big wooden box afloatin' in the bay" gets him curious and he decides to find out what's inside (of himself). He pulls it in, opens it up and much to his surprise he discovers "the THING." But he likes it—he's "as happy as a king." The trouble is nobody else does—nobody else wants it. They all tell him, "Get outa here with that _ _ _ and don't come back no more!" Until finally he tries to take it beyond the pearly gates and Saint Peter tells him, "Get outa here with that _ _ _ and take it down below."

The THING symbolized the guy's human creation, nonthreatening to his subjective self but recognized as dangerous by everybody in town, even his wife. This THING had to be boxed because it was overpowering—too overpowering. It was the unknown something to be feared, shunned, damned and definitely avoided at all cost—yet neatly neutralized by a harmless song and the thoughtform of the subconscious, the astral sea, with a floating compartment that sealed away the undesirable desire. An attempt, admittedly meager, to deal with relics of Atlantean geneticists that—bad news to the world—are still around today.

So if you find one of those THINGS, put it in a box and seal it tight. It's the only thing you can do with any THING that's out of hand in this day and age! That's the way people feel. So they box up their fears in subconscious disposable containers and go singin' down the street, their noise box annoying all the way. That's how they get your attention—and your energy.

(Strange isn't it, when you come to think of it, that this Homo sapiens itself was designed to be the disposable container. I believe "expendable" is the term "they" use for "them." Have you ever had the feeling that Big Brother had you numbered and that you were dispensable to his designs?)

No wonder some claim ownership—"That's my THING! Leave it alone. That's *my* human creation!" They want to take it with them all the way to heaven. They never heard the line, "Ya can't take it with ya when ya go!"

You see, people really can't see what's offensive about themselves—offensive to the Light, that is—and they want a human saviour that will take them the way they are—all the way through the seven heavens of the seven chakras. That's what's known as unconditional love. They want the universe to step aside and make way for their human creation—the whole kit and caboodle!

The False Gurus

That's why so many follow the false gurus. They tell them they can do anything they want to and still have God consciousness. Beware of them. They are no part of the Great White Brotherhood and the true Guru/chela relationship sponsored by Jesus Christ, Saint Germain and the Ascended Masters.

Yes, the aliens are in the temples made with hands.[14] Some are the false pastors of Christendom. In them the truth that "Jesus loves you" becomes a palliative and so they suffer their human creation instead of seeking and finding his Love through the fervent heat of alchemical transmutation and the fiery trial. And so people say,

"Jesus loves me just as I am. I don't have to change." But Jesus doesn't teach that. His path is one of change, daily change, all the way Home.

Then you see the false gurus of the Indian Black Brotherhood. They never exact *the* price, nor do they pay *the* price for your salvation—the balancing of your karma and the ennoblement of your soul. I know, they're telling you they're doing both—but remember, God placed his immortal Spirit inside of you: You don't need a fallen angel disguised as Christ or Guru to impart to you what you already have. But if you do choose to fall *for* them and *with* them, oh yes, you will pay false sacrifices in the service of their human personality but they won't teach you the true path of sacrifice, first of the THING, the human creation, and then of the spirit through the Work and the Word of the LORD.

Their false teaching is that you can do it all by raising the Kundalini and chakra meditation. These are techniques which when lawfully practiced under a true Master (even an unascended Master of the Himalayas) can afford balance and mastery; but salvation and the transmutation of karma by the Saviouress—service on behalf of the Mother's children and the violet flame—is another path entirely.

Someone must pay the price. Jesus did. Someone—the true Guru must bear your burden until you are able. The true Guru will teach you how to pay the price—every jot and tittle—and this is the crux of Jesus' Lost Teaching, the missing ingredient without which your alchemical experiment in the laboratory of the soul will not succeed.

There are false Christs in every world religion today as well as in the various sects. You must examine them and base your evaluation not on their outer personality or words and more words, but on this criterion alone: Do they have the capacity to get you where you want to go? Will they lay down their life for you? Are they able to pay the price and do they wear the true mantle of Jesus Christ, Saint Germain and All Saints who comprise the Great White Brotherhood?

The saddest of all indictments of our society is that those who know and know better are still not curtailing the black magic of the fallen angels carried on in the name of science and in the name of religion.

If the sons and daughters of God do nothing to stop them in the remaining hours of the twentieth century but join them instead in their false religions and their pleasure and personality cults, seeking new thrills playing on and in their bodies in a rerun of old and vile experiments, then the cosmic forces of Nature will deliver their judgment as they always have—through wind and wave and "lightnings, and voices, and thunderings, and an earthquake, and great hail"![15]

And humanity will know firsthand and too late the karma of doing nothing (they have a momentum on it, don't they!) about the molestation of Life, precious Life, by the aliens in their midst.

With one voice, on cue, we shall hear the anguished cry of the mankind, Homo sapiens: "The thing which I greatly feared is come upon me."[16] And their betrayers will echo it.

And the aliens whom they have lifted up to be their kings and priests in the earth,[17] officiating between them and the LORD God—what of them?—and the great men and the rich men and the chief captains and the mighty men and every bondman (mechanization man and the false chela who serves and idolizes the false gods) and every free man? Shall they all not hide themselves, according to prophecy, in the dens and in the rocks of the mountains? Shall they all not say to the mountains and rocks:

"Fall on us, and hide us from the face of the Ancient of Days that sitteth on the throne and from the wrath of the Lamb. For the great day of his wrath is come; and who shall be able to stand?"[18]

It happened before and it can happen again: Came the flood of Noah, the Great Deluge that wiped all this from the face of the earth, "for it repenteth me that I have made them..."[19] And the cataclysm that ensued sank the entire continent of Atlantis—supposedly.

And the fiat went forth from GOD (through Elohim) which trembled the web of light that passes throughout the universal substance: "Henceforth, let every seed bear after its kind." And, as in all cases of divine fiats uttered from the heart of the Solar Logoi, the seed, the DNA chain, obeyed; and human beings remained fixed to human beings, not to animals.

Had Man not compromised his Light through his interchanges with fallen angels and their laggard scientists, who were tampering with the creation of GOD out of sheer fascination for the robots and THINGS of Atlantis, and through his unrestrained curiosity to cohabitate with them ("Let's see what it's like, let's do it, let's find out for ourselves!")— had the Man whom Elohim made remained his loving, obedient servant-Son, all blessings lawful unto his spiritual/intellectual/emotional growth and human/divine happiness would have been added unto him in due course.

But he did not. He would not. And for the moment, the fallen angels had their way—lusting as they did after the creative powers (the Christic Light) of the Sons of God, taking them by force, torture, and even in bloodletting rites performed in the "synagogues of Satan"[20] upon the bodies of the holy innocents—and upon their prisoners of war on the battlefields of earth.

Ultimately the betrayers among God's children who joined the god-scientists and false priests would pay dearly in the stultification of the spiritual/physical development of their own genetic lifestream. To the present, the lost spiritual faculty (gene) has not been fully restored, nor the negative genes removed. This is the real reason why Jesus said, "Ye are not all clean."[21] For the very reasonable karmic reason that the children of Israel have not fully forsaken their secret desire to be wed to the machine![22]

And he prophesied also of the religions who fail to set before their flocks the goal of the alchemical marriage to the Universal Christ. Who needs a computerized mate, for the love of Christ, when you can access the Mind of God and be fused to it!

While child-Man gropes with alternating allegiance to reestablish his personal relationship with God, the Nephilim—who have become more defiant *because* of the LORD's judgments, never humbled but only more cunning—continue their genetic experiments unchecked, to create superhumans, supermice[23] and a superrace of gods among us: Deus ex machina!

All of this which we have only touched upon is so far forgotten, so deeply buried that many today who actually have a threefold flame—who, throughout this planetary dark night of the soul, have retained the divine spark—do not believe (having enjoined themselves to the lie of the laggard races) that they can enjoy a personal relationship with God, with Jesus, on their own.

They have fallen for the multiple deceptions of the sons of Belial who have inserted themselves between Man and God, mediating where only Christ can mediate, sitting in the seat of Guru that belongs to him alone.

It is for this lie of the interlopers, and their perpetuation of the lie in their false "theology" in Church and State, that some do not believe that

God exists at all. Furthermore, they have believed the lie that they must go through someone else with superhuman psychic powers to get to "reality." Having no self-identification in Christ and no apprehension of what is Real, they go after the sky-gods who summarily seduce them in all their chakras!

Having taken up their karmic evolution side by side with earthlings—through intermarriage and other importunate alliances, all the better to disguise themselves from *you*—the sky-gods maintain that certain disdainful presence which evokes worshipful admiration even while it projects revulsion, alienation and dire fear.

Such as these comprise the false hierarchies of embodied fallen angels who operate in the religious and pseudo-psychic, cultish fields, who are also seen prominently displayed as trendsetters in the media and on the political scene, blunting movements of the people and spiritual revolutionaries or any poor Joe that should ever raise a cry or a hand to demand an audit of their status quo of power—never to rise again.

Watch out for them. They're in the banking houses and networks of international crime and drug trafficking, in the media and among the feigners of piety—and wherever there is the smell of money or human blood.

And they've done a switcheroo: They sponsor mass movements that seem to successfully challenge their forces of control, when they themselves in fact are in control and always benefit from any social upheaval, war, economic crisis, or sudden shift in the market. Just when you think you're on the Right side, you're on their side.

No strangers to the lists of government are these: from sophist to socialist, pagan to communist to conservative right, these gods over men have created their metaphysical speculations by specious reasoning—"isms" which have no practical bearing whatsoever on feeding the hungry, healing the sick, raising the dead, cleansing the genetic lepers and casting out devils from the economies of the nations, from the body politic and its collective world conscience. Their angle in money manipulation on an international scale is to amass wealth, huge wealth, for power—for control, of the people.

And none of it—no matter what the window dressing—has any bearing whatever upon the realities of the ongoing War between those forces of Light and Darkness which have chosen sides: whether the cosmic solution of the Divine Mother or the anti-solution of the UFOs—the spiritual-suicide solution of the fallen angels beckoning mankind to "heaven" from their everywhere flashy, metallic, mechanization-concept spacecraft.

In contrast to this Babylonian nightmare hovering like the moon and the moon people and the people of the shem[24] and the plutocrats and plutonians, the unassuming children of the Light understand that Christ is come to restore by the Holy Ghost that which was lost through genetic engineering and other genesis entanglements with the seed of the Wicked One.

They know and know well (for they are partakers in his Communion) that only through the heavenly hierarchy of the Universal Christ can the relationship of Man and God be guaranteed. And they know him to be the One who was and is the Mind of God present in Christ Jesus and all Ascended Masters—and in the Higher Consciousness of every issue of the seed of God yet unascended.

It is easy to see that many of the original plans of God have been distorted and that life is not as it should be on planet earth today. The powers that be—that were and still are among the alien gods—literally monkeyed with RNA and DNA, and they produced whatever genetic results they wanted to without having the genetic knowledge or the integrity of the Holy Spirit that a scientist of this capacity ought to have had. Yet they had the power. How they got it is another story, not for this volume.

Did you ever wonder how it is that, although everything upon earth was destroyed during the Flood, the evils of Atlantis are still with us? I used to, but I don't anymore.

The answer is quite simple when you know it. You see, the gods who commanded the skies and ruled the mankind of earth in those days were not about to be overturned by the Deluge. Experienced karma-dodgers were they, accustomed to using the technology and the resources of the Divine Mother stolen from the Sons of Sanat Kumara to escape their fate. And that is exactly what they did in the midst of this planetary judgment unleashed through planetary forces by Solar Logoi.

And so the answer is twofold: (1) the gods took off in their spacecraft, circled the earth till the devastation was spent, landed when land appeared, and took up once again their scheming and subjugation of the survivors;[25] and (2) the rest of the Atlantean evolutions who fell into their camp reincarnated (their power severely curtailed by the Lords of Karma in the cutting or cutting back of the crystal cord); moreover, the laggard evolutions who had spawned a race of soulless flesh-and-blood robots carried with them—in the astral code of their genes, of course—their proclivity to do evil. Yet, the power of their overlords was also reduced— a fact which, to the present hour, they have gone to great lengths to conceal.

They can be had. They can be turned back. The hour of their Final Judgment is come. Archangel Michael and his hosts are here to do the job. Your call compels their answer.

"Fear not, little flock, it is the Father's good pleasure to give you the kingdom."[26] Take Jesus' hand. This is his message of the Everlasting Gospel. Sons and daughters of God, take your stand; you are the LORD's instruments. To him be the Victory.

The Corrupt and Powerful Brought to Judgment

"Power tends to corrupt and absolute power corrupts absolutely" was an utterance made quite a few years ago, and the truth of it is before us still. And spiritual power can come under this heading as well as economic power, social power, and even psychological power.

We certainly should not consider the creation of so-called manikins that walk and talk and the interference with humanity's genes to be apart from such abuses of power and say, "Well, we're not concerned," because here we are talking about the power to create a kind of life in a test tube and to alter this synthetic life in a test tube.

The pages of *Time* magazine and others have portrayed the intentions of our modern-day geneticists who are of the opinion that individualized freedom, genetic freedom, is bad for people. The question is, bad for what kind of people? Theirs or ours?

Are the Nephilim gods, who have used humanity for aeons, attempting to establish ground rules for their created race come again or for the children of Light? This much we know—they are yet determined to bottle and combine the genes of God's children (in their recombinant DNA experiments) with the synthetic genes of their synthesized half-animal, half-machine, half-human, half-god creations.

One article reported that genetic researchers have devised tests to detect hereditary diseases in pregnant mothers. If the tests show that the unborn child is seriously affected, the mothers-to-be are advised to have "therapeutic abortions." One family with a history of a certain hereditary nerve disease, for which such a test has not yet been developed, is being urged by doctors not to have any children.[27]

And then you have people like Dr. H. Bentley Glass, an eminent geneticist, who was quoted in a popular science digest as predicting that leaders in the future will decree that parents "have no right to burden society with a malformed or a mentally incompetent child."

The article went on to describe Glass's view that "the future will be a far more regulated society" and that "screening of adult carriers of defective genes will make it possible to warn them against or prohibit them from having offspring." Glass believes this "will be inevitably forced upon us by our exponential rates of increase." "The once sacred rights of man must change in many ways," he decreed.[28]

As the English would say, "Balderdash!" It is ridiculous to even make such a statement. Yet the ridiculous are holding the bag—of your inheritance and mine. Our genes are in their court. They hold them by the power of our life-force which they have corrupted. We've got to get them back. That's all there is to it! And Archangel Michael can do it. And he *will* do it in answer to our call.

Let the sons of Belial who cannot hide behind their serpent skins be challenged by the Sons of

God in embodiment! These are the disciples of the Universal Christ who are "occupying"—as he said, "Occupy till I come"[29]—planet earth until his Second Coming and until the fallen angels, themselves genetic tares sown among the wheat, are bound by the hosts of the LORD.

Before leaving you somewhat discomfited by my subject, let me give you another angle on it— one which, though starkly, even frighteningly real, is both comforting and hopeful in the end.

In 1965 the Master R—founder of the original Hungarian House of Rakoczy, adept of Atlantis whose retreat, the Cave of Light, is in India, Teacher of the illustrious, including El Morya and le Comte de Saint Germain with whom he worked behind the scenes in eighteenth- and nineteenth-century Europe—contacted me to set forth his treatise on "The Mechanization Concept."

His twenty-four-chapter discourse, dictated to me weekly for twenty-four weeks, includes a section germane to our discussion. I shall read to you, then, from the archives of the one known as the Great Divine Director. (His name is actually the title of his office in hierarchy by which he is respectfully addressed by his students who matriculate in the universities of the Spirit under that office.) Following are his words:

"Lord Bulwer-Lytton in his writing called *The Coming Race* revealed certain facts concerning the creation of mechanical man—i.e., the creation of automatons.[30] Those who wish to read the story which he told concerning the descent of a young man into the earth and his finding of a strange city and its exalted inhabitants may do so if they are so inclined. . . .

"Now, the dear Christian Scientists maintain that there is no reality in evil or death, yet in their grand newspaper called the *Christian Science Monitor* they do bring before the public many of the untoward conditions which are occurring upon the planet today. I cite this in passing to show that even that which is known to be unreal to the Godhead has its effect upon the world scene and the consciousness of man even though, admittedly, it be a temporary effect.

"And so you may consider that these old histories of past civilizations where the powers of both Good and Evil entered in are relatively unimportant to you today, but this is hardly true even as such conditions existing today are not unimportant. For it is well that mankind understand the origin of Evil, seen as they understand the origin of Good, in order that they may effectively eliminate the cause and core of 'that which seemeth to be but is not.'

"Long ago, from a certain system of worlds there came bands who descended to earth, the hordes of shadow who were invited here by mankind (for mankind thought by the power of good example to elevate the consciousness of the laggard bands).

"Now it is not so well known that these laggards were accompanied by some who were not invited.

Some of these brought knowledge to mankind and to the earth, and some of this knowledge was degenerative and destructive. In addition, they also brought with them strange creatures of their own creation—seemingly intelligent beings not created by God, however, but by advanced scientists on other systems of worlds.

"The extent of the evil of these hordes and that of their mechanical creations has been very great, and the oppression they have wreaked upon mankind has been terrible to behold. The infiltration of the planet by these creatures is indeed a manifestation of human creation, not of the divine creation. God did not create Evil, neither did he create destruction nor hatred nor egoism nor any form of vanity whatsoever....

"...I do not bring forth this information in order to frighten any, but to warn mankind that there are beings among them who are not the creation of God, who are not possessed with the same beautiful electronic pattern and causal body with which a manifestation of God is endowed.

"I propose no so-called witch hunt. I propose that no one search out specifically these beings for identification....I urge that the result of this release of knowledge shall be that you will turn more and more to God for your supply of every good thing, that you will determine more than ever to be alert to assist the mankind of earth in overthrowing absolutely all that is darkness and shadow and pain upon the earth planet. In order to do this and to break the monstrous plots which the sinister strategies have launched upon mankind, harmony and unity must remain the forte of all who love the Light....

"The existence upon the earth planet of what we may term 'simulated man' is a fact carefully hidden from the masses of mankind. Although it is the knowledge of the few, it may become and perhaps should become the knowledge of the many. Yet great care must be used in the dissemination of this knowledge, for it is never the desire of the ascended hosts to do anything except that which would result in the greatest blessing and the release of mankind from every binding condition....

"Therefore, great care must be exercised by mankind today in ferreting out upon the planet those individuals who belong in the classification of 'the wicked' lest the innocent lambs suffer for their deeds. It is our hope that the heinous crimes perpetrated against all humanity by those so classified can, in the name of cosmic justice, be corrected without the undue suffering of mankind en masse.

"Through the power of infinite freedom and relieving the consciousness of the gross mechanical sense, we believe that the purposes of God can be fulfilled by divine edict—without the interference of human fanaticism and untempered zeal. It is our hope to squeeze out blind injustice and negation by saturating the planet with those necessary reforms which, by divine love, will remove the bane of that oppression which the wicked rulers have for generations instituted upon the earth.

"At this point a better definition is in order. You will recall that Jesus, in his parable of the wheat and tares, announced that an enemy had sown tares among the wheat.[31] These tares are the counterfeit man. Jesus said they were the children of the Wicked One which exist apart from the original creation of God. And yet, inasmuch as nothing cannot create something, that which was created must have been created by some one who at some time some where drew forth the necessary information to so create.

"In many cases in the New Testament it is recorded in the life of Jesus that he referred to certain individuals as a 'generation of vipers,'[32] as 'hypocrites,'[33] and as 'sons of Satan,' addressing them in these words: 'Ye are of your father the devil, and the lusts of your father ye will do. He was a murderer from the beginning, and abode not in the truth, because there is no truth in him. When he speaketh a lie, he speaketh of his own: for he is a liar, and the father of it.'[34] This reference obviously does make a distinction between all men and some men.

"Let me hasten to assure you, then, that there do exist upon the planet creatures who did not come forth from God—who are the counterfeit of the real manifestation. Many of these are consciously in league with the insipid and insidious purposes of the powers of darkness. They seek through conspiracy and plot to ravish the world of its good, to set brother against brother, to confuse, disturb, and destroy harmonies wherever they exist.

"These function on the physical plane, utilizing and directing their energies in a concerted effort against the Light. They are, however, the pawns of 'spiritual wickedness in high places.'[35] And the league of the spiritually negative forces with these embodied wicked individuals has resulted in the slaughter of many noble souls down through the ages.

"I am not so interested in identifying and describing these individuals as I am in calling to your attention that they do exist. John the Baptist, as he preached the coming of Christ, foretold the end of this race of mechanical men when he said, 'O generation of vipers, who hath warned you to flee from the wrath to come?' Again referring to the barrenness of this counterfeit creation he said, 'Every tree therefore which bringeth not forth good fruit is hewn down, and cast into the fire.'

"He prophesied the coming of one who would baptize with the Holy Ghost and with fire (with the sacred fire and the purifying power of the violet transmuting flame): 'Whose fan is in his hand, and he will throughly purge his floor, and will gather the wheat into his garner; but the chaff he will burn with fire unquenchable.'[36]

"Needless to say, these human automatons are the chaff and their final end can come through only one process: transmutation. For this is the only approved method whereby the wicked shall be removed from the face of the earth.

"In the Bible these soulless beings are referred to throughout as 'the wicked,' for they have seen to it that all more specific descriptions of their race have been removed—lest mankind discover them and rise in righteous indignation against their overlords. And thus the death of John the Baptist and that of Jesus the Christ were brought about by the counterfeit race who for thousands of years have set brother against brother, race against race, and have caused the children of God to blame one another for the murders of the saints.

"Today, as always, they occupy positions of authority and financial power. They have gained control of the destiny of empires, and they seek ever to thwart the pure purposes of God. The injudicious use of taxation exerted by their direction has placed an unconscionable yoke upon the neck of humanity.

"Their control of entertainment media and the trends of youth toward dissonant art forms and discordant music has perverted noble attitudes and spawned a race of delinquent rebels whose code, or lack of it, has gnawed at the vital future of America and the people of many nations.

"Modern means of communication and distribution of the printed word, the spoken word, and the dramatic word through television and motion pictures have caused ideas to span continents and the world almost with the speed of light. Like a prairie fire, the dry grass consumes itself to the roots of the hopes of mankind which are blighted, then, by the searing infamy of wasted energy and emotion.

"It is my opinion that through correct action

negation can be overruled. I believe that through the power of prayer as evoked through beloved Jesus' 'Watch With Me One Hour' service,[37] through the conscious use of decrees, and through the increased distribution of Ascended Master material and true cultural knowledge, the yearnings of mankind for the golden age will be so strengthened that those who have wrong and selfish thoughts will be exposed as Darkness against Light reveals its true nature.

"The mechanical man is the wolf in sheep's clothing[38] who may defy detection for awhile, but we know how to expose all those who deliberately or in ignorance perpetrate any form of sinister strategy against mankind....

"There is a very old and wicked spirit which has consistently sent forth the ignorant to completely distort the truth. And the lies of mankind uttered in self-conceit, self-defeat, and delusion are sometimes so great that they sway the faith of those who should immediately recognize the foolishness of human nonsense in its crudest manifestations.

"Blessed ones, when will mankind awaken to the fact that the Spirit of God is peaceable, gentle, easy to be intreated, and victorious?[39] When will they recognize that those who produce the biting, stinging statements against their fellowmen are but patterning after their father who was known of old as the accuser of the brethren.[40] Now let us for all time put an end to attitudes of negation. Let students of the Light cease to be the pawns of negative ideas....

"Arise, then, to meditate Truth for yourselves, O mankind! For Truth is above and beyond the bane of mechanicality and carnality. Truth and freedom are synonymous. For Jesus has said, 'The Truth shall make you free.'[41]

"Your freedom lies in putting negation forever behind you. To look back upon the burning Sodom is unnecessary. The mount of attainment is ahead. A gentle spirit is not of necessity docile when great causes are at stake.

"I AM determined that the fire of heaven shall flood forth through the student body of this activity to assist them to throw off the weight of human effluvia—to become, if necessary, more like Master Morya rather than less.

"Beloved Jesus expressed many of these aspects, for the description given in the New Testament clearly describes him as one who spake, not as the scribes, but as one having authority.[42] You must first take authority over yourself, then you must take authority over the thoughts that come to you that are not right because you know within yourself that they are not right.

"Then you must take authority over those individuals who come to you either with a spirit of inharmony or with a vocalization of negation. Then you must take authority over the world itself and the mass effluvia of human thought. And it is God in you who will give you your victory. . . .

"A better world will be built. The builders of that world must one day begin. 'Behold, now is the accepted time; behold, now is the day of salvation."[43] The great bonds of cosmic charity which are expressed by the cosmic masters and the entire Great White Brotherhood cannot be refuted by the action of a few individuals or even the many, but the effectivity of right action is in the acceptance of the preceding right thought so that when action goes forth it is guided by holy wisdom....

"We have directed you in love, in honor, and in purity of motive in order to secure for you that eternal grace which is your birthright. Be satisfied with nothing less. Be satisfied with the excellence that we give you, which is as much your own as it is ours. Be unafraid to challenge those who bring strange tidings. But remember the balance of the law, for oftentimes truth is stranger than fiction.

"In this release I have tried to compound many subjects: a mountain of truth, a solid bedrock of faith beneath the mountain, a sense of courage for the climb, a dash of mighty wisdom for the battle of life, and the love that translates into power when it is needed. You are our children, Christ-illumined and oriented. To you is given the admonishment and understanding of the phrase *To Know, To Dare, To Do, and To Be Silent.*

"The battle lines are being drawn for the invisible victory. The peril of the world is not all gone, but continues to hover like the sword of Damocles over civilization. The need for protection and advancement continues to be very great, but we have not forsaken our chelas nor will we leave you comfortless.[44]

"The end of division and separation, the end of destructivity, of inhumanity among men is at hand, even at the door. As the sullied garments are laid aside and the clean white linen of Christhood are lovingly enfolded around the children of the Light, the Sun of Eternal Righteousness shall show forth a coming race without spot and without blemish. God wills it so!"[45]

Thus spake the Great Divine Director.

The remainder of his twenty-four-week series is published under his title: "The Mechanization Concept: Mysteries of God on the Creation of Mechanized Man." It is one of the most important pieces of writing you'll read in this lifetime—from my estimation.

And so, in the name of the Great Divine Director, we say:

People of earth, descendants of the Central Sun, this is your hour of decision: To ratify or not to ratify on earth the original judgment of the All-Father to cast out from the heaven world the rebels against the Creator, the usurpers of his office. Upon your decision rests the genetic fate of all future generations of this planet as well as untold others.

Let the children of the Law of the One espouse the Ancient of Days' code of cosmic compassion and reverence for Life, even while they neglect not their merciful offering to the Father in the daily recitation of the Judgment Call—"They Shall Not Pass!"—which we herewith set forth.

This powerful call was dictated to us by Jesus Christ from the LORD's judgment seat—for the sparing of the little children of Jesus' heart from their frightful fate at the hand of the descendants of the Wicked One. For much is at stake, as Mother Mary told the Catholic world in her Fátima message, even the very spiritual survival of these precious ones.

Wherever you are, worlds without end, O my beloved disciples of the Universal Christ in the Universal Age, won't you stand in honor of all who have ever lost their lives in the contrived wars and concentration camps of the rivalrous Nephilim gods and demand the judgment by the LORD God Almighty of the interplanetary conspiracy of the fallen angels and their mechanization man. From the plane of Light we offer it with you now.

The Judgment Call
"They Shall Not Pass!"
by Jesus Christ

In the Name of the I AM THAT I AM,
I invoke the Electronic Presence of Jesus Christ:
They shall not pass!
They shall not pass!
They shall not pass!
By the authority of the cosmic cross of white fire
it shall be:
That all that is directed against the Christ
within me, within the holy innocents—
within every son and daughter of God—

by the Nephilim gods, their genetic engineering, population control, and contrived wars,
slaughtering the Sons of God and children of
the Light on the battlefields of life—*

Is now turned back
by the authority of Alpha and Omega,
by the authority of my Lord and Saviour
Jesus Christ,
by the authority of Saint Germain!

I AM THAT I AM within the center of this temple
and I declare in the fullness of
the entire Spirit of the Great White Brotherhood:

That those who, then, practice the black arts
against the children of the Light—
namely, the entire interplanetary conspiracy of
the fallen angels and their mechanization
man—*

Are now bound by the hosts of the LORD,

Do now receive the judgment of the Lord Christ
within me, within Jesus,
and within every Ascended Master,

Do now receive, then, the full return—
multiplied by the energy of the Cosmic Christ—
of their nefarious deeds which they have practiced
since the very incarnation of the Word!

Lo, I AM a Son of God!
Lo, I AM a Flame of God!
Lo, I stand upon the Rock of the living Word
And I declare with Jesus, the living Son of God:

*Here insert your specific call for the hosts of the LORD to take command of
conditions of personal and planetary injustice which you name.

They shall not pass!
They shall not pass!
They shall not pass!
ELOHIM ELOHIM ELOHIM[46]

Beloved of the Light: Work while you have this Light, this Life, and this Opportunity to use the spoken Word for world goodwill. For they are Christ's own gifts and graces to you in this hour of planet earth's maximum peril.

Summon, then, the courage, take heart! Give this Judgment Call with your own inserts appropriately composed on behalf of the children of God whenever and wherever you become aware of personal or planetary situations of injustice, especially those pointed out in our preceding discussions of the strategies of the dark ones.

Jesus' warning was never more acute, never more accurate: "Fear not them which kill the body but are not able to kill the soul: but rather fear him which is able to destroy both soul and body in hell."[47]

This "fear" must be translated, as the Great Divine Director admonishes us, into the action of dynamic decrees for the Coming Revolution in Higher Consciousness—reversing the tide of the fallen angels' power (the so-called Gentile world power) and transmuting, by the just judgments and sacred-fire alchemy of the Holy Spirit, all opposition to world freedom under the God-government of the true inheritors of the seed of Christ through the Ancient of Days.

Christ forewarns the wise of the factors of failure on the part of the people of Good that spell imminent danger and even doom if we do not tangle with them *now:*

1. *Failure* to control the reincarnated Atlantean laggard scientists, not only the geneticists but also the zombies in their war games, pitting against the children of Light their computerized robots—now proliferated into a class of mindless, godless, heartless subhumans who kill on command with diabolical delight and not even a supercilious sense of their own passage, in repetitive deaths, to the mists of astral hell holes where they are spawned and respawned—supplying endless bodies for devils to do their dirty work century upon century

2. *Failure* to deal with the destroyers of the earth in every class and rank, whose earmark, like the mark of Cain,[48] is always the denial of God Truth as the animating spirit of the seed of the Universal Christ—and the denial of that God Truth as the solution/resolution in every heavenly and human equation

3. *Failure* to confirm the LORD's judgment of the dead who clutter the earth with their cults of Death, who serve the gods of Sin, championing causes which abort the cycles of Life of the sons and daughters of God from womb to tomb[49]

4. *Failure* to overcome personal and planetary fear by the perfect Love of the Holy Ghost, who has delivered into our hands the full power of the Word in the dynamic decree to the violet fire and the mandate to use it.

All this is in our power to do. The Goddess of Liberty, "our noble Lady with the Lamp," passes to every American and citizen of the world the torch of true Freedom founded upon true Wisdom of the spirit. Let us seize it and run with it ere this generation and the dreams of a planet be dashed once more upon the rocks, or rockets, of the toilers' pride.

By the sign of the seventh angel[50] we conquer. By Saint Germain and the violet flame, our sole weapon and battle cry, let us call to Archangel Michael and the hosts of Light to rid the earth of the curse of every creeping, crawling antichrist.

Individual Freedom Is the Key to Godhood

For all of this, and still weightier matters, even God, the Great Creator of Life, has always been concerned first, last and always that we the children of the Light, we the Sons of God should have our individualized freedom—even to our individualized hurt.

Why? Because individual freedom is the key! It's the key we can turn to become responsible creators in our own domain, friends of God like Abraham,[51] yet subject to the bounds and laws of our habitation—definitely survivors in the Aquarian age! By attaining to the knowledge of those spiritual powers with which he is divinely vested, the heir of the promises may chart the course of his own individual life without doctrinal interference from others.

Freedom, true freedom, is the power to create and to re-create oneself after the Divine Image. This teaching on spiritual alchemy and the laws of transmutation governing change in both the physical and spiritual universes[52] is the forte of the Ascended Master Saint Germain, who champions individual freedom because he knows that individual freedom is the key to Godhood. And he knows it is the key to the God-government of the nations vested in the Sons of God—wrested by the fallen angels, soon to be superseded by the coming I AM Race of Christed ones.

Creativity vested in the Godhead is also partially vested in Man's head. That means you. Each and every one of us—whether or not we know what we ought to know—is still given the prerogative of making his own decisions and taking control of the creative energy allotted to him from the Divine Presence. It is entirely up to us, then, to determine what use we will make of that energy.

What, then, are some of the factors of control, human and divine, apparent in the relationship between Man and God?

I find a passage from Saint Paul on the internal strife of our two natures that goes like this:

> For that which I do I allow not: for what I would, that do I not; but what I hate, that do I.
>
> If then I do that which I would not, I consent unto the law that it is good.

Now then it is no more I that do it, but sin that dwelleth in me.

For I know that in me (that is, in my flesh) dwelleth no good thing: for to will is present with me; but how to perform that which is good I find not.

For the good that I would I do not: but the evil which I would not, that I do.

Now if I do that I would not, it is no more I that do it, but sin that dwelleth in me.

I find then a law, that, when I would do good, evil is present with me.

For I delight in the law of God after the inward man:

But I see another law in my members, warring against the law of my mind, and bringing me into captivity to the law of sin which is in my members.

O wretched man that I am! who shall deliver me from the body of this death?

I thank God through Jesus Christ our Lord. So then with the mind I myself serve the law of God; but with the flesh the law of sin.[53]

Saint Paul plainly spoke of a force within ourselves quite foreign and altogether inimical to the divine intent. He spoke of malevolent influences almost beyond our control that have the power to alter our will to the detriment of the inner design. Yet once upon a time we let them in.

Through his relationship with the God flame in Jesus, Paul became aware of latent thoughtforms and negatively charged forcefields, of astral infections picked up from the lowest levels of the natural man spreading through the subconscious of the race.

He understood the mechanism whereby we automatically outpicture in our lifestreams that which is from beneath, producing those unwanted patterns that are to be found in the garbage dump of world thought and feeling, now existing within ourselves side by side with spiritual alchemical formulas, the untapped treasure—as if we had two planes of manifestation. (And we do—and more than two.)

Such is the danger of free will in the unbridled unconscious of the individual who has not submitted the totality of himself to the will of Christ and the God-control of his Christ Self—sealing heart, head, and hand with the Lord's fiat that seals the place where evil dwells, the place of the uncontrolled passions, the solar plexus.

This chakra at the navel is either the gate of peace or the gate to the astral underworld (of the electronic 'asteroid' belt of every man's untransmuted lower nature). It is the opening, if man allows it, to the demons that rupture through the four lower bodies in riptides and tirades of emotional behavior. Or it is the Open Door for you to release Christ Peace to all life which no man can shut[54]—except thyself.

The Lord's fiat for this "place of the sun" which the solar plexus is intended to be—the Open Door to the Sun of Righteousness who comes with healing in his wings[55]—which we would give to thee is HOLINESS TO THE LORD.

This is the fiat which the LORD instructed to be engraved in gold upon the mitre placed upon Aaron's forehead for the sanctification of the offerings of the people and to commemorate the special relationship between God and the seed of Light (Israel).[56] HOLINESS TO THE LORD. Thus it is written and thus it is worn by the High Priest, your Holy Christ Self, as he officiates at the high altar of the Holy of Holies in your inmost being.

But in the return of the LORD in glory, in the coming era signified by the descent of this beloved Holy Christ Self into each man's temple (the reign of the Universal Christ in all hearts), Zechariah prophesies that HOLINESS UNTO THE LORD shall be written on the bridles of the horses—"Yea every pot in Jerusalem and in Judah shall be holiness unto the LORD of hosts."[57]

This LORD of hosts is none other than the Great Guru of the seed of Abraham, YAHWEH (the Yod He Vau He), the I AM THAT I AM whom we know in his personification as the Ancient of Days, the LORD Sanat Kumara.

He is the most ancient of Avatars, revered in Hindu tradition as Kārttikeya—leader of all the hosts of heaven. He is celebrated throughout the solar systems and far beyond as the One who has stood with the planetary evolutions in the face of the Great Rebellion of the fallen angels, standing between the children of Light and their intergalactic adversaries. Throughout all ages of our remembering before and beyond, the LORD Sanat Kumara is the 'Guru-guarantor' of Man's relationship to God.

Sanat Kumara is the sponsoring hierarch of all avatars who have ever come to earth on a rescue mission to rescue the children of Light. And he will sponsor every Light-hearted one who is determined on the path of Love.

It is Sanat Kumara (whose name and office have been feared and misinterpreted by religionists without true knowledge) who has taught us with the Masters Jesus and Kuthumi, the Buddhas Gautama and Maitreya that in this hour of personal and planetary Armageddon each child-Man of God through his inner High Priest (Peter's "hidden man of the heart"[58]) may take the *Holiness Mantra* to sanctify his life and consciousness, his children, his habitation and his possessions—and his very soul.

This teaching is a corollary to the New Covenant which Jesus interpreted to us as we have set it forth in Chapter 9.

Thus, when confronted with the leftover unholiness within the "members" of our four lower bodies, as noted by Paul, the law of Moses and Christ requires that we give the fiat:

HOLINESS TO THE LORD
In the name I AM THAT I AM!

Rejoice, O Israel, in the pure power of God released through your spoken Word! For your most reverent recitation of this divine decree will truly work wonders of God-control and soul-liberation in your life—yes, real God-control over that human that has controlled you too long—whenever you let our God who is the all-consuming sacred fire speak through you, indeed, our God who is always the Giver and the Receiver of the Word.

Nor did Paul leave us or himself in the pitiful plight of sinful man. His resolution of our duality, inherent in our sensuality, found in the eighth chapter of his epistle to the Romans is the alchemy of Comfort to the Son of God who is fully the heir of the Universal Christ. It is the foundation of the Everlasting Gospel, the scientific statement of what Man's true relationship to God can be here and now—on earth as in heaven:

> There is therefore now no condemnation to them which are in Christ Jesus, who walk not after the flesh, but after the Spirit.
>
> For the law of the Spirit of life in Christ Jesus hath made me free from the law of sin and death.
>
> For what the law could not do, in that it was weak through the flesh, God sending his own Son in the likeness of sinful flesh, and for sin, condemned sin in the flesh:
>
> That the righteousness of the law might be fulfilled in us, who walk not after the flesh, but after the Spirit.

For they that are after the flesh do mind the things of the flesh; but they that are after the Spirit the things of the Spirit.

For to be carnally minded is death; but to be spiritually minded is life and peace.

Because the carnal mind is enmity against God: for it is not subject to the law of God, neither indeed can be.

So then they that are in the flesh cannot please God.

But ye are not in the flesh, but in the Spirit, if so be that the Spirit of God dwell in you. Now if any man have not the Spirit of Christ, he is none of his.

And if Christ be in you, the body is dead because of sin; but the Spirit is life because of righteousness.

But if the Spirit of him that raised up Jesus from the dead dwell in you, he that raised up Christ from the dead shall also quicken your mortal bodies by his Spirit that dwelleth in you.

Therefore, brethren, we are debtors, not to the flesh, to live after the flesh.

For if ye live after the flesh, ye shall die: but if ye through the Spirit do mortify the deeds of the body, ye shall live.

For as many as are led by the Spirit of God, they are the sons of God.

For ye have not received the spirit of bondage again to fear; but ye have received the Spirit of adoption, whereby we cry, Abba, Father.

The Spirit itself beareth witness with our spirit, that we are the children of God:

And if children, then heirs; heirs of God, and joint-heirs with Christ; if so be that we suffer with him, that we may be also glorified together.

For I reckon that the sufferings of this present time are not worthy to be compared with the glory which shall be revealed in us.

For the earnest expectation of the creature waiteth for the manifestation of the sons of God.

For the creature was made subject to vanity, not willingly, but by reason of him who hath subjected the same in hope.

Because the creature itself also shall be delivered from the bondage of corruption into the glorious liberty of the children of God.

For we know that the whole creation groaneth and travaileth in pain together until now.

And not only they, but ourselves also, which have the firstfruits of the Spirit, even we ourselves groan within ourselves, waiting for the adoption, to wit, the redemption of our body.

For we are saved by hope: but hope that is seen is not hope: for what a man seeth, why doth he yet hope for?

But if we hope for that we see not, then do we with patience wait for it.

Likewise the Spirit also helpeth our infirmities: for we know not what we should pray for as we ought: but the Spirit itself maketh intercession for us with groanings which cannot be uttered.

And he that searcheth the hearts knoweth what is the mind of the Spirit, because he maketh intercession for the saints according to the will of God.

And we know that all things work together for good to them that love God, to them who are the called according to his purpose.

For whom he did foreknow, he also did predestinate to be conformed to the image of his Son, that he might be the firstborn among many brethren.

Moreover whom he did predestinate, them he also called: and whom he called, them he also justified: and whom he justified, them he also glorified.

What shall we then say to these things? If God be for us, who can be against us?

He that spared not his own Son, but delivered him up for us all, how shall he not with him also freely give us all things?

Who shall lay anything to the charge of God's elect? It is God that justifieth.

Who is he that condemneth? It is Christ that died, yea rather, that is risen

again, who is even at the right hand of God,
who also maketh intercession for us.

Who shall separate us from the love of
Christ? shall tribulation, or distress, or per-
secution, or famine, or nakedness, or peril,
or sword?

As it is written, For thy sake we are
killed all the day long; we are accounted as
sheep for the slaughter.

Nay, in all these things we are more
than conquerors through him that loved us.

For I am persuaded, that neither death,
nor life, nor angels, nor principalities, nor
powers, nor things present, nor things to
come,

Nor height, nor depth, nor any other
creature, shall be able to separate us from
the love of God, which is in Christ Jesus
our Lord.[59]

Knowledge of Spiritual Self-Defense Is Necessary

As we have seen, the same Law that works
together for the good of them that love the Light is
subject to abuse by such as the Atlantean scientists
reincarnated in our midst. Divine Science, the gift
of the Divine Mother, taught by Moses, Aaron, the
prophets, Christ, the apostles and the Eastern
adepts, is imperiled by the same ones—the extraterrestrial scientists who for tens of thousands of
years have set themselves to the task of engineering
earthlings to their uses.

Now we see those who "fell," in rockets or spacecraft or by their own karmic weight (technically, the Nophelim), and those who were "cast down" by the right arm of the LORD's archangel, Michael (the Nephilim, general term used for both[60]), turning to their advantage the present dark cycle of mankind's returning karma—this most difficult transition we are passing through as we move from the Piscean to the accelerated Aquarian vibration.

Therefore, understand the Great White Brotherhood's concern for your safety and survival unto the fulfilling of *your* mission on planet earth—what with the dangers of invisible poisons that penetrate the astral as well as the physical planes of earth's atmosphere, including radioactive fallout, along with the pesticides and chemical pollutions, germ warfare and yellow rain, harmful cosmic rays and the unknowns of UFOs, all of which can be picked up to contaminate not only the physical envelope of man and beast but also the aura and the energy field.

We would remind you to re-create daily the beautiful tube of light, your shower of radiant energy from the heart of God that Jesus invoked and that can be invoked by you, as we have already taught you to do in Chapter 6—for your protection in all planes of consciousness.

It's high time, in this age of agents and aliens and astral entities, that you made a habit of this tube of light—for it is the habit (customary dress) of the religious devotee and the undergarment of the saints.

Call it down around yourself and your loved ones as an effective shield against the intrusion of all unwanted energies—from the psychotronic manipulation of brain waves and the nervous system to psychic projection, mass hatred, the common cold and virulent viruses and, yes, interference with your genes through drugs, vaccinations, fetal experimentation, etc., etc., and whatever other madness they may come up with as the century presses on to its tensely coiled conclusion.

You have to learn your own system of spiritual defense. Because it's the basics in holding on to the relationship of Man and God. It's the only way—given the world situation as it is today—to be a survivor, spiritually, mentally, emotionally and physically. This system is based on the principle of harmony—God-harmony in your members— practiced all ways.

I am convinced by my knowledge of and experience with cosmic law that human beings who are unhappy—who are bored with life, who have a warped view of life, and who are not getting out of life what they ought to—are suffering purely as the result of their own wrong act of not spiritually defending themselves against the negative vibrations of the world.

"Well," you say, "they have never heard of the tube of light and so they must be very vulnerable to those negative forces that afflict the mind and soul with depression and nihilistic tendencies." And I would agree with you.

At this juncture of the 1980s, teenage suicide is the second major cause of death among our youth. Suicide is becoming a way out taken by increasing numbers of adults without recourse to the Godhead. Is anyone else offering a solution that works?

That is the reason why this organization exists: to disseminate the knowledge of cosmic law to the people of earth, because people need to have a basic knowledge of spiritual defense to protect themselves—not by fighting at the drop of a hat to defend their domain, but by a cosmic invulnerability.

I'm talking about your invulnerability to the forces of Death and Hell that are lurking both inside and outside of your psyche and aura, which invulnerability the tube of light gives you when you call it forth from your Beloved Mighty I AM Presence.

You need to sustain your tube of light around your physical form. Don't be chary about repeating this decree as many as nine times, or renewing your call several times a day. Discord will shatter the forcefield of this "crystal fire mist solidified," so when you rupture your tube of light by inharmony of any kind, including self-pity and self-condemnation as well as emotional outbursts or unkind words, you must call upon the law of forgiveness and reestablish your harmony by the violet transmuting flame which transmutes all discord on contact by your fervent decree; and then reinvoke your tube of light.

So let's engage in a moment of Universal Oneness and stand and face the Chart together as we give El Morya's abbreviated but highly effective "Tube of Light" decree. Since Morya says, "Time is not," we can share a cosmic moment as we look through God's eye and 'see' this white-fire cylinder (it helps if you visualize it as a cylinder of white fire nine feet in diameter, sealed all around on the outside in the blue-flame shield of Archangel Michael) drop down from our own Beloved God Presence and then 'see' ourselves standing in an inner tube of violet fire that transmutes and consumes the subconscious records of past lives and race memories interfering with our current acceleration.

Let's give it four times for the sealing of the Trinity (in our threefold flame) and the Universal Mother (her light in our chakras) within our four lower bodies

Together:

> Beloved I AM Presence bright,
> Round me seal your Tube of Light
> From Ascended-Master Flame
> Called forth now in God's own name.
> Let it keep my temple free
> From all discord sent to me.
>
> I AM calling forth Violet Fire
> To blaze and transmute all desire,
> Keeping on in Freedom's name
> Till I AM one with the Violet Flame.

We are not dealing with a new concept but we are dealing with an old concept, as old as the hills—the concept of Man's relationship to God. I think the greatest thing in the world we can think about when contemplating this relationship is the concept that each one of us has a crystal cord.

Remember that it's an 'umbilical' cord of light, connecting your heart and soul and four lower bodies to your I AM Presence. The spiritual energy that flows through this cord beats our heart, keeps our lamps (chakras) burning bright and nourishes our entire lifestream. And that cord goes all the way back to the heart of the living God whence we came.

So often we bump into these disconnected, discombobulated people wandering around the world who tell us what an awful, miserable life they're having. They don't have to have misery in their life. Sometimes they're too far gone to know they're having a miserable life—and they can be cured of that, too, so they'll become sensitive enough to their own deplorable state to want to do something about it!

But, if they do have the type of misery that karma produces, the formula to cure the misery is already in existence. God has said, "I will not allow"—*I will not allow*—"you to be tempted above that you are able to resist." That is a promise.

God is faithful. He "will not suffer you to be tempted above that ye are able"—Paul spoke from personal experience—"but will with the temptation also make a way to escape, that ye may be able to bear it."[61]

You see, there really is no excuse for allowing density and darkness and noncomprehension of our relationship to God to continue in our world. So let's promise each other that we'll invoke our tube of light every day and call to Archangel Michael to protect us from both the wiles of the tempter and his frivolous temptations—making us believe we have so many physical and psychological needs and then convincing us that the satisfying of these needs is worth the compromise of our honor, when it's our honor— and God's cosmic honor flame in the pillar of fire (i.e., tube of light) that goes before us[62]—which we need more than anything this world has to offer!

The following simple fiat will compel this Captain of the LORD's hosts and his blue-lightning angels to your side instantaneously. Try it and see if you don't feel his presence or at least notice its powerful effect.

Pause to center in your heart, there to amplify your love for this heart-Friend of the ages. Establish your connection to him by the love currents from your heart chakra to his. Meditate on Love's two-way action in the divine interchange and then, just before you recite this decree, offer your personal prayer to God in Archangel Michael's name for yourself, your loved ones, and all oppressed peoples of the world. This decree works best when you give it nine times—giving you the power of the Three times the Three.

Lord Michael before, Lord Michael behind,
Lord Michael to the right, Lord Michael to the left,
Lord Michael above, Lord Michael below,
Lord Michael, Lord Michael wherever I go!
I AM his Love protecting here!
I AM his Love protecting here!
I AM his Love protecting here!   (9x)

May the angel of the LORD be with you always, my beloved.

The Living Truth Is Both Teacher and Teaching

We have the Lost Teachings of Jesus by God's grace; and therefore we do not have the need, as some have, to create an illusion before any man, whether concerning Christ's pure doctrine or our own personalities. It's simply not necessary, for the living Truth is both the Teacher and the Teaching. And when you have that, my friends, you have everything.

And that's what I'm here to give you so that you can make it your own. And when you do, you won't need me or any preacher to tell you what to do and what not to do, because the standard of Truth and the Standard-bearer will be in your heart. (Now, don't forget his name. For THE LORD OUR RIGHTEOUSNESS *is his Name!* And we know it because God revealed it to our friend, the prophet Jeremiah.)

Nor are we here to try to tell any preacher in the world that he is wrong and we are right and we're the only ones who have the only way. Christ is the only way and Christ *in you* is the hope of glory. And his Truth is available to all by the Holy Spirit.

So let the people who come to us for spiritual guidance make up their own minds as to what is Truth and who has it. That's the important thing—that you ponder Truth in your heart and learn to love Christ Truth as a part of your Real Self.

We try to do everything we can to create blessing and love and friendship in our gatherings even though it profits us not, from a human standpoint. But it does profit and fatten our souls to know that we can call to God to bring his Love down into this world and that he answers our daily calls for you in miracle upon miracle of his grace.

And do you know something?—a lot of people don't know this—if you don't make a call to God for his Love, the world may not get it. Why is that? Because when God sent your twin flames as man and woman to evolve in the physical octave, he gave you free will and told you to take dominion over his "footstool" kingdom, as Isaiah calls the planes of earth.[63]

In other words, you and your twin flame are supposed to master the material universe and time and space and your own consciousness suspended in the midst of it. And he gave you the gift of his infinite Love to share, in order that you might meet and conquer every opposition to your love by his flaming flame of Love.

By losing their tie to the God Presence through disobedience to the Law of Love, as we have said, man and woman lost their position of authority in the earth and became more the victims of their karma than the masters of themselves and their environment. And that's when they let the fallen angels get the best of them!

You see, whenever you fail they're always right there with their alternative, nice 'n' easy—their shortcut methods: ride somebody else's coattails, buy now pay later, play the lottery, recite some worded formula, get the mark of the beast stamped on you—rub your belly and pat your head, and life outside the initiatic path of the Cosmic Christ will be a charm. Yes, they're waiting for your fall, or if they can catch a roving eye, they'll present their deal and it'll be your turn to say:

"No deal!" I'll take Maitreya and his chastisement and any hardship, whatever it takes to reestablish my solid relationship with my Father. I may have failed him, but he'll take me back. And I'm willing to pay the same price Jesus paid to be delivered. "No deal, ye serpents! Get thee behind me!"

Wherever you go, beloved, you can never escape the daily choice and confrontation between their way and God's way. In order to choose God we have to get rid of the desire to want something or someone more than we want him. Inordinate desire is what makes you take up the "deal" of the archdeceivers.

If you want any thing in this world more than you want Christ and his Consciousness in you, well then, you see, they've got your number, and sooner or later they'll hatch a plot you'll fall for. And you'll be trapped in another round of karma with the serpents, trapped by your own Achilles' heel: inordinate desire.

The way to overcome this is to realize that "your Mighty I AM Presence is the fullness of all you desire." Saint Germain has said it often. What does that mean? It means that God will give you everything you could ever want or need in his good time, and timing. If you want to do it God's way, lawfully, you have to be willing to labor and to wait.

So when you re-tie yourself to your God Presence, you become once again the authority for your world because you act for God. You're his agent. And when you do this, God will act through you because you have given him—by your free will—the freedom once again to use you as his instrument.

And this is the purpose of religion (from the Latin *religio, religare* 'to bind back')—to bind man and woman back to God again, to reconnect the lost crystal cord, to reestablish the blessed tie that binds us to our God Presence and to our twin flame, so that after a long night of misunderstanding we may once again take up our divine plan in partnership with God and the dearly beloved (divine counterpart of our soul)—by free will.

Man Was Created to Be the God of His Universe

Do you remember the destruction of Sodom and Gomorrah? Did you ever hear what happened when the angels came down to destroy it? They made contact with Abraham and Lot, didn't they? And the LORD did not hide from Abraham what he was going to do.[64]

Now, Abraham didn't like the idea because Lot was living there and Lot was close to him. So he said, "Well, LORD," he said, "I know you've got the power to do it. You can destroy this city if you want to. But," he said, "just supposing, LORD, that there're fifty good people living there. Would you destroy the city then?"

God looked at him and he said, "No," he said, "if there're fifty good people there, I won't destroy it."

Abraham spoke again, and he said very zealously, "Well, what if there're forty-five good people there—would you destroy the city?"

"No," he says, "I wouldn't destroy it if there were forty-five good people there."

He asked again for thirty and again the LORD acceded.

So, finally he got down and he said, "LORD, I don't want to make you angry. You're the Creator of the universe. You're the Judge of all the earth. You have all the wisdom." He said, "If there're just ten, ten good people there, will you spare the city?"

The LORD looked at him and he said, "If

there're ten good people there, I'll spare the city."
But there weren't. And the emissaries told Lot to
get his family out of that place because "We're
going to destroy Sodom and Gomorrah."

So Sodom and Gomorrah went down the
drain into the desert. It was fused by atomic
energy.[65] Some people might say, "What? Did you
say by atomic energy? Why, that wasn't even created back then! They'd never heard of it. They'd
never heard of nuclear fission."

Well, I said *atomic energy* and I meant it!
Because that's exactly how it was done. It was
the same situation as Hiroshima and Nagasaki in
World War II when they dropped the bomb. Sodom
and Gomorrah were destroyed by atomic energy.
Because listen, dear folks, this earth is not the only
world in space.

Go out under any canopy of heaven, in any
hemisphere, and look up at the sky and take note of
the myriad stars that are there and remember the
words of God to Abraham. He said, "I will multiply thy seed as the stars of the heaven and as the
sand upon the sea shore innumerable."[66] This is
what God said.

And I will tell you something. Man, the
product of Divine Love, was created in order to
become a god of his own universe. He was not
created to be a controlled being, controlled by
anybody's whimsy or by the karma of circumstance
or by environment or by destructive desires. He was

created to master his desires. And with God, I tell you, all things *are* possible.

You can say to me, "Well, I don't believe it's possible for *me*," and I can tell *you*: Change your state of consciousness by turning it on to Christ.

Change your state of consciousness by recognizing that you have a Presence, individualized for you—that you have a Holy Christ Self, the Universal Christ who said, "Here is the whole loaf. Take, eat: this is my Body, which is broken for you."[67]

The true Lord's Supper is the recognition by man that he has an individualized Christ Self and that that Christ Self is central to his life—as far as mediatorship goes, as far as communion goes—along with his Divine Presence. The Christ Self has a direct contact with every soul on this earth. No one need fear. Everyone can open up wide and say, "Well, thank God that there is a Universal Christ individualized for every one of us!"

What is this Universal Christ? John the Beloved wrote, "All things were made by him, and without him was not any thing made that was made." Well, you say, "How can this be? Christ lived two thousand years ago."

I tell you, nay. Christ has always been. "For by him all things *were* made, and without him was not any thing made that was made. In him *was* Life, and the Life *was* the Light of men."[68]

So, what are we talking about? We're talking about Light! What did Einstein tell you about energy and light? In his famous energy-mass equation, he told you that matter could be converted into an enormous quantity of energy. And he revolutionized the theory of light with his postulation that light is composed of individual quanta, called photons.

And you know about the Law of Conservation of Energy that says energy can be neither created nor destroyed—it just changes form. Well, all things can be molded, can they not?

And that is the term we use in thinking of creativity. We think of the great Master Potter who sat before the potter's wheel of life as it was turning, and he began to mold and shape each individual. And he gave you a pure and beautiful, radiant lantern of a soul—a lantern that can light the whole world. Any one of you can do it. What Christ did, you can do.

His message resounds from Bethany's hill: "If you believe that I AM the Christ, the things that I do shall ye do also, and even greater things than these shall ye do because I go unto my Father."

And what do you have today but a ministry that blasphemes and accuses you of blasphemy if you say, "I believe that God can do this through me," or "I believe that God can live in me and perform his marvelous works through me."

Do we have people trying to keep it all for themselves without sharing his broken Body with all of us? We all need his broken Body. It's a Body of forgiveness when you need forgiveness. It's a

Body of strength when you need strength. It's a Body of resurrection when you need to be resurrected. It's a Body of zeal when you need zeal.

This is a Body of purpose. And it is an orderly purpose. It transcends all this world. It transcends all human personality. We are nothing without Christ, nothing without the Beloved, the I AM Presence. Without our contact with this Presence, we humans down here would not even be able to produce the violet transmuting flame of forgiveness. Why, the human monad would not even be able to play out the role of his human self. He couldn't even function as an animal without the perfection of God!

Now, look at yourself. Some years ago they ran a series in *Life* magazine. And what did they show? The marvels of the convolutions of the brain and the various components. They showed the cerebrum, the cerebellum, and the cerebral cortex. They showed the thalamus, hypothalamus, the pituitary gland, and the pineal body! They showed the dura mater and the pia mater with a beautiful liquid light flowing across it.[69]

But what they didn't show you is the great harm that people do to their brains by their disbelief—and even by physical tarry substances taken in through chemical air pollution, cigarette smoke and nicotine, for example, and especially pot.

Do you know that man's brain was originally golden? Today we refer to it as "gray matter." Gray matter! No wonder El Morya came out with the statement that was in complete refutation of that business on gray matter. "Oh yes," he said, "there are gray ones upon this planetary body."

You see, matter is innocent. It's not matter that's gray, it's the consciousness without Light that's gray! And when the mind is gray, eventually the brain matter takes on the color and vibration of the aura, and so does the rest of the body. You've seen people who look gray all over either from smoking habits or from serious illness. It's the astral body so affecting the physical, and the physical so contaminating the astral, that the overall appearance is just that.

And what did Saint John write from "the Amen, the faithful and true witness" unto the Church? He said, "Because thou art lukewarm and neither cold nor hot, I will spue thee out of my mouth."[70] That's Jesus' definition of the gray ones.

They're neither black nor white—here nor there. And their ambivalence becomes a chronic karmic condition readily apparent, yet readily curable by the violet flame. Yes, if there is a will—a determined will to change—there is a way.

God wants people who are either on fire for him or on fire for whatever they're on fire for. Because if they're that way, you see, there is a chance. Then, if you get one of these people who are on fire for everything that they shouldn't be on fire about and you get them into the kingdom of heaven, they turn right around and they're on fire for God just as they were on fire for everything else.

But you take some of these half-baked people

who never seem to come to the point of browning on top. They just sit there. And you put all the heat on and they dry up. And finally they come out like a bad batch, all burnt and no good, and you say, "Take it out of the oven!"

So God wants somebody who has a spark, somebody who sparkles with his zeal for Love.

It's easy to criticize the other fellow. But you want to remember one thing. The French have an old saying, "Qui s'excuse, s'accuse": whoever excuses himself (makes excuses) accuses himself. I've also heard it said that whenever you point the finger at somebody else, you've got three fingers pointing at you. Isn't it true? So let's learn the process of divine forgiveness and not act as an impediment to the other members in the Body of God.

For we were born to rule more than ourselves. If you don't believe me, believe David as he spoke to the LORD in the presence of the Beloved:

> O LORD our Lord, how excellent is thy name in all the earth! who hast set thy glory above the heavens.
>
> When I consider thy heavens, the work of thy fingers, the moon and the stars, which thou hast ordained;
>
> What is man, that thou art mindful of him? and the son of man, that thou visitest him?
>
> For thou hast made him a little lower than the angels and hast crowned him with glory and honour.

Thou madest him to have dominion
over the works of thy hands; thou hast put all
things under his feet.[71]

The Judgment of Men's Sins Before and After

I have always believed that God created this
world out of Love, and that he had a high and a
beautiful purpose, and that that purpose must be
revealed. Now it's coming out through the Lost
Teachings of our elder brother Jesus set forth by
the Lord and by the Ascended Masters. God's holy
purpose is not a product of our poor little brain.
How could anybody think that? It's a product
of Jesus and El Morya and Saint Germain and
Mother Mary and all the true Teachers of Wisdom,
one in the Mind of God, and of their Teachings, to
which we aspire with you.

We have these get-togethers so that we can
discuss the Christian mysteries until "every eye
shall see him"[72]—because the mysteries are unveiled to each one by Christ himself through the
Holy Spirit, the true intercessor in our midst.

Yes, I expect this organization to supplant the
false doctrines of the Church completely. I expect this organization to sweep every lukewarm,
half-baked church there is in the whole world out
of existence—ultimately. I mean every single word
I say.

And do you know why? Because they're going
to have to either lick us or join us, one of the two.
They won't have a chance to remain lukewarm or

half-baked because the *Truth* will prevail! And the Truth is that God is in Man.

And the people want the Truth and when they have it, they'll run with it. And they'll run right out the door of the old dispensation. And they won't sit still in their pews for Error any longer! And it is the Truth that will make them free, not I or you.

So the pastors, they turn around and they tell you how evil you are. They tell you about all your passions for evil. They tell you about all the wickedness that's in the world. They tell you about all the negativity that's in the world. They tell you about all the wars and rumors of wars and the time of trouble[73]—but we can read all about that in our daily newspaper. We don't have to hear about it in church.

They tell you about what you already know and then they say, "Two thousand years ago a man came down by the name of Jesus Christ and he died for your sins." And by that very statement they are telling you that God is a God of anger and that he is a God of wrath against people and that he punishes the innocent and rewards the guilty.

They are telling you that by the crucifixion of Jesus Christ on the cross, that by that act (and I say it happened—I didn't say it didn't happen) God is going to forgive everybody forever for everything they've ever done. And they're telling you that God himself demanded it.

They are telling you that if you have twelve

friends and one of them is without sin and the rest of you are sinners, in order for the sins of the twelve of you to be forgiven the thirteenth will have to submit to a blood sacrifice—a sacrificial murder rite. And only by so doing will your sins be forgiven. Even our own systems of justice, corrupt as they may be at times, have not even conceived of punishing the innocent (by death, mind you) for the crimes of the guilty while the latter go scot-free.

Now, the author of Hebrews (that divine document ascribed to Paul but perhaps the work of our Lord) comes right out and says it: If you turn around after you've heard the teachings of the Truth, the good news of Christ, and you go right back willfully into the same sin you were in before, he says, there remains for you no more sacrifice for your sins, no hope except a certain fearful looking for of judgment and fiery indignation which, he adds, will devour the adversaries of Christ Truth.[74]

Paul, who preached this doctrine, knew exactly what he was talking about because this was the inner Teaching of Jesus. But a lot of people have misinterpreted that. They think that that means if they make one little blasted mistake, just one, after they have been "saved" (according to the perceptions and conceptions of some religious people), then they're damned forever and they're going down to hell. And they think that's what it means.

It doesn't mean that. It means that judgment must come to you—and that that judgment may or may not be pleasant. And here's what the judgment is. It plainly states in the Bible: "Some men's sins are open beforehand, going before to judgment; and some men they follow after."[75] This means that everybody does not have the same acceleration or the same handling, or systemizing, of their sins.

Some people are so conscientious that they want their sins to go to judgment daily—like some of the tribes of the American Indians. They used to sit around the fire at night and they'd take all of their misdeeds of the day and they'd see them— just momentarily—in their mind and they'd say, "Great Spirit, Gitche Manito, the Mighty, please, take these sins unto thy Self."

And they'd mentally cast their sins into the fire, asking the Great Spirit to consume the records and the hurt of their misdeeds and forgive them. And they believed. They believed in the consuming fire of the Mighty One.[76] And once they put their wrongs into the fire, they accepted it done. And it *was* done. And they slept in peace and at dawn they arose to a new day of opportunity.

These are people whose sins are open beforehand, going to heaven *before* to judgment—because they are conscientious. They don't want to be indebted to God or Man. They want to pay as they go. And so they are grateful for the daily reckoning of their accounts, even if it sometimes spoils their plans or makes life a bit inconvenient. This, then, becomes a daily judgment and a daily penance.

But a lot of people don't want a day of reckoning, and so they keep on saying, "O Lord, *please, please, please* forgive me for all the wrong I've done! And don't punish me for any of it!" And so they pile up a huge mountain of debt. And then one of these days when they come back into this world and find all that mountain sitting there, they look at the mountain and they say, "Oh, what is that? I don't want to look!" And they turn away from it.

But they built the mountain, you know. They put it there. And then they say, "I don't want to look!" But it was God's mercy that allowed their karma to pile up because they kept on asking about it. They said, "Please don't punish me," and so God didn't. And then it all comes due. And there it is. It's got to be paid. The bill must be paid. "I am de bill collector," you know.

And so the Lords of Karma are the bill collector. And a man comes to the point where he says, "Lord, now I want to enter into the kingdom of heaven." The bill collector's standing there and he says, "Well, your mansion is waiting, but," he says, "you do have a mortgage against it. So I'd like you to pay this mortgage off first and then you can enter in," you see.

And that's exactly how karma works, but everybody doesn't handle his karma the same way. And so Paul says, "The good works of some are manifest beforehand; and they that are otherwise cannot be hid."[77]

You have Saint Bernadette with tuberculosis of the bone and a tumor the size of a child's head on her knee. The pain was so bad that she could hardly stand it—but she kept it a secret because she wanted to keep on working as a nurse in the infirmary. We all remember her scrubbing the floor of the cloister on her knees in the movie *The Song of Bernadette*[78] and hiding her "thorn in the flesh" for the love of the Lord's Work through her. This is the way she chose to deal with her karma. So each one must choose.

Look at Saint Thérèse, who also suffered greatly with tuberculosis. At the end of her life she was racked with pain. Yet she heroically faced all her trials, and she made it—all the way up the spiral staircase to heaven. She made her ascension. And ever since her translation at the tender age of twenty-four, many people have been assisted and healed—often with the lingering fragrance of roses—by a simple appeal to Saint Thérèse of Lisieux.

This is an interesting fact, because someday you may be in their position. Not that you'll have tuberculosis, I trust not, but that you might have a chance to get up to heaven, to in fact make your ascension through this very Work of the Lord— the Ascended Masters' Summit Lighthouse activity. And when you get there, you may assist some of the people who haven't yet made it. That's what it's all about. This Teaching and this Path is all about people helping each other in their relationship with God and with the God flame in one another.

The Imitation of Christ Produces Miracles

There's nothing wrong with Jesus Christ. Don't get me wrong. He's the greatest Master I've ever met, but he expects all of us to fulfill the same role. We're supposed to become living Christs. Well, we're not going to become living Christs by just worshipping Jesus, because worship does not produce the miracle. Imitation does. We have to imitate him in the regeneration.[79]

He didn't do it for you, but he proved what you can do—get your own victory over the astral plane[80] and the *false* hierarchy set up by the fallen angels to counteract the Word and Work of Jesus Christ's own *true* hierarchy—that of the LORD's hosts who comprise the Great White Brotherhood. And he'll help you get your victory over the conspiracies of the antichrists, and he'll teach you, but he won't do it for you. Because he's not allowed to by cosmic law! And even if he were, he loves you too much to deprive you of the joy of your own victorious overcoming of the beast and all that was and is and is not.[81]

You see, it's not—your human creation is not real. And your victory lies in knowing it's not real and proving it at every turn in the road of reaping (reaping your positive and negative karma) by right *motive*, right *reason*, right *decision*, and right *action*.

In this generation, we have to learn to put the seal of God—his sacred name—on our forehead *and* in the palm of our hands. Shall I tell you what that means? Putting it in your forehead means that you've got it in your mind. And putting it in your hand means that you put it to work in action. Do you understand? That's all that means. It's a mystical symbol. That's what God told Moses.

"And it shall be for a sign unto thee upon thine hand [the sign that you must take righteous action in his name, as his representative], and for a memorial between thine eyes [focused in the third eye], that the [authority of the] LORD's Law may be in thy mouth: for with a strong hand hath the LORD brought thee out of Egypt."[82]

This commemoration of the deliverance of the LORD's people from the Egyptian taskmasters[83] preceded and was preparatory to YAHWEH's new covenant with his chosen people spoken through Jeremiah. The words of this new covenant bear repeating—they are a mantra from your Mighty I AM Presence. So you should write God's promise on your memory—heart, head, and hand—and affirm it with joy:

> . . . I will put my Law in their inward parts and write it in their hearts, and will be their God and they shall be my people.[84]

Well, the purpose of the laws and observances and teachings given to us by the Prophet Moses and the Saviour Jesus Christ is really very simple. They are given to us not as ritualistic formulas to become an end in themselves but as the means, step by step, to the exercise of Godhood. Yes, we are being initiated for the putting on of the mantle of our Godhood.

Now, that doesn't mean we're a religion of people vying to be "gods many" in the pagan sense of the word. On the contrary, it is the path of the mystics, the way of the beloved of every world religion, of all religions who fear not the Father, who love him and desire union, whose divine spark tells them he has ordained that union of Love of Father and Son. These have approached the altar of ineffable Light and have made the choice not to reject the Light but to enter into the Light, to be enjoined to its bliss.

Unless this be our goal from the start, unless this be our daily reason for being on earth—and all others subordinate to it—unless we can be the LORD's instrument, *as himself*, unless we can pursue the Spirit of his prophecy and his miracles, *as ourself*, how can we save ourselves or our generation from the perils of repetitive Evil such as occurred in the holocaust of the Nazi concentration camps and as is still going on in the labor camps of the Soviet Union? Or from the Evil possession of everyday people in everyday situations that affect us deeply, with groaning and travail as we wrestle with demons?

We of our human selves cannot solve the huge moral equation of our time without the I AM Presence with us and the angel of the LORD— Archangel Michael. We can't forgive, forget, and forsake the past without God's all-consuming violet flame that brings mercy and justice to all through the Holy Spirit, even as it erases the records of our pain and our outrage at the fallen angels' blasphemy against Jew and German alike, and British, American, Russian, Polish, Hungarian—all humanity and the children of Light—or against ourselves personally as we have wrestled with the Liar and the Murderer in a loved one.

Exercising Godhood means we're reaching for the auric emanation of our Mighty I AM Presence. It means we want to wear the Light because we love the Light and God is Light. We want to surround ourselves with spheres of God's holiness—the concentric spheres of our causal body of rainbow Light. We want to wear the Light as a garment of service, a priest's habit, a monk's hood. We just want to be frocked in Love and to put on royal robes of righteousness woven of good deeds and our lawful exercise of the Word.

For we understand this garment, this aura, to be the extension of God's consciousness—the clothing wherewith we were clothed in heaven and with which we shall be clothed again. Because we know we are heirs of the promises. The Light within us bears witness of the Light of God that we are his Sons. "Naked came I out of my mother's womb," said Job, "and naked shall I return thither."[85]

Moving onward on the Path, the Sons of Light declare, "We shall not return to the LORD naked, we shall come to the LORD of glory bearing the harvest of our lawful sowings. For we shall have put on our God-*hood*, our inheritance of Light wherewith we shall be clothed forevermore." This is our lawful exercise of Godhood. This is why it was not robbery for Jesus to make himself 'equal' with God.[86]

What is done to one is done to all. The message of all the world teachers and the sufferers of the infamous torment of the fallen angels is: "What they have done to us, they will do to you, unless you unite under the I AM Presence and call upon the LORD without ceasing for his true and righteous judgments."

They have not stopped and they will not stop until you raise up God's Light within you.

As Moses raised up a fiery serpent of brass and set it on a pole in the wilderness and all who had the snakebite and looked upon it were healed,[87] so you must raise up the sacred fire in your spiritual centers (chakras) and on your spinal altar.

You must conserve the life-force of thy heavenly Father and thy earthly Mother within thee, if you, too, would be the instrument of the Master's healing. You must expand and balance the three-fold flame in your heart, internalize the Word I AM THAT I AM in your forehead, in your heart and in your hand—as God's Power/Wisdom/Love in action—if you, too, would save the world for future generations.

And you must know that *God in you will do this holy thing through you.* Yes, beloved, when you give yourself to him, the LORD will perform his perfect Work both in you and through you for the saving of *all* Lightbearers on planet earth.

This you must do because the fallen ones will not stop their destructivity as the destroyers in the earth[88] until that Christ be raised up in you, who is the true deliverer of your households and nations. The Light of the I AM in you must be sealed in your forehead and in your hand for the devouring of the agencies of absolute Evil, whether astral or physical. This is the spiritual work that belongs to all God's people as they serve side by side with the holy angels and Ascended Masters.

The victims of the fallen angels in every century must be the grim reminder that they will not fade away. *They* have not said, "Never again," but carry on their stealth wherever they are left unchallenged and unchecked by the determined decree of the people.

Let the seed of Abraham's Christ exercise the power of the Word not for revenge against the enemy—for the LORD has said, "Vengeance is mine, I will repay"[89]—but for the soul liberation, the spiritual/emotional healing and the karmic freedom of the victims of the seed of the Wicked One, who in every generation are still suffering the tortures of the damned somewhere on planet earth.

Unless we can do the things that Christ did, we're not going to be regenerated. And we can start whenever we want to. It doesn't matter what church or synagogue you belong to or what doctrine you believe. It's the Truth that will make you free[90] — if you know it, and if you do it!

And the Truth is that man was born once as the issue of God in the heart of the Great Central Sun. Then he was born into a veil of flesh for the first time. And after his initial round of so many cycles in the Matter spheres, he didn't make it. So the spiritual guardians of the race marked on his card "Failed to pass the grade"—he's got to take it over again.

So he comes back and he eats more oatmeal. And his mama nurses him again. And he learns to crawl and toddle around. And then he takes on the challenge of the world all over again and he still doesn't make it. So he comes back and back and back again and winds up as General Patton!

And I imagine that one of these days old George will be back, too. And I daresay that if the man ever turns to the Light a hundred percent, he'll be as zealous for the Light and as great a winner for God as he was in the battles of World War II.

A man's character is all that he really has. *Your* character is all that *you* have, it's what you are—until you are changed into the same image of Christ from glory to glory by the Spirit of the LORD.[91] Then you're awake, you're no longer asleep in your little human self; and you realize that the real you is a great being. And then when you harness your character to that great God-free being that you are, well, you're really going to go places!

You have a marvelous potential! And that potential is no more and no less than God. And there is no reason in the world why you can't experience it—except the reasons that you create in your mind or that somebody pops into your mind, that you hold there, that say, "I can't do it."

Of course you can do it!

You say your neighbors are not going to like it if you take up the study of the Light. One man was telling me about how a minister called this religion a cult. Don't be alarmed—that's standard procedure. They have to call it something! It kind of gets in their hair. They don't like it.

But we're not creating this organization so people won't like it. This organization was created by God to help people. And that it will do. So don't be afraid of what anybody calls us or what anybody calls you. It doesn't matter what they call you.

You know, we used to say, "I don't care what you call me as long as you don't call me late for breakfast!" (Now, of course, my mentors have told me that I should try to cut down on my breakfast and eat two meals a day!)

But don't be afraid of public opinion or what it says about you. When I was seven or eight years old, I used to take clocks and telephones apart. And my neighbors have never forgotten that to this day. When I return to my hometown—like when Jesus returned to Nazareth and they said of him, "Is this not Joseph's son?"[92]—they say, "Here comes the clock taker-aparter" and "Here comes the telephone destructor."

People never forget the wrongs you do or have done. Don't worry about it. Be glad that God forgets them. That's all that counts. And *you* forget it, so *you* don't get hung up on it!

Don't get hung up on your ideas of yourself— of how small you are or how little you are or how impractical you are, how this or that person doesn't like you or how this or that person has misunderstood you, or how you don't have as much money as you want and you wish you had more talent.

Oh, you can wish for so many things! Don't worry about playing the wishing game. If you get God, you've got it all. It's just a matter of time and you'll be able to work out your relationship to him in every area of your life.

I never thought that I would ever be standing up here at this lectern in this chapel in this mansion. In fact, I never had any idea this place would exist. But when I was thirty years old, living entirely in another state and clime, doing an entirely different job, I had a vision of myself in Colorado Springs in a huge house. And I couldn't understand it, but here I am!

So none of us know just what we're really going to be doing in the decades ahead. But don't worry about it. The biggest problem that men create is the problem of creating worries. Man is a creator. He can create worries, can't he? If he can create worries, that means he can create evil as well as good, can't he?

Well, go ahead and create evil if that's what you want to do. But you'll pay for it. And if you create good, you're going to receive good in return. And you'll be rewarded. That's the Law and it's guaranteed.

Abraham saw many wonderful things. One time he saw the LORD in a vision with a great shield. And the LORD spoke to him and he said:

"Fear not, I AM thy shield and thy exceeding great reward."[93]

If everybody would stop to consider the I AM Presence as both their shield (shielding them from the full impact either of the blasts of the fallen angels or of their own returning karma for their misuse of the Law) and as their reward (rewarding them for putting the Law to good use), they'd try to relate to the universe.

Because you can count on the Law of the One being fair to everyone—universally equal, no respecter of men's persons[94]—always the shield and the exceeding great reward of the godly.

Don't try to be separate from the universe. Don't try to be separate from humanity. We're all one. Try to relate to everyone through the I AM Presence.

You know how those Christmas-tree bulbs work? You pull one out of the socket and all the rest of them blink out. You put it back in and they all go on.

Maybe it's that way with you. Maybe the world needs your light. I think it does. Start putting it out. Realize you can make a bigger body-bulb or you can produce more current or you can get a brighter light. Just strike a little flint into the tinder and create your light. Let your candle glow! Let your light shine![95]

Stop all the human nonsense of worrying over what's going to happen—concern with your family, concern about your economic future, concern about the problems of your country. Rest assured that you can do a little bit about it—and sometimes some of you may be able to do a lot about it. But don't *worry* about it, because worry doesn't produce anything!

"Take no thought for the morrow, for the morrow shall take thought for the things of itself" were the words of the great Master who also said, "Sufficient unto the day is the evil thereof."[96]

And what does that mean?

Well, Jesus told us what it means. He said, "The evil is the 'energy veil', or net, of the fallen ones that lies in wait to trap thee."

He said, "It's already there so don't worry

about it, but rather be concerned about maintaining a strong tie to your Mighty I AM Presence who will guard you against the snares of the wicked."

Then the Master said, "The evil is also your own energy veil—it's the cocoon of illusion that you've already surrounded yourself with: it's your karma. And," he said, "that's already there, too, and it comes up daily for your transmutation by the Holy Spirit's sacred fire. So don't worry about that either, because it'll be there as sure as the dawn until you've cleaned it all up. And then you'll be clean, every whit.[97]

"But have that lawful concern that your mind and heart stay steadfast, waiting upon the LORD your God, so that the day's allotment of karma and tests don't trip you up and you find yourself at day's end worse off than when you started."

So that's the whole meaning of "Sufficient unto the day is the evil thereof." It's a sufficient challenge, it's premeasured, and you can beat it with the I AM Presence and the LORD's angel, Archangel Michael.

So the message is: Don't worry—if you've got God, you've not only got everything, but with him you can beat anything that tries to tear you from him—especially your own karma and your own vulnerabilities to the traps of the negative force.

You see, the words of Jesus won't help you a bit unless you listen to them, understand them, and heed them.

And so we're bringing you some insight on the

relationship of Man and God according to the Lost Teachings of Jesus.

Consider: God is the Creator in the first instance. He gives you the right to create as he did in the second instance. So here you are, the Son, a co-creator with the Father. And by his creative power in you, you find you've created either good or ill.

If you've created ill, you're reaping the harvest of that. Yes, we've said that. But I'm saying it again because I don't want you to become a worrywart about your past karma coming down upon you like a house of cards. Because you can do something about it. You can turn the tables on it. And you can start right now.

Not Human Sacrifice but Offering Oneself to God

I didn't say that Jesus didn't die on the cross. All I'm saying to you is the same thing that God's angel said to Abraham.[98] Abraham carried his only son, Isaac, out into the wilderness and he built an altar. He wanted to please God and he was going to offer his son Isaac on that altar. He took a knife in his hand and he was going to slay him and burn him for a burnt offering as God had told him to do—to test his faith, you see.

Which of you, having a son or a daughter, would do a thing like this? But Abraham was a good man, a man after God's own heart. He was acting in faith. He thought he was doing right. But he never did it, because in the end God did not require it of him. Just remember that.

The angel of the LORD came along and said, "Abraham, Abraham, do it not!" And so he offered a ram that was caught in the thicket there in his place, and Isaac was let go. So, it was his fear of the LORD and his obedience to God that was proven in his willingness not to withhold his son—his only son, who himself was obedient to his father in all points of the Law.

And I'm telling you now that the same is true of Jesus Christ. God did not demand that Jesus be the propitiation for the sins of man by dying, but he did demand that he be the propitiation for our sins[99]—for world karma, in fact—*by living!* The most important event in Jesus' life was his offering of himself to God. Like Isaac, he withheld nothing from his Father, he made himself a living sacrifice unto death thereby proving the Seventh Ray law of universal transmutation. And he expects you to do the same.[100]

You see, the Lamb of God slain from the foundation of the world is the true and acceptable offering. The ram in the thicket symbolizes the soul wed to the antahkarana of eternal Life. When in a distant embodiment some three thousand years later Isaac was to merge fully with that Light in Christ, the Light itself would suffer the flame, and the soul wed alchemically to the Light would not suffer loss but become the Immortal One.

Thus, when we are ready the LORD offers us his initiation, he does not offer us as sacrifice. For through the assimilation of the initiatic Light, we, too, may bear the sins of the many as we make daily 'sacrifice' in the temple, offering dynamic violet flame decrees for the transmutation of world karma. And we also gladly 'sacrifice' our own karma to the violet fire burning on the altar of the Temple of Man in order that we might then bear one another's burden—until it, too, be consumed by our God who is the consuming fire of our devotion, to which Moses attested.

Yes, Jesus bore world karma in the Piscean dispensation. He even fell under the weight of the Piscean cross of Death and doubt and fear and the world torment of that Hell created not by God but by the reprobate angels:

It was not his crucifixion, not death that conquered Death, but his obedient, loving sacrifice in Life, which he gladly made and continues to make unto the Final Judgment of the false hierarchy of the fallen angels. By Jesus' Life, this seed of the Wicked One (who had slain the Lamb again and again in each incarnation of the Word throughout millions of years of galactic history) incurred the LORD's Judgment and they continue to incur it cycle by cycle to the present hour.

More than that, it was his enduring Love and the sacred sword of Christ Truth that he bore unto the resurrection and the eternal Life of the Sons of God worlds without end that got the Easter Victory.

Beyond the sight of all participants in the drama of the Lord's passion, it was the initiatic flame of the resurrection in its all-suffusing Light that fastened the Son of man to the cosmic cross of white fire formed by the I AM THAT I AM.

'Twas not by Caesar's cross on Golgotha but by the initiation of *the Tree of Life* that the Son of man, fully assimilated in the Light of the Son of God, was assumed unto the Lamb of God who is the Universal Christ.

This is the mission of the Universal Christ in each one of us. Jesus' garment is one we must be willing to wear, his role is ours. His Path and his Christhood are ours uniquely to imitate.

Gently he foretold our hour and the power of his Light with us: "Take my yoke upon you—my path of personal Christhood unto the full initiation of the I AM THAT I AM—and learn of me; for I am meek and lowly in heart: and ye shall find rest unto your souls. For my yoke is easy, and my burden is Light."[101]

"Wist* ye not that I must be about my Father's business?"[102] were his words spoken to his mother and father when he departed from them as they were returning from the feast of the Passover in Jerusalem.

So, you see, he was about his Father's business. He did everything that he told us to do. He went into all the world and he preached the gospel to every creature. He healed the sick. He cleansed the lepers. He raised the dead. He cast out devils. He performed all of the works of God among men. Freely he received the Light of his Father, freely he gave it.[103]

Wist means "know"—"know ye not."

All this he did—not for us, but so that we would go and do likewise and fail not to fulfill every requirement of the Law for our resurrection and ascension into the God Presence.

Yet people hated him. He was "despised and rejected of men, a man of sorrows and acquainted with grief," says Isaiah.[104] Yet people feared him and they knew that he had a power and an authority that was not his own. As he said in the end: "All power is given unto me in heaven and in earth."[105]

It was a power and an authority that came from the living God. And it came from the same authority and source that spoke to Moses in the burning bush: I AM THAT I AM.[106] We should learn to understand this and have faith in the great God-power that is in ourselves.

This is not a lie. It is Truth. We have a God-power in ourselves! And we have a Christ in ourselves.

What do men do with him? They crucify to themselves the Son of God afresh, and put him to an open shame.[107]

Jesus' Teaching on Sin, Karma, Reembodiment

You see, the crucifixion of Christ—had that been the means of wiping the slate clean—would have meant the end of sin. In other words, you've got a slate over here, and on it is written a word. It says "sin"—s-i-n. And it says, "You did it."

According to the teachings of most of the churches, Christ came along and by his death he put the eraser on that board and wiped it clean. And following this theory to its logical conclusion today, there shouldn't be any more sin. Of course, we know there is.

But that's exactly what they say it says in the Bible, but they don't really understand it. "He put that eraser on the board and erased it all," the pastor says, "because it says, 'As in Adam all die, even so in Christ shall all be made alive.'"[108]

But what does that really mean?

What it really means is that "if a man is made alive in Christ, he is a new creature. Old things are passed away; behold, all things are become new."[109] The man has to be quickened and reborn by being "in Christ" and *by Christ being in him.*

And that is a matter of sacrificing his old carnal nature to the living power of the regenerate God that is also within him. He's dual. Man is both demon and God. He's got to get rid of the demon and keep the God.

What is the demon? The demon in man is the personal demon that people have when they say, "I'll have this!" or "I'll have that! And nobody's going to stop me—not even God." Well, you know that isn't the way we should talk. That isn't the way we should be.

We need to figure out what our responsibilities are and what are God's. This is essential in any relationship, but nowhere more so than in our relationship with God.

For instance, God isn't going to come down

and pull a little child out of the fireplace. A little golden-haired babe is creeping into a red-hot fire. If the child reaches the fire, her hair'll be scorched, over 40 percent of her body will be burned, and she'll die. No angels materialize. No God materializes. If the parents put the child there and leave her in the room near the burning fire, God isn't going to interfere. Man has free will. This is Law. And the purpose of it is to teach man.

Somebody says, "Well, I can't remember that I was ever here on earth before. I don't remember my embodiments."

But your soul does.

You see, God is interested in preserving not the mystique of your physical body, with all of its paint and powder and mascara. God is interested in preserving the reality of your soul!

But, "the soul that sinneth, it shall die."[110] This, you recall, was the word of the LORD that came to the prophet Ezekiel. And it makes sense, as we have discussed, that if the freewill endowment has the potential for divine selfhood on the up side, then it has the prospect of the ultimate self-denial on the down side.

This the soul knows. And that's why the soul learns its lessons through the experiences we have, even if the outer mind doesn't catch on so quickly.

But people don't want to deal with the consequences of their actions. It's a stigma of the race. We want someone else to pick up the tab. And so we let the hirelings create a theology that suits our psychology of nonaccountability. But it's not biblical. The doctrine of vicarious atonement for sin through the crucifixion of Jesus Christ is simply not what Jesus taught.

It's not a matter of the body at all. It's a matter of preserving the soul. So the soul truly does know the law of karma as the LORD explained it to Ezekiel:

"The son shall not bear the iniquity [karma] of the father, neither shall the father bear the iniquity [karma] of the son: the righteousness [good works, i.e., good karma] of the righteous shall be upon him, and the wickedness [evil works, i.e., bad karma] of the wicked shall be upon him."[111]

I could write a book on karma and reincarnation as taught and experienced by the personages who move through the pages of the Old and New Testaments and the history books and the akashic records—and someday I shall, God willing, but for now I'll leave you to contemplate Jesus' own words to John the Beloved from the oft-quoted book of Revelation.

I am going to quote to you from chapter 22, which ends with the warning from Christ himself that if any man shall add unto the words of the prophecy of the book, God shall add unto him the plagues that are written in the book, and if any man shall take away its words, God shall take away his part out of the Book of Life and from the Holy City.[112]

Now, those interlopers who invaded the

Church early on have not only changed the meaning of this chapter 22, but they have also distorted the true image of Christ and of our Father and of their Divine Doctrine, which the scriptures and the prophets and the LORD and his Holy Spirit have declared to our hearts from pre-biblical history to the present hour.

Jesus' Teaching on the Judgment and Salvation

Hear, then, the message which Jesus Christ sealed for our edification and our salvation—with the penalty of spiritual death to any who would touch it:

> He that is unjust, let him be unjust still: and he which is filthy, let him be filthy still: and he that is righteous, let him be righteous still: and he that is holy, let him be holy still. [113]

The meaning of this pivotal text is parallel to the teaching of Ecclesiastes, "Where the tree falleth, there it shall lie." [114] Both tell us that at the hour of the Final Judgment we will be what we will be.

This Judgment takes place at the conclusion of individual cosmic cycles as well as at the conclusion of 2,000-year dispensations under the hierarchies of the Central Sun and at the turning of the *manvantaras* and *pralayas*. [115] It so happens that we are at the ending of just such a 2,000-year cycle called the age of Pisces, standing at the threshold of new beginnings in the next age called Aquarius, and we are experiencing new opportunity side by side with the old weight of personal and planetary karma which must be reckoned with.

We believe the Day of Vengeance of Our God prophesied by Isaiah[116] is the Final Judgment of many souls at the conclusion of this age, the Piscean. These are the lifestreams who have been around the longest (some of them having been reembodying on these planetary homes for several million years!) who are scheduled to graduate from earth's schoolroom—victoriously in the resurrection unto the Universal Christ and the ascension to the heart of the Father through the I AM Presence. Others, such as the unrelenting rebels against the Sons of God, must stand trial before the great white throne and the Four and Twenty Elders at the Court of the Sacred Fire.

This Jesus has told us, and this we have personally witnessed as the Lord has taken us—our souls in the etheric garment—to bear testimony before the Court at the trials of the seed of the Wicked One, who have never ceased to blaspheme God and his little ones since the day they turned away from the throne of grace.

The two types, or classifications, of souls who appear in the last day of the given karmic cycle are profiled in Daniel 12:

> And many of them that sleep in the dust of the earth shall awake, some to everlasting life, and some to shame and everlasting contempt.

And they that be wise shall shine as the brightness of the firmament; and they that turn many to righteousness as the stars for ever and ever. [117]

The Final Judgment, it must be understood, is distinguished from the judgment that takes place at the conclusion of each embodiment, which is conducted in the form of an inquiry into the actions of the soul and a review of her preceding life's record.

In this evaluation of your performance made in the presence of your Christ Self (your advocate before the Father) by a hierarch of Light—it could be the Ascended Master who sponsored you in that embodiment—you see how you did, you are told by the Lords of Karma what you left undone, what you must go back and do or redo, and what you accomplished of lasting worth for family, friends, nation and the planetary evolution. You are even shown films of your lifestream's highs and lows, so you can observe how others saw you, were blessed or cursed by you, and judge for yourself how you did on life's tests.

All of us are here today because we have unfinished business to take care of. Nevertheless, all of us should assume we are in the round of finishing up and that there is a strong possibility (because it's the end of the age) that we will be facing our final exams at the conclusion of this present life.

Even if we get an extension on our threescore and ten or we get to come back again, it's best to make the most of every day to balance our karma and serve to set all life free from theirs, so that in the next round, if indeed there need be another, we ourselves will be freer to be more the manifestation of who we really are in order to serve God better.

Thus the Day of Vengeance of Our God is the day of karmic reckoning when each soul is weighed in the scales of divine justice according to his cumulative record of all incarnations in the Matter spheres on the various planets and systems of worlds.

Following is Jesus' Teaching on the Final Judgment of the soul before his Maker. Those who plan on reembodying should take to heart that even the inquiry and review at the end of this life before the Lords of Karma can be a stiff initiation. And whatever you do today and tomorrow is determining your astrology and your karma, your health, your genes, and your family in your next life. Furthermore, the same Law which governs the Judgment in the ending applies to each concluding cycle of your embodiments along the way. And the penalties accrue and penance is assigned day by day and lifetime by lifetime.

It is our hope that you will be smart enough not to get stuck in the mud of your karmic cycles any longer, and that you'll stop making karma and start balancing it by the acceleration of the violet flame in your world. For your enlightenment by the Holy Spirit and your salvation in Christ we lovingly give you this Lost Teaching which the Lord Jesus has given to us for you:

> He that is unjust, let him be unjust still: and he which is filthy, let him be filthy still: and he that is righteous, let him be righteous still: and he that is holy, let him be holy still.

He that has been unjust in his dealings with God and Man, and in his exercise of free will, will be counted unjust before the Four and Twenty Elders at the Court of the Sacred Fire and before the great white throne; death itself will not produce a just man out of an unjust man. As the fruit ripens on the vine, so will it be in the harvest and so is the individual the sum of his word and his work.

According to the choices he has made, man is either unjust or filthy or righteous or holy. And so he shall stand as he is before the LORD God to give accounting for his exercise of free will in the opportunity of perhaps millions of years of soul evolution in this continuum of Matter.

And when he shall have concluded his own defense and reviewed the records of his deeds lifetime after lifetime shown to him by the Lords of Karma and the recording angels, the Lord Jesus Christ will pronounce before the Court:

> Behold, I come quickly; and my reward is with me, to give every man according as his work shall be.

Then the Lord and Saviour will identify himself as the Universal Christ—as the Word. From the beginning to the end of this cosmic cycle:

> I AM Alpha and Omega, the beginning and the end, the first and the last.[118]

Next comes the final word on who may and may not inherit eternal Life:

> Blessed are they that do his commandments, that they may have right to the Tree of Life and may enter in through the gates into the city.
>
> For without are dogs, and sorcerers, and whoremongers, and murderers, and idolaters, and whosoever loveth and maketh a lie.

These verses 14 and 15 of Revelation 22 are most revealing because they deny the doctrine of instantaneous salvation by the *profession* of Christ and confirm the doctrine of karmic accountability by *accession* unto divine Sonship.

Now, let me explain it to you. If it were possible for anyone to be saved on his deathbed by confessing Jesus Christ as his Saviour—when his life is spent, he's made his choices, and the opportunity to assimilate Godhood lifetime after lifetime is passed and the sands in the cosmic hourglass have run out—if it were possible for Jesus Christ to take unto himself all of our negative karma of millions of years, don't you think he would do so?

If the Father's law allowed it, undoubtedly our dearest Jesus would dissolve our sins on the instant.

But the fact is the Great Law does not allow it. Because, you see, that karma is also our cumulative self-awareness. It's what we are.

So if Jesus took the cosmic eraser and erased the record of millions of years (or even of one lifetime) of our sowings, he would also be erasing the consciousness that conceived it and carried it out—that's you or me—and there'd be nothing left of us to inherit the kingdom. Because the sinner and the sin are one; and the righteous soul and his righteousness are also one. Yes, we are the sum total of our words and our works, our thoughts and our feelings, our desires.

Now, you may say there's more to you than your karma and your free will, and that would be only partially true. It is true that God is in you and that God is your absolute Reality and that the Whole is greater than the sum of its parts, *but* until the soul is wed to this Light, until the soul receives the 'engrafted' Word[119] by the element of free will, you see, it cannot Self-realize itself (its inner divinity). It can only know itself as the lower self, which has taken the low road by choice.

Therefore the "dogs, sorcerers, whoremongers, murderers, idolaters, and whosoever loveth and maketh a lie" cannot be saved at the gate by the mere profession of Christ. They are what they are—homogenized, there's no cream to separate out. The sin and the sinner are one, stained through and through. From the inside to the outside, they vibrate the nature of their sin. They're the "saturated" or "supersaturated solution."[120] There is, in fact, nothing left that is salvageable; their freewill choices have permeated all of the substance they're made of.

Inasmuch as they have not taken the opportunity afforded for the accession unto divine Sonship, receiving and accepting the engrafted Word lifetime after lifetime, their Final Judgment and second death is predictable—as prophesied in Revelation.

This conclusion, stating the end of those with good karma and bad karma, is also inherent in Revelation 21:7, 8. Here again it is a man's works and not his profession of Christ or his prior favor that determines his destiny:

> He that overcometh [all things from beneath] shall inherit all things [from Above]; and I will be his God, and he shall be my son.
>
> But the fearful, and unbelieving, and the abominable, and murderers, and whoremongers, and sorcerers, and idolaters, and all liars shall have their part in the lake which burneth with fire and brimstone: which is the second death.

Take note that Jesus does not say anywhere that those who cry, "Lord, Lord," at the last minute will enter into the kingdom (consciousness) of heaven (the highest octaves of Light). But the Master does say those who *do* "the will of my Father" will have earned certain divine rights, the most notable being the "right to the Tree of Life."

He even says, as Matthew 7 records, that those who prophesy, cast out devils and do wonderful works all in his name will not enter in to Christ's dominion—unless they have the right spirit, and the pure heart and vibration.

The LORD requires the deep desiring of our hearts unto the glorification of God, enlivening and sanctifying our righteous deeds, else in the Day of Judgment, I the Witness and the Judge of the Quick and the Dead will profess:

"I never knew you: depart from me, ye that work iniquity!"[121]

This Doctrine of the Word and Work of the LORD—the LORD's mantle of responsibility, worn gladly, squarely on the shoulders of his best servants—is *the key* to salvation *today* in the Aquarian age.

Take note, ye false pastors who destroy and scatter the sheep of my pasture[122] with your false doctrine of nonaccountability in the blood of Christ, that Jesus' own doctrine, not yours, *is the doctrine of the law of karma!*

Yes, karma! defined as all cause/effect sequences we have set in motion in or on all worlds wheresoever we have been stationed by the Holy Spirit.

Karma: our word and our work—the means and the ends of all change we have effected for good or for ill.

Karma: our actions and the consequences thereof.

Karma: our life record, our personality, our attitude, how we relate to one another—our genes, our laughter, our jars full of jelly beans.

Karma: our raison d'être—our reason for being, living, loving, achieving, and ascending to God's heart.

Sowing and reaping the Lord's words and works on earth, engaging in his so-called 'Karma',* which is actually his burden of Light (since he is a karma-free being), we, his beloved, do enter into his consciousness, we do put on and become the Universal Mind that he also put on and became—by our right choice, our right calling, and our right comfort to all life.

Matthew 25 describes the scene of Christ's judgment of the nations when he shall sit upon the throne of his glory with all the holy angels with him.

> When the Son of man shall come in his glory, and all the holy angels with him, then shall he sit upon the throne of his glory:
>
> And before him shall be gathered all nations: and he shall separate them one from another, as a shepherd divideth his sheep from the goats: And he shall set the sheep on his right hand, but the goats on the left.
>
> Then shall the King say unto them on his right hand, Come, ye blessed of my

---

*In this case, because the Lord is the karma-free Piscean Avatar, we call his Word and Work the *Dharma*, which translates from the Sanskrit as the Teaching, the Path, the Duty to be God in action through engaging in the LORD'S Word and Work (see Book Three, page 275).

Father, inherit the kingdom prepared for you from the foundation of the world:

For I was an hungred, and ye gave me meat: I was thirsty, and ye gave me drink: I was a stranger, and ye took me in: Naked, and ye clothed me: I was sick, and ye visited me: I was in prison, and ye came unto me.

Then shall the righteous answer him, saying, Lord, when saw we thee an hungred, and fed thee? or thirsty, and gave thee drink?

When saw we thee a stranger, and took thee in? or naked, and clothed thee? Or when saw we thee sick, or in prison, and came unto thee?

And the King shall answer and say unto them, Verily I say unto you, Inasmuch as ye have done it unto one of the least of these my brethren, ye have done it unto me.

Then shall he say also unto them on the left hand, Depart from me, ye cursed, into everlasting fire, prepared for the devil and his angels:

For I was an hungred, and ye gave me no meat: I was thirsty, and ye gave me no drink: I was a stranger, and ye took me not in: naked, and ye clothed me not: sick, and in prison, and ye visited me not.

Then shall they also answer him, saying, Lord, when saw we thee an hungred, or athirst, or a stranger, or naked, or sick, or in prison, and did not minister unto thee?

Then shall he answer them, saying,
Verily I say unto you, Inasmuch as ye did
it not to one of the least of these, ye did it
not to me.

And these shall go away into everlasting punishment: but the righteous into Life
eternal.[123]

Once again, the criterion for entering into the
Life eternal is words and works: sharing the Lord's
burden—his Light/Energy/Consciousness in action
as our sowings and our reapings on earth.

And the reason that those who do charitable
deeds unto the "least of these my brethren" receive
the same reward as if they did them unto Jesus is
precisely because the same Christ is in the least as
is in the greatest of God's sons and daughters.
Because the Word is the Light which lighteth *every*
man-ifestation of God. Therefore are we the servants of this Universal Christ in all of God's
children.

Even so, my children, I gratefully bow to the
Light within you, and that's why I'm talking to
you—because I want to restore your relationship to
God based on the reality of your True Self and your
mission to embody the message of this Everlasting
Gospel of Jesus Christ.

So the Lord makes plain that doing God's
commandments, fulfilling his Law by becoming
the conscious embodiment of that Law, eating his
flesh and drinking his blood[124] in the spiritual

sense, is the prerequisite to having access to the fruit of the Tree of Life: We must first become and put on the garment we would wear.

In order to see him as he is in Reality, we must first be like him.[125] Through the golden-age consciousness we enter the gates to the heavenly city shining in the splendor of the Lamb's Light.

The Judgment Day is the Day of the Divine Bestowal to all who have elected to become the Real Self, who have forged and won their God Identity, overcoming all "things"* through the Word and Work of the LORD right down here in these 'decelerated', 'de-evolved', 'de-valued' veils of time and space.

It is written, "Every man shall bear his own burden."[126] And that means every manifestation of God must work out his own karma and carry the weight of his own destiny: "Work out your own salvation with fear and trembling."[127]

Thus Paul preached Christ's doctrine of balancing one's own karma to the Lord's followers at Philippi in Macedonia. For only by so doing, exercising right choice, *corrective choice*—righting the wrongs of the past by works and inward groanings and prayers and fastings—can he forge his individuality (work out his soul's elevation, i.e., *salvation*) unto God.

Jesus, the Son of man, in his Gethsemane,

---

*We now know that the term "things" takes in a lot, including the Atlantean conspiracy still with us and the entire collective unconscious of the race. These are the sorts of things that must be confronted by the one who would "inherit all things" from Above.

his hour of working out scientifically the problem of being—your being and mine—did, my beloved, sweat "as it were, great drops of blood" which fell to the ground.[128] Should we, then, his followers all the way to the cosmic cross of white fire and the Tree of Life, expect the initiations of our karma and our individualization of the God flame to be any less arduous?

Not if self-mastery through dominion over the elements of self and Selfhood be our goal. Not if the ascension is the Star of Hope we follow. Not if graduation from earth's schoolroom by the cosmic honor flame be the reward we seek. Surely not, if we're planning on being Ascended Masters in the world to come.

The unredeemed sinner has no identity in God, for he has created himself not after his image, but after the image of the Man of Sin.[129] Therefore Ezekiel was right on—he knew Christ's Truth from the Logos: The soul that sinneth, and sinneth without repentance and interior self-correction, it shall die the second death in the Day of Judgment. For negative karma without redeeming words and works is self-canceling. And the zero cancels itself out.

Nothing cannot suddenly become something: "He that is filthy, let him be filthy still..."

Jesus says that "every idle word that men shall speak, they shall give account thereof in the Day of Judgment. For by thy words thou shalt be justified, and by thy words thou shalt be condemned."[130]

I ask you, can the false pastors tell me where the Master says that the blood he would shed in the hour of his crucifixion would negate this inexorable law of karma?

Even the astute author of Hebrews upholds the Law of the Holy Ghost in this matter:

> It is impossible for those who were once enlightened, and have tasted of the heavenly gift, and were made partakers of the Holy Ghost,
>
> And have tasted the good word of God, and the powers of the world to come,
>
> If they shall fall away, to renew them again unto repentance; seeing they crucify to themselves the Son of God afresh, and put him to an open shame.
>
> For the earth which drinketh in the rain that cometh oft upon it, and bringeth forth herbs meet for them by whom it is dressed, receiveth blessing from God:
>
> But that which beareth thorns and briers is rejected, and is nigh unto cursing; whose end is to be burned. [131]

On the other hand, this scholar of Christ's calling teaches that the law of karma is just as faithful, just as diligent in seeing to it that the good is rewarded and furthermore that by good works the saints work out their salvation and inherit the promises:

But, beloved, we are persuaded better things of you, and things that accompany salvation, though we thus speak.

For God is not unrighteous to forget your work and labour of love, which ye have shewed toward his name, in that ye have ministered to the saints, and do minister.

And we desire that every one of you do shew the same diligence to the full assurance of hope unto the end:

That ye be not slothful, but followers of them who through faith and patience inherit the promises. [132]

The Master told John the Revelator that in the Last Judgment the dead would be judged "every man according to their works." He said, "Death and Hell [and all who embody the consciousness thereof] were cast into the lake of fire. This is the second death." [133]

The lake of fire is a vortex of sacred fire, the all-consuming sacred fire of God which consumes on contact the cause, effect, record, and memory of the souls, together with their karma, who have not availed themselves of the continuing opportunity to glorify God in their body and in their spirit.

Yes, beloved, if it were possible, even these would be saved, but they themselves have not willed it so; therefore God cannot will it so, for in so doing for one, he would be abrogating his covenant of free will for all.

Yet, in the face of this clearly written Truth,

Jesus must still rebuke the hypocritical scribes and Pharisees who, as Isaiah said before him, still worship him, the true incarnation of the Universal Christ, in vain, "teaching for doctrines the commandments of men."[134] And so it is the case today in the churches called Christian. But his Word will outlast the leaven of the Pharisees still being mouthed in the temples and mosques and sanctuaries of Abraham's seed.

Inasmuch as the Bible in its unfoldment of the mysteries of God under his progressive dispensations through the words and works of the LORD's emissaries is perceived to be self-contradictory, those seeking to prove their doctrine of favoritism or nonaccountability on the basis of "we are the chosen" or "we are the saved" seem to have no difficulty, as they omit the *weightier* matters of the Law (karma can get pretty heavy when you're preaching on the wrong side of the Law), in wresting the scriptures to their own destruction[135] and to the intended destruction of God's children.

You can read for yourself Matthew 23 to hear Jesus' judgment of the false pastors which we ratify today in his name. His concluding invective tells them what they already know and tells us what they have cleverly concealed from their flocks these many thousands of years:

> Ye serpents, ye generation of vipers, how can ye escape the damnation of hell?
> Wherefore, behold, I send unto you

prophets, and wise men, and scribes: and some of them ye shall kill and crucify; and some of them shall ye scourge in your synagogues, and persecute them from city to city:

That upon you may come all the righteous blood shed upon the earth, from the blood of righteous Abel unto the blood of Zacharias son of Barachias, whom ye slew between the temple and the altar.

Verily I say unto you, All these things shall come upon this generation [the genetic descendants of the fallen angels who have continued their wickedness unto the present through the planetary network of their false hierarchy]. [136]

Jesus wanted us to know what they could no longer keep a secret: That the false pastors in every generation are of the original bands of fallen angels who invaded the Church and befrocked themselves with stolen robes—that they are a generation of devils who have branched out into every field, destroying the Lord's harvests through his own, and that they will not escape the second death in the Last Judgment.

Meanwhile, beloved, "Go ye not after them," [137] but with Mary of Bethany sit still in the house of Truth, [138] meditating in the secret chamber of the heart, and wait for the coming of your Bridegroom. With the woman (was she Magda?) go and find him and wash his feet with tears of repentance and anoint his feet with an ointment that in his Love thy sins may be forgiven. [139]

Salvation through the Everlasting Gospel

In conclusion, Jesus preaches his doctrine of salvation based on sacrificial works—unceasing and untiring selfless service unto the fulfillment of the Lord's *Dharma*. This was *his* prescription for being saved.

The disciples were astonished when he told them, "It is easier for a camel to go through the eye of a needle than for a rich man to enter into the kingdom of God."

And they looked at each other and they shrugged their shoulders and they said, "Who, then, can be saved?"

Jesus then revealed that it is impossible for generic man, Homo sapiens, to save himself, "but not with God: for with God all things are possible." [140] Again, not the dead but the quick, alive with the "flaming Flame that shall not be quenched," [141] carry with them the threefold-flame potential for salvation.

Yes, beloved, these are able to meet the real requirements for salvation taught by Jesus himself, not by the do-it-yourself-kit pastors, who call you to the altar down that old sawdust trail and guarantee that if you confess the Lord Jesus Christ you will be saved from all your karma from here to eternity. The Lord said:

There is no man that hath left house, or brethren, or sisters, or father, or mother, or wife, or children, or lands, for my sake, and the gospel's,

But he shall receive an hundredfold now in this time, houses, and brethren, and sisters, and mothers, and children, and lands, with persecutions; and in the world to come eternal Life.

But many that are first shall be last; and the last first.[142]

This is the calling and the credentials of the true disciples of the Ascended Master Jesus Christ. So, if you're tough and ready for sacrifices and the Lord's abundant return on all you give, if you're tough and ready for persecutions and the path of self-mastery unto Love's victory that will come by them, if you long to take the vow of poverty, chastity and obedience along with that of the defense of Mother Church, becoming the servant of all, then take it straight—take Jesus' own doctrine as Brother Francis and Sister Clare did, and know with them that because you did at least one voice besides your own will hear and understand.

The New England bard and scribe of the immortals yet in our midst, Henry Wadsworth Longfellow, gave us Love's key to the heart of Francis and his Lord. Let's take a moment to meditate on the heart of his sermon together:

The Sermon of St. Francis

Up soared the lark into the air,
A shaft of song, a wingèd prayer,
As if a soul released from pain
Were flying back to heaven again.

St. Francis heard: it was to him
An emblem of the Seraphim;
The upward motion of the fire,
The light, the heat, the heart's desire.

Around Assisi's convent gate
The birds, God's poor who cannot wait,
From moor and mere and darksome wood
Come flocking for their dole of food.

"O brother birds," St. Francis said,
"Ye come to me and ask for bread,
But not with bread alone to-day
Shall ye be fed and sent away.

"Ye shall be fed, ye happy birds,
With manna of celestial words;
Not mine, though mine they seem to be,
Not mine, though they be spoken
    through me.

"Oh, doubly are ye bound to praise
The great Creator in your lays;
He giveth you your plumes of down,
Your crimson hoods, your cloaks of brown.

"He giveth you your wings to fly
And breathe a purer air on high,
And careth for you everywhere,
Who for yourselves so little care!"

With flutter of swift wings and songs
Together rose the feathered throngs,
And singing scattered far apart;
Deep peace was in St. Francis' heart.

He knew not if the brotherhood
His homily had understood;
He only knew that to one ear
The meaning of his words was clear.

Our words to you are the Everlasting Gospel
of Jesus Christ and our greatest desire is that to one
ear—your own—their meaning will be clear. For it
is the true Gospel he gave to us for you, beloved.

For the cause of Truth he came into this
world and to this day he thus denounces the
false witnesses and defends the true—for thee, for
thee alone.

From the vantage of the mountain of God
where all is One and the Law of Love resolves the
inconsistencies of the valley, there are no contra-
dictions—not in the psychology of our soul all-
one, not in the complete and unadulterated Lost
Teaching of Jesus.

Let us understand, then, that we can be
washed and purified by Christ, we can be immersed

in the violet flame baptismal fount, receive forgiveness for sin and our karmic past; and our burdens can become Light by universal transmutation.

Yes, all of this can come to you. But it'll be God's way, and you'll have to play your part—among the multitudes, truly feeding the sheep, healing the sick, ministering to the poor, the rich, the exalted and the debased. And you'll do a lot of fasting and praying, self-examination and self-purification with powerful decree work—and work it shall be—in the Sanctuary of the Holy Grail and in the secret chamber of your heart.

And you'll come full circle and you'll understand that the sacrifice of Christ is that "my Body was broken for you." That's the "Cosmic Communion." Well, it is already self-evident in the fact that there's a Holy Christ Self for everybody. And so the Body of the Universal Christ is broken. And one day when "they shall all know Me, from the least of them unto the greatest of them, saith the LORD,"[143] it'll all come together again in a unity of purpose. And all the godly will begin to live and love together in one universal harmony and be as God wants them to be.

And what's more, they'll recognize one another as such—not as members of this or that church or country club or elite corps, but as communicants of the LORD's Light gathered together in a great company before the throne in heaven as on earth (for the twain shall be one), saying "Alleluia! Salvation, and glory, and honour, and power, unto the LORD our God: For true and righteous are his judgments."[144]

Let me tell you something. At that moment, all of the beautiful creative acts of Elohim who created universes without end and shining stars and spiral nebulae and little streamers of light and even asteroids in space will come into focus in Man. Because Man now self-realized as the Son of man will suddenly begin to understand that there's a plan behind the whole works.

And that plan is so beautiful and so lovely and so involved with us right now that we don't have to wait. We don't have to wait till tomorrow. It works right now today.

People can be healed. They can be sealed. They can be enlightened. They can be lifted up. They can be brought into happiness and joy and the character of God just by a thought—God's Thought: just by a word—God's Word.

Because God's Thought and God's Word is a powerful seed of Light planted within every man. You can have that, you can be that, and you *are* that.

Now rest in that giant Faith.

Chapter Thirteen

THE VIOLET FLAME FOR GOD-REALIZATION

The Violet Flame for God-Realization

It must be realized by all that no man at any time, even in the sleep state, ceases to create. If he does nothing more than sit with his mind disengaged even from a sense of reality, whiling away the hours, boring himself without concentrating constructively on anything, he is still creating.

People do this. They radiate boredom into the universe.

Millions of schoolchildren all over the world are thinking of summer vacation. They hear the hum of the bees. They see the streams and new green meadows and they want to roam the hills, and in their minds they are through with their lessons for the year. So their minds, no longer thinking of anything in particular, lazily drift out the window, daydreaming and wandering in the channels of willy-nilly thought.

People do not realize that they have the stream of God's energy pouring down through the top of their heads every minute—even when they're sleeping, otherwise their heart would stop.

And so this energy of idleness and daydreaming becomes an activity which is purposeless. It has no purpose, but it consumes energy and it becomes like a flytrap. It catches other people in its nets and they, too, begin to put their minds in what we have called "idle gear."

Of course, to disengage oneself from the tensions and responsibilities of the daily routine and to consciously allow the inner mind to take over while the outer mind is at rest and restoring itself is a necessary re-creative ritual. This may occur when the mind and body are spent for the day and one is falling asleep—or in a more controlled approach to meditation.

But I would point out that in the waking state it is not healthy constantly to indulge in reverie; it can even be a dangerous thing, a means of escape from the lever of decision and the shuttle of conscious self-determination in which we must engage our forces—not only to be a winner in life, but to interact meaningfully with the Godhead and with our friends and neighbors.

Alas, such idle reverie, while avoiding the tests of the hours, thus wasting the measured beat of life's opportunity, tends to remove the soul from its centeredness in the divine prerogative to be— and to be conscious.

Thus, let us beware of undisciplined mental states that breed spiritual stagnation and mental stultification when we are not exercising our God-given authority over the domain of the mind—our greatest endowment, our potential for unlimited creativity.

Centeredness in the Mind of God is the mark of the true Master of Wisdom and when such attainment is balanced by integration in the fiery heart of Love, the force of masterful, compassionate action follows. This is the difference between the God-oriented and the humanly distracted (and distracting) individuals who allow themselves to be the victims of life. They're the victims of mass thoughts, of mass entities, of mass demons: they do not understand the disciplines of concentration on the Law of the One that are ultimately necessary in order to achieve God-mastery, physically, mentally and spiritually—which disciplines are taught in the retreats of the Great White Brotherhood.

Achievement is the natural estate of man, who can, if he will, assume authority over his world and over himself. But it takes finding your center and then staying on course when confronted by aggressive mind-suggestions that come to disturb your meditation on Light and on Light's achievement of God-realization within you. Recognizing this, let us understand the role that is played by the Seventh Ray, the violet ray, which was released by God as the highest aspect of Light.

The Alchemy of the Violet Flame

As we all know, if we take a prism and hold it up to the sun, directing the refracted light upon a screen, we see the breakdown of the white light into the primary and secondary colors appearing as a vibrant rainbow playing upon the screen. Sometimes the play of sunshine through a crystal chandelier or a gemstone will cover a wall with myriad dancing threefold flames of ardent primary fire. Or the ruby, gold, apricot, and deep sapphire blues will suddenly bring to focus the amethyst, emerald, aquamarine, and purple—depending on the cut of the crystal.

Now, as you know, the highest color that can be seen in any rainbow display is the violet. And if you've ever studied the gorgeous double rainbows that have appeared over our retreat and in the Rocky Mountains, you've noted that the violet seems to trail off into infinity as though there were more to the rainbow than meets the physical-eye spectrum. And this is in fact so.

The violet disappears into a higher frequency violet ray akin to the light of the Seventh Ray and dispensation, the wavelength of Aquarius. And that power, mathematically speaking, is comparable to the number nine, the highest numerical aspect, having almost infinite transformations with its magical formulas, as mathematicians and numerologists know.

So we begin to take note of what the ancient alchemists understood as the power of the Three—and the Three-times-Three—the Trinity of spirit, body and soul in the microcosm of man corresponding to, and being multiplied by, the Trinity of Father, Son and Holy Spirit in the Macrocosm of God.

According to Saint Germain, the early alchemists who were initiates of the Great White Brotherhood through guilds, secret societies and mystery schools knew that they were dealing with the power of the Trinity times the Trinity, as Above so below, symbolized in the six-pointed star of David.

In their experiments they sought to imitate the works of Christ, their guiding light being the mystic mason himself, Saint Germain, who for tens of thousands of years, and more recently in a series of embodiments from the Prophet Samuel to Francis Bacon, has been the all-pervasive mind, laying the empirical foundation for the Enlightenment, pushing back the barriers of limitation in the physical and spiritual sciences.

Well before he as the Wonderman of Europe outpictured the quintessence of the alchemists' dream for all to see, Saint Germain was directing and inspiring devotees of the sacred science in his life as Roger Bacon—medieval philosopher, educational reformer and harbinger of modern science. Renowned for his investigations into alchemy, optics, mathematics and languages, he earned the title Doctor Mirabalis ("wonderful teacher") and a reputation as a wonder worker.

The miracles of Jesus and the feats of Saint Germain (who also had close ties to the sixteenth-century Swiss alchemist Paracelsus) represented to these alchemists a standard of spiritual and scientific adeptship which they felt called to emulate. As forerunners of Francis Bacon's Seventh Ray science, they communed with elemental life and took their first steps in alchemy through concentrating on the mastery of earth, water, air, fire and ether by the threefold flame of the heart.

These practitioners of the 'All-Chemistry' of God were indeed 'wholistic' in their approach as they meditated on the principles of cosmic law as well as the mysteries behind such demonstrations as turning the water into wine, multiplying the loaves and fishes, healing body and mind, raising the dead, techniques of regeneration (by herbal formulas and other means), perfecting the elixir of life, changing base metals into gold, or simply repairing the flaws in gemstones.

For them alchemy was a means to an end—the spiritualization of Matter, whose accomplishment would signify that, as Above so below, they had entered the mind of the Great Alchemist who had created both the physical and spiritual universes. Their successes were far greater than the moderns credit them with, but their goal was beyond the reach of today's avant-garde in the academies of science. They sought nothing less than the self-realization of the inner man of the heart and the perfecting of the physical matrix according to the Divine Image. Their desire was to achieve immortality in the footsteps of Christ through the control of physical and spiritual forces.

They were the keepers of the flame of the science of the spoken Word and the religion of the sacred fire which had been practiced on Lemuria and Atlantis prior to their decline and in previous golden ages when the life and evolutions of planet earth were less physical. Their vision was one of the union of science and religion.

Following the example of the master alchemists Jesus Christ and Saint Germain, they actually exceeded in some areas the most advanced accomplishments of twentieth-century science. And when they shall have synthesized its developments with their own inner attainment, these very lifestreams, reincarnated, shall be the ones to bring forth from the Cave of Symbols, Saint Germain's etheric/physical retreat in Wyoming, those inventions and discoveries presently being guarded for the future benefit of mankind.

This technology of the Aquarian age Saint Germain has said he would release when the nations shall have put behind them the destructive uses of science and religion to accept the challenge which lies at the heart of both—to enter the secret chamber of the heart and the nucleus of the atom and to harness therefrom the unlimited spiritual/physical resources to establish the golden age.

The alchemists' sacred key is the violet flame. This is the gift of Jesus Christ and Saint Germain whereby man can approach the Holy of Holies, the sacred fire behind all manifestation—the inner cause, noumenon, behind the spiritual and physical phenomenon. The application of the violet flame in daily usage and in the exercise of the authoritative power of the spoken Word is the means to reestablishing contact with the eternal flame and its harnessing for man's fulfillment of his fiery destiny, hence his return to the plane of causation.

The violet flame is the missing ingredient without which the mason is not able to perfect the thirty-three degrees of initiation. It is the flame that endows all physical achievement with the unity of purpose, fusing the visible and invisible worlds. All of this history of the alchemists on the Path is a part of the violet spectrum and the quality of universal transmutation associated with the Seventh Ray of which, step by step, you, too, must strive to become the master.

We know of no better course of instruction for your achievement of God-realization through the violet flame than Saint Germain's collected works on alchemy. These we must one day assemble as the foundation of a major course on freedom at the Ascended Masters' University. Meanwhile, our pocketbook *Saint Germain On Alchemy* is the stone not to be rejected by the student striving for the attainable goal of adeptship in the Aquarian age.

Truly, among the brothers of the White Lodge, there is no higher authority on the rituals of the violet flame for the soul liberation of a planet than the beloved Seventh-Ray Hierarch who comes to us in the tradition of Melchizedek, a priest of the sacred fire serving humanity at the altar of science and religion in their rituals of the internalization of the God flame of freedom.

In his "Trilogy On the Threefold Flame: The Alchemy of Power, Wisdom and Love," published in *Saint Germain On Alchemy*, Saint Germain meticulously sets forth the concept of the Trinity, so essential to the alchemist.

From this study we move to the understanding that the action of the violet light and the violet flame is comparable to the action of Lord Shiva in the Brahma/Vishnu/Shiva panoply. It is comparable to the Third Person of the Trinity, East or West—the Holy Spirit being the multiplier of the Father and the Son in the temple of man. The Holy Spirit acts as the divine magnet to magnetize the Eternal Feminine, the Shakti, who then releases the power of the Masculine Tri-unity out of the Spirit cosmos into the Matter cosmos. So too, your raising up of the Mother flame within the chakras will accelerate the release of the violet flame from your causal body into your four lower bodies.

Purification and the Trial by Fire

The Holy Spirit in the Person of the Great Initiator of our souls—the Comforter, the Counsellor, the Advocate—delivers God's baptism to you by Jesus Christ *"with sacred fire"*—"whose [winnowing-]fan is in his hand," preached John the Baptist, his messenger, "and he will throughly purge his [threshing-]floor and gather his wheat [the seed of Light] into the garner [barn]; but he will burn up the chaff [the debris of Darkness] with unquenchable fire."[1]

When the disciple of the Holy Spirit invokes the LORD's fiery baptism—an initiation which must come to all who would establish dominion on earth in the four planes and elements as well as in the heaven world—it is the violet flame aspect of the sacred fire that separates the chaff (the negatively misqualified energy) from the wheat (positively qualified words and works blessing lifestreams and glorifying the Life-Principle) and consumes it in the floor of consciousness—gathering the good wheat and sealing it in the individual's heavenly storehouse, or causal body.

Who amongst us dares to say that we require no purification? Who amongst us dares to say that we are masters of our world? If we are beset with such assumptions, believing them to be true, then we should also tell ourselves that we should not be here. We shouldn't be in this world at all, for there are many better places than this world that exist and if we are masters, we ought to be there—because by our achievement of God-realization we should have readied ourselves for those masterful conditions.

Jesus pointedly made us aware of our limited state when he said, "Which of you by taking thought can add one cubit unto his stature?"[2]

And then he gave the simple solution to the human condition: "*Seek ye first the kingdom* [consciousness] *of God and his righteousness* [the scientific application of the Universal Law to the mastery of self in time and space], *and all these things* [achievements] *shall be added* [multiplied by the alchemy of the Holy Ghost] *unto you.*"[3]

Elizabeth and I have never ceased to bear witness to the reality of this promise in our lives. Putting God first in the raising up of his consciousness and his law, scientifically applied in his Word and Work, we have found that every goal of our lives, physical and spiritual, has always been achieved, by his grace.

Now, if we didn't need refinement of soul and mind and the purification of our hearts and the cleansing of our four lower bodies as a prerequisite to our achievement of God's consciousness, then why would Malachi have given the LORD's prophecy of a messenger who will come "like a refiner's fire and like fullers' soap" to "purify" and "purge" the sons of Levi?[4]

The *spiritual* descendants of the original Levites who did not pollute and profane the altar or the table of the LORD[5] are the inheritors of the priestly office tending the eternal flame of the Holy of Holies. And are we not also keepers of the flame of Life—of liberty and of freedom? In Aquarius every male and female initiate under the Great White Brotherhood must stand before the altar of his God, a true Levite, sanctified for his Seventh Ray calling to be the bearer of the threefold flame of individual Christhood on behalf of them that worship in the temple of God[6] on each of the seven rays.

Taking first steps first, then, the very fact that we are here on planet earth—a schoolroom for the many who, for one reason or another, haven't made it into the next dimension—indicates that we are to be placed in the role of either teacher or pupil—if not teacher, then certainly pupil, one of the two. In one sense, in the totality of our lives, we are all pupils and all teachers at the same time.

By the initiations of the Seventh Ray we fulfill both roles and mount the ladder of attainment, bringing with us all who are beneath us on that initiatic ladder as we accelerate with all who are above us. Without the Seventh Ray Masters and the Seventh Ray order of transmutation of our karma and the world weight thereof, we would not, could not, enjoy the freedom to master the stairs of the degrees.

Furthermore, our freedom to create and to be creative and to teach others to do likewise, even as we imitate our Seventh Ray mentors both with us in the flesh and beyond the veil, is entirely dependent upon our saturation in the violet light, the violet ray, and the violet flame!

And so, when invoked, the violet ray descends from the heart of God through the I AM Presence, becoming in the plane of invocation and in heart of the devotee the violet transmuting flame—while the violet light is the by-product in Spirit and Matter of the action of both the violet ray and the violet flame, even as sunlight is the by-product of fusion in the physical sun.

This violet flame is the key ingredient of the trial by fire[7] that must precede the fiery baptism of the LORD taught in scripture. Whenever it is invoked regularly with intense devotion, this violet fire as the agency of the Holy Spirit consumes the nonproductive, negative records of past lives, balancing karma, blessing all parties to each specific karmic equation. It forgives sin by erasing cause, effect, record, and memory of the offense, the offender, and the offended.

But each one so involved in an act of sin must forgive the other(s) and himself; for the violet flame will not free the nonforgiving party. You need only invoke it to find out for yourself that in all ways the violet flame produces the alchemy of both spiritual and physical transformation as well as healing and resolution to all parties to an altercation.

Now, we all have a formation of certain atomic and molecular structures and substructures in our four lower bodies and in our thought processes, which comprise the building blocks of individual identity. These blocks—which are geometrical in form, like the tetrahedron, the hexahedron, the octahedron, the dodecahedron, and the icosahedron—are merely manifestations that duplicate and arrange themselves according to some composite pattern. This pattern, preordained from the Divine Image in the etheric blueprint and mirrored cell by cell in your individual lifestream, is unique to you and your twin flame.

These structures that are both etheric and physical, spanning the spectra of light and matter through the four dimensions and beyond, are geometric vessels, if you will, chalices of crystals formed of organic matter and spiritual light, bio-chemical in one phase of their functioning yet transcending all physicality in another. Though he knows it not, man is a physical/spiritual being in form.

You, then, the alchemist of the Seventh Ray, apprenticing yourself to the angels of Lord Zadkiel, who are your tutors in the science of Spirit/Matter transformation, must come to know yourself as a conductor of Seventh Ray energy to the physical universe. You must see yourself as a sun center of violet flame blazing—consisting of billions of microscopic flame-flowers leaping and dancing from the nucleus of every atom and cell—creating sine waves of dazzling emanations, charging your soul and spirit and mind, that of your families, neighbors, friends and communities, with the power and the will to be free!

The invisible geometry of man and womb-man—the veritable grid of light that forms the wedding garment, silhouetting the soul veiled in her etheric body—is the forcefield you can build upon even today to weave your Deathless Solar Body and to begin to imitate in smallest measure, and then greater, the alchemical feats of the Count Saint Germain, the Wonderman of Europe.

When we understand that man is involved in a living alchemy, that he is constantly in a state of flux, or change, we realize that change can be either the change of notion—n-o-t-i-o-n, just notion—or it can be what we call the "directed change."

We realize that all change is ultimately subject to free will, to consent or nonconsent to the principle of Life. This takes place at conscious, subconscious, and superconscious levels of man's being. However, without the geometry of Being, which is God, neither controlled change nor the trial by fire could take place. Seek and ye *shall* find, for the kingdom (consciousness) of the Seventh Ray is verily within you.[8]

Aladdin's Magic Lamp

Today most people who are at all interested in understanding themselves on the spiritual path recognize that they have to give some sense of direction to these powers-that-be at work in their 'members' through the creative Word that is released according to their 'numbers'.

Now, keeping the mysteries of the Seventh Ray in mind, suppose that God—or a Master or a beggar—handed you Aladdin's magic lamp in this very moment and said, "Rub the lamp and the genie will appear, and when he does, tell the genie what to do and he will do it." Well, would you tell the genie what to do? Or would you just say to the genie, "Do whatever you want to do"?

Remember when you were a child and someone told you the story of Aladdin and his lamp—and how a clever magician disguised as a merchant went through the streets hawking, "New lamps for old!

New lamps for old!" and how Aladdin's wife fool-
ishly traded his old lamp for a new and shinier one?

About that time you probably thought that
the most wonderful thing you could have in the
whole world would be Aladdin's magic lamp and a
genie—all yours and only yours to command. Why,
you'd be the envy of the neighborhood, you'd lead a
charmed life forever!

Well, the fact is, you do have a magic lamp—
it's your great, great, great, great Grandfather Abe's
"burning lamp"!⁹ It's the flame of God burning on
the altar of your heart, and when you 'rub it' with
devotion and faith in anticipation of the appearance
of the Lord in glory,¹⁰ suddenly he comes into
your temple.

Your Christ Self is the directing intelligence
of the genie of your mind! He's the Magician that
is a real Magus, and like Aaron, his divine magic
will outdo all the magicians at Pharaoh's court.¹¹

Yes, your genie (the lower mental body) is
there to carry out the genius of your own higher
intelligence, ready to go into action at your command. Left to itself, this genie does not have the
discriminating intelligence of your Christ Self. It
must be told what to do, trained and disciplined, or
else it may get into mischief, like when you let it
idle or daydream.

So you do have to tell your genie what to
do. You do have to make your mind the obedient
"slave" of your Christ Self, who tends the threefold
flame of your 'magic lamp'. Thus, by your spirit's

leave—your free will which it is the prerogative of your soul to exercise—your Real Self holds in tow, subject to the law of the I AM Presence, the genie of your mind. It sees to it that it will perform only those scientific feats of God-control over natural forces which are consistent with your divine plan *and* the constructive Good of all life.

The story of Aladdin teaches two important lessons for our mastery of the Seventh Ray. First, that there must be a conscious and conscientious direction of the individual life of man—by himself through the guiding force of his Higher Consciousness, akin to God. And second, that the gifts of free will and the genie demand a daily, carefully considered exercise of choice.

For, whatever we choose, powerful forces at our disposal (some subconscious, some superconscious) move to fulfill our demands upon life. If we submit our desires to the sifting of the eternal Logos (the Universal Christ individualized in our own Christ Self), we will be protected from the folly of idle wishes working idle wishcraft upon others with an ensuing weight of karma.

But if we bypass the Christ, who stands at the Door of Higher Consciousness—"the open Door which no man can shut"[12]—seeking to gain access to cosmic forces by climbing up some other (unlawful) way or means, we become a thief and a robber[13] of God's power with full karmic accountability for our actions and their consequences to every part of Life.

Thus, the Universal Christ spoke through Jesus and said I AM the Door[14]—I AM the Way, the Truth, and the Life; no man or woman cometh (lawfully) to the Father (gaineth lawful access to his power) but by me.[15]

This Universal Christ (individualized in the Master Jesus and in your Holy Christ Self) is therefore your Saviour from all misguided deeds (i.e., sin)—past, present, and future. *If* you subject your life and soul, mind and will, your whole heart and desire to the Law of the Logos and apply the violet flame to every unfortunate, unlawful misuse of God's Light on record in your book of life, the same Universal Christ will work with you and through you for the universal freedom of this world—and your own.

I trust you are beginning to see that in order to spiritually survive this world and gain entrance into the next, you must know the whence, how, and whither of your lifestream; and if you do not, you must know that a higher power does—even your Higher Consciousness, who is your Christ Self—and have the good sense to apprentice yourself to this Person of the Godhead.

Finally, you must understand that the means to this goal of self-transcendence through Jesus is the discovery of the Master's Lost Teachings on the violet flame and the Seventh Ray. This is the science and the ritual of the Melchizedekian priesthood, perverted to this hour by false priests in science and religion.

In the Temple of Purification now on the etheric plane over the island of Cuba, Archangel Zadkiel and his complement, the archeia Holy Amethyst, trained initiates in the priestly offices of the Seventh Ray. Both Melchizedek and Saint Germain studied here in the physical retreat prior to the sinking of Atlantis when the focus of the violet flame was also withdrawn to the etheric plane and temple. Under the tutelage of Lord Zadkiel, the Chohan of the Seventh Ray perfected the science of longevity which he demonstrated in his elixir of youth as the Wonderman of Europe.

All who serve as representatives of the Great White Brotherhood in the world religions officiating at the altar of God who are also willing initiates of the sacred fire are received by these hierarchs of the Seventh Ray at inner levels to be God-taught for temple service. They are shown the synthesis of science and religion at the altar of the sacred fire, for the Law requires that the one who stands as high priest representing the people before the Holy of Holies must have attainment in the sacred science of alchemy equal to that of his demonstrable mastery of the precepts of religious doctrine.

Thus when a priest of the Order of Lord Zadkiel breaks bread and blesses the wine, as did both Melchizedek and Jesus, there flows through his hands, his heart and third-eye chakra the violet ray for the alchemical transmutation of substance. This alchemy of the Word is known as transubstantiation.

Jesus was an adept of this priesthood, which is why it was pronounced upon him during a certain initiation not recorded in scripture, for it took place in Zadkiel's retreat: "Thou art a priest forever after the Order of Melchizedek."

Jesus used the violet flame in the performance of spiritually scientific and physically alchemical miracles. It is the Master's greatest desire to bring this knowledge of the sacred science to his twentieth-century disciples and saints from all ages and religions who have reembodied for the sole purpose of mastering the Seventh Ray and making their ascension with their twin flame in the Aquarian age.

Ask God What You Ought to Pray For

Because of our incomplete self-knowledge, beloved Jesus pointed out to me that we should ask God to teach us what things we ought to pray for. We need to know who we really are, what we ought to have, and what means are available and lawful in attaining our goals. And I have found great value in consulting the Higher Consciousness in this.

I was amazed one time to find out how little I really knew about what I ought to pray for. This was part of my own training by the Masters. I said, "Well, I ought to pray for good health." Yes, that sounded alright. "I ought to pray for supply so that I will be able to do God's will to a greater extent." Yes, that's good. But then when you come to the point of achieving true spirituality, that's the rub.

Very few people really understand what specific

things they ought to ask for, even when they are blessed with an extraordinary light. It's really something to think about—the idea that you could have access to all of God's power and still not know just exactly how God would want you to use it.

So in order to know what we ought to have and what we ought to pray for, we must study cosmic law—God's promises, his covenants (binding contracts) made between himself and his children, who were given the divine spark in order that they might earn the spiritual right to be joint-heirs with Christ of the divine Sonship.[16]

Paul likewise wrote to the Romans (as we have read in connection with our discussion of duality) concerning Christ's indwelling Spirit, whom he acknowledged as our Intercessor in prayer:

"The Spirit also helpeth our infirmities. For we know not what we should pray for as we ought, but the Spirit itself maketh intercession for us with groanings which cannot be uttered. And he that searcheth the hearts knoweth what is the mind of the Spirit, because he maketh intercession for the saints according to the will of God. . . . It is Christ. . . who is even at the right hand of God, who also maketh intercession for us."[17]

And so, being called according to his purpose, foreknown of him, predestined to be conformed to the Image of the Son—called, justified, glorified, as Paul taught the non-Jews of Rome—we must also avow, "If God be for us, who can be against us?"[18]

For all these reasons set forth by Christ's apostles and in his personal witness to us today, we are compelled to invoke the violet flame's transmuting action to clear from our worlds all these notions of our nonimportance and all this idleness of mind that says it doesn't matter whether I focus my mind or not, because what I think or don't think doesn't affect anybody anyway.

These states come from our nonawareness of the indwelling Intercessor and the Image of the Son. What we are and do is of supreme importance because the prophesied Immanuel[19] is God with us and in us.

Let us know that God made us to be co-creators with him. And if that wasn't enough, he gave us free will to be, to think, to declare "I AM" and to act in his name. This self-knowledge alone must impel us to call to God inwardly and to make the inner determination—an agreement together in Christ Jesus[20]—that we are going to be vested with the garment of understanding and we are going to know by the Holy Spirit how to be about our Father's business.

The author of Proverbs, perhaps Solomon himself, tells us, "Wisdom is the principal thing; therefore get wisdom: and with all thy getting get understanding."[21] And he didn't say that because it wasn't important. He said it because it was important.

Do you remember the story of the woman who was given three wishes? The first thing she wished for was a million dollars. And almost immediately they came from the mill where her husband worked to tell her that he had had a terrible accident and had been killed and that the insurance policy that he carried was coming due and she would receive a million dollars. So she had one of her three wishes fulfilled.

Then she had two more. The first thing on her mind was the terrible tragedy that had befallen her, so she wished her husband alive again, thus taking up the second wish. Within the hour she heard his footsteps on the porch as he was coming toward the door; immediately she wished him back in his grave, using up the third wish.

The woman was frightened by the power of the three wishes.

And so, not knowing what to ask for can prove to be very critical. We ought to give a good deal of thought to this. Not that we try to solve it by thought, but by prayer, by the Lord's intercession, and by the recognition that what is of supreme importance to us in life is God.

I don't think it should be too hard to figure out where to begin. Just look to the greatest needs and burdens—both physical and spiritual in your family situations and personal relationships.

You can take a piece of paper and write down some of your problems, consecrate it with a prayer from your heart to Jesus, put it in your Bible on your private altar in your bedroom or on your mantle and then watch how one by one they disappear. They disappear because you bring to bear upon each problem the crux of Light; this cross is formed in the meeting of the Mind of God (the descending vertical bar) with the mind of man (the horizontal bar)—your consciousness one with Jesus at the nexus.

There must be a conscious blending of the forces of God and man. This is what is meant by "matrix." It is the pattern, the grid of Light, sustained in the womb (fecund Mind of the Mother in Matter), providing the place of the cross where Father and Son meet.

Learn to Command the Powers of the Universe

As my wife was saying to you this morning, "Understand the power of your word as it is written in the Book of Isaiah: 'Command ye Me!'" Those verses contain a splendid statement of the omnipotence of the I AM THAT I AM and of the LORD's Sons—even the seed of Light who bear the unfed flame—to command the Light concerning his work on earth and the activities of his Sons:

> I am the LORD, and there is none else, there is no God beside me: I girded thee, though thou hast not known me, that they may know from the rising of the sun and from the west that there is none beside me. I am the LORD, and there is none else.
>
> I form the light and create darkness [the alternating cycles of Alpha and Omega]: I make peace and create evil. [Through my

law of karma the evil as well as the good
return upon their creators.]

I the LORD do all these things....

Thus saith the LORD, the Holy One of
Israel and his Maker, Ask me of things to
come concerning my Sons, and concerning
the work of my hands, *Command ye Me!*[22]

This is the invitation of the LORD, acting
through the individualization of the God flame
focused in your Mighty I AM Presence and spiritual centers, to participate as a co-creator with
him when it comes to eventualities concerning his
Sons and happenings involving his works through
them on earth.

This you can accomplish through the science
of the spoken Word taught to us by beloved Jesus
and Saint Germain. The divine decree confirming
God's will on earth and challenging all that is
counter to that will is yours to affirm in the name
of the Universal Christ.

So learn to command the powers of the universe in the name of GOD I AM THAT I AM,
subject to his will adjudicated for us through the
mediatorship of the Universal Christ. This is the
cornerstone of the Path that will lead you safely and
lawfully to the achievement of God-realization.

Don't be a puppet dangling on a hapless string
or a will-o'-the-wisp blown by every wind. Learn to
command yourself! If you don't, you are dispersing
the talents that God has given you, and needlessly.

That's why we are here today—because in our

past lives we have failed to apprehend all that we are. We need not fail. There is no reason for it whatsoever. I sometimes think that when people are very far behind their peers on the road of worldly or spiritual achievement, when they're way down in the dregs, they seem to get more deliverance only because by contrast to their former state they now appear to be saved to the utmost.

But as you get closer to God, you come to the point where your problems are not all material but they begin to be spiritual. In other words, you have certain spiritual problems you're solving apart from your everyday physical needs; and these problems *must be solved.* You can't ignore them (because they won't go away); and you can't accommodate them, because if you do, pretty soon the 'camel' will be on the inside of your tent and you'll be on the outside.

And until you take a stand and defend your spiritual right to be in your tent on your patch of earth, until you affirm, "I am who I am and I am where I am and I have a right to be doing what I'm doing—which is God's Work through his Word in me"—why, you won't make another inch of progress on the path of God-realization, not now or a thousand years from now!

And that otherwise vegetarian pet camel of yours—the force of the not-self that you dote upon and sacrifice your true self for—why, it's going to have all the beef and you're not going to have any!

Now, take my jokes and learn of me because

I'm speaking on many levels to many levels of your mind. Because there's more of you that needs this Truth than you're aware of. And the whole man must be made whole and the violet flame that we bear in our message and song, our auras and dynamic decrees is the Refiner's fire that will help you as nothing else can.

And these challenges you are facing today and you don't know what to do about are a necessary part of what we call the refining process. It's the testing of the spiritual mettle of your soul. It's getting you through difficult and complex levels of your own karma, and leftover lessons that tediously repeat themselves again and again. It's your Holy Christ Self forcing you to deal with situations you've managed to get away with in the past, but the Great Law won't let you do it any longer—not if you want to make real progress on the path of God-realization.

Now, when you come to the point where you are refining yourself, having seen there is nothing else to do but accept the Refiner's fire, when you're really serious about fitting yourself for a true, high spiritual office—then watch out, because that is the real problem area. That's where your tests get testy and exacting, demanding a greater and greater excellence of the spirit with each new soaring.

I want to mention in passing, and a word to the wise will be sufficient, that many people wonder why when they start out upon the Path they have problems, and why when they get further still upon the Path they have even more problems.

I want to point out to you that the human race taken as a whole is a very large group of people and that among this very large group of people, some fail spiritually. People fail in every generation. They take upon themselves vows of holy orders and they fail.

They start out with God and worshiping God, escaping the pollutions of the world through the knowledge of the Saviour, and they go back and get entangled in the same ignorance and superstition that they came out of. Peter explained it according to the true proverb: As the dog is turned to his own vomit again, and the sow that was washed to her wallowing in the mire, so a fool returneth to his folly. [23]

It often happens that people do these things. Sometimes, for all practical purposes, they never come back to the Light. Sometimes people reach the point where they're on the verge of real attainment, and suddenly they disappear in the night—of their karma.

And this is the dark night of the soul when they feel worthless and rejected by Christ, though he awaits at daybreak to receive them. And if they would have doggedly pushed through that dense substance, that dark night of their human creation (accumulated and hardened from many past lives), vigorously applying the violet flame instead of wallowing in self-pity, they would have found just around the bend the dawning day of their own individual God-mastery.

Yes, I know that it appears as a boulder on the pathway of life—sometimes a boulder of pride, a hurt ego, or a huge sense of injustice toward the Teacher. But no matter what the situation is, don't stop—you've got to press on and have your victory!

Yes, learn to command the powers of your universe!

Brothers of the Shadow

Others, knowing they have reached a degree of personal adeptship, take the left-handed path instead of the right-handed path, consciously dedicating their control of elemental forces to the lower ego. Do you see the point? They knowingly become black magicians, or something very close to it.

They want superhuman power and mastery over others rather than mastery over themselves— and they manipulate the laws they have learned and the Light they have stolen from the altar to achieve a 'personality-godhood', so to speak. When this happens, their failure is marked in the akashic records as well as on the ethers.

And so they become a part of those we call the brothers of the shadow. And they pursue the left-handed path as false chelas of the false gurus. And when they see you, any one of you—the little disciple of the Master beginning to succeed—what is the first thought that comes to them? "I will stop him!" That's their thought. They don't want you to succeed where they failed.

Does that make any sense to you? And these

are beings that in many cases roam the astral realm or they may still be in physical embodiment, preying upon the unsuspecting neophytes serving under the Great White Brotherhood—"seeking whom they may devour,"[24] as John also notes in Revelation 12.

By forfeiture, they have lost the divine spark, their original endowment of God Identity, and they have by conscious choice become a part of what we call the powers of darkness—which, of course, have no power in Reality.

In the Presence of God they have no power, but they do retain considerable power where human consent or vulnerability is involved. In other words, where people by the lever of free will—consciously or unconsciously by a choice or a not-choice—give them power, they exercise power over them.

Thus, by their fears and superstitions and fanaticisms, people themselves empower the sinister force, when they could just as well vanquish it by a call to the Mighty I AM Presence.

Jesus explained another corollary to this Law, giving the Devil his due, when he said, "This is your hour and the power of darkness."[25] But disavowing the Devil's power over his Christed being, he said, "The prince of this world cometh, and hath nothing in me."[26]

This is a case where the fallen angels are given the opportunity to play out their hand; as they freely exercise their murderous intent toward the Sons of God, so they are judged.

In order to fulfill his fiat, earlier discussed, "For judgment I AM come into this world," Jesus allowed himself to be taken, tried, condemned to death, and crucified—that the fruits of the Evil One and the parent tree might be taken for their Final Judgment—but not until they were fully exposed before all the world. For by his example the Lightbearers must also anticipate the day and the hour of their own right choices for Light's victory over Darkness and the dark ones besetting their age and their world.

These forces, in their jealousy of the Sons of God, take their stand to try to hinder the aspirant after God's Light. And so, the Ascended Masters want you to know when you enter the spiritual path that sooner or later you are going to encounter these brothers of the shadow.

And do you know when you will get the greatest onslaught of negative energy from them? I'll tell you. It's when you come to the point where you are about to truly realize God. You must understand this. When you are very, very close to your God-realization, that is when they will work to try to hinder you the most.

And, oh yes, they will work in many strange and mysterious ways. Sometimes they work through fatigue and emotional stress; then again, they work through boredom and a loss of zeal for the quest. They deliberately create circumstances to steal your joie de vivre. (Their nickname is "killjoy bluejay"! Smile.) Then again, they work through distractions and a host of sudden 'manufactured' problems that "can't wait."

C. S. Lewis in his *Screwtape Letters* wrote a satire on the hierarchy of devils who plot the demise of aspirants on the Path—with meticulous planning and cunning performance. Although it seems Lewis didn't believe in embodied devils, he was an astute student of their psychology (and of that of the Christian neophyte) and their modus operandi. I recommend this book, as do El Morya and Jesus, for new chelas on the Path.

And, of course, the most clever tool of all is the tool of discouragement. They say the Devil carries a little satchel, you know, and that he has one very sharp tool. And people ask, "What tool is that?" Well, the Devil himself will tell you, "That's discouragement." Because when the dark ones fail to get us through any other means, they will use that tool—the tool of discouragement. Sometimes they use it at the very precise moment when people are about to achieve.

I learned this a long time ago. You get disheartened by something someone very close to you does or says. You feel dejected because you're disappointed—you see, you've pinned your faith or your love on someone, and you get the idea that they've failed you just when you needed them most. And if you don't watch out, depression sets in and then when subconscious (or conscious) anger gets stirred in, you've got an admixture which can result in a nervous breakdown.

Despondency and sleeplessness (or the escape to excessive sleep) are signs of unresolved inner conflicts which all began when you fell for the Devil's discouragement plot. They even project thoughts of suicide. But what the false hierarchy really wants is to get you to abort your mission in this life by committing spiritual suicide. And remember, these discarnate entities bent on your failure will keep playing on your weakest point until you or they win.

And this is a contest, mind you, in which only you can decide the winner.

Those who betray the Light within themselves betray the Universal Christ everywhere in the lambs of God. The deed done, they feign oh so great pity, with loud protestations and weeping and wailing and deprogrammings Soviet-style, for those whom they now, in their "enlightened state," consider to be mindless, will-less brainwashed followers of the Ascended Masters' Teachings.

Next they display a seedy disdain for God's children, whom they view as just so far beneath them on the "real path." Then follows contempt. And when they finally realize that all their antics to sway the lambs of God from their true Shepherd are to no avail, it's all-out war against both the followers of God and the seat of the Godhead itself (occupied by the Guru in Spirit and in Matter)—and the entire chain of the heavenly hierarchy in between.

Jude learned from Jesus, and so did we, of the apostate princes who enter the Path forming their circle of admirers, a personality clique, or cult, drawing to themselves those who prefer the praise of men to the perfect praise of our Lord Christ Jesus:

> For there are certain men crept in unawares, who were before of old ordained to this condemnation, ungodly men, turning the grace of our God into lasciviousness and denying the only Lord God and our Lord Jesus Christ. . . .
>
> These are murmurers, complainers, walking after their own lusts; and their mouth speaketh great swelling words, having men's persons in admiration because of advantage.
>
> But, beloved, remember ye the words which were spoken before of the apostles of our Lord Jesus Christ;
>
> How that they told you there should be mockers in the last time, who should walk after their own ungodly lusts.
>
> These be they who separate themselves, sensual, having not the Spirit.[27]

Carrying on as "the accusers of the brethren," whom Archangel Michael with his unbeatable legions of Light cast out of the higher octaves into the lowest octaves of the earth, these embodied fallen angels continue to accuse the lambs of Christ "before our God"—right in his very Presence—"day and night," as John the Beloved wrote Jesus' testimony in Revelation 12.

John also discloses that it is characteristic of these roving bands of fallen angels to blaspheme GOD, his name I AM THAT I AM, his tabernacle and them that dwell in heaven. (The latter is also translated "his heavenly Tent and all those who are sheltered there."[28])

Jesus has shown us that it is the canopy of the LORD's consciousness (his kingdom), encompassing the saints in heaven and on earth—in other words, the entire Spirit of the Great White Brotherhood, including the Ascended Masters and their unascended devotees on the path of personal Christhood—that is reviled and assailed by the original betrayers of the Word cast out of heaven into earth by Archangel Michael and his legions.

Jesus has told us not to close this volume without forewarning you of your soul's encounter with such as these. For all who would enter his kingdom (the circle of Christ's presence and dominion) must first defeat this adversary of their own Christhood and his. As Jesus denounced his "woes" upon them, so in his name, must you also confirm his true and just judgments:

Woe unto you, scribes and Pharisees, hypocrites! for ye shut up the kingdom of heaven against men: for ye neither go in yourselves, neither suffer ye them that are entering to go in.

Woe unto you, scribes and Pharisees, hypocrites! for ye compass sea and land to make one proselyte, and when he is made, ye make him twofold more the child of hell than yourselves.[29]

Seventh-Ray Ministration to Life

Concerning the task of ministering to every part of Life, keeping oneself unspotted from the world, uncompromised by its temptations, and strengthened to defend the lambs of God while maintaining inner communion with the Shekinah glory, Jude offers this Seventh Ray counsel of his Lord to the Masters' disciples:[30]

1. *"To build yourselves up in the Faith"*

This is the fortification of the soul in the knowledge of Christ's Lost Teaching that you be not overcome by the taunting of the revilers of the Word.

2. *"To pray in the Holy Ghost"*

This is to take unto oneself as a garment of sacred fire the essence of Christ's Spirit, entering into the Third Person of the Trinity as one would join forces with a heavenly Friend and Teacher, knowing his counsel is always at hand to divide the words of men, separating Truth from erroneous doctrines—yea, from the blasphemy of men who are devils. Pray that the Holy Ghost speak in your heart the warning and the corrective word of caution for those who are led astray from the heart of Jesus.

3. *"To keep yourselves in the Love of God"*

Love for God and for the living flame of Love shared by the soul wed to Christ in the alchemical marriage overcomes all pulls and preferences of the world and its senses. "Preferring one another" in God's love to the temptations of serpents for the pleasures of self-indulgence and the dissipation of the Light of the chakras in their cults of death and worldly success, the saints overcome the 'beast' of the false hierarchy by the 'blood', i.e., Life—or Light—essence, of the Lamb and the Word of their testimony.[31]

4. *"To look for the mercy of our Lord Jesus Christ unto eternal Life"*

This mercy imparted in the ritual of Communion through the transubstantiation of the bread and wine as well as the dictations of the Ascended Masters necessitates our conscious and willing assimilation of the Body and Blood of Christ imparted through his Lost Teaching. For his Word is Life.

This transfer of the Light-essence of the Universal Christ is the means whereby we take in the Alpha/Omega, Spirit/Matter, or Father/Mother Consciousness. The Body and Blood of Christ is the Universal Light in the masculine (Blood) and feminine (Body) polarity of his androgynous Being. Yet, the physical flesh and blood of the Son of God was indeed fully charged and saturated with that Light of the Seventh Ray which he transferred to the bread and wine at the Last Supper—a ritual of the Seventh

Ray performed traditionally by the priest-hood of Melchizedek.

Today, though we continue to observe Holy Communion in full recognition of the LORD's celebration with us, we understand that the violet flame, as the highest vibrating agency of the Holy Spirit, is also present at the heart of this transfer of the 'Body' and 'Blood' and, by its transmutative power, purifies our souls and four lower bodies even as it imparts more and more Light as the disciple is able to receive and retain it in his finer bodies as Jesus did.

Fully endued with the violet flame of Christ's Body and Blood by daily devotion in the giving of dynamic decrees to the violet flame, the communicant is literally clothed upon with royal robes of purple/righteousness and joyous self-immolation, consuming the shadows and gloom of a world enslaved to itself, entering the full liberty of Christ's Sonship, which he ordained.

5.   *"To compassionately reassure those beset with doubts and fears"*

Give from the sacred cup of your Christ flame and office. Confirm your witness by love, teaching, and the power of heavenly invocation to the saints, strengthening the one burdened by the illumination of your communion in Christ, reinforcing the presence of holy angels and heavenly virgins—Faith, Hope, Charity—and divine self-knowledge in the Word.

6. *"To pull out those who must be saved from the fires of hell"*

Call upon Archangel Michael to cut free souls ensnared by devils who are in danger of hellfire, and pray fervently for the binding of evil spirits who prey upon children. Go to them yourself and physically remove them from all hazard.

7. *"To others, be kind with great caution, keeping your distance even from outside clothing which is contaminated by vice"*[32]

Beware of those committed to the powers of darkness. When attempting to save a Lightbearer so entrenched, put on the whole armour of God in dynamic decrees to Archangel Michael, the holy angels, and seraphim. Give Archangel Michael's Rosary and the Lord's Ritual of Exorcism[33] in advance of taking decisive action and let the Light (of the violet flame) decontaminate their forcefields.

Such is the wise counsel of the World Teachers who would give ministering servants worldwide effective training in serving the needs of those beset by the burdens of an age marked by the accelerated return of personal and planetary karma and devils stalking, knowing they have but a short time[34] before the Judgment of the Gentile (Nephilim) world powers.

Put It into the Violet Flame!

The violet transmuting flame is just waiting for you to call it into action to free yourself from the attic or basement debris of your consciousness. So before we do just that, let's find out what this debris is all about so we can then put it into the violet flame!

You know, you can have debris in your basement, but you can also have it in your attic. How is that? Well the basement is where the lower order of human thoughts materialize. Suspicion is one of these. If I look at my friend, or I look at the stranger, and I decide perhaps he has a bad motive, I may be suspicious of everything he does. So as I am suspicioning what he is doing, I begin to deal with the basement side of life.

And there are so many attitudes of mind besides suspicion. There are all types of thoughts that are all too human—subtle prejudice toward various types where you don't even recognize the beast of prejudice as such. Then there are the more insidious and malicious types of thoughts, such as covetousness and criticism, which you entertain even before you know they're in your head. These things are involved with the basement side of life and the dark debris that is in the unlit corners of the sublevels of the mind and feeling worlds.

But some people have the idea that when we come to the attic of life, which is the side where we aspire to something higher, then we're free of all of that. Not so when you're in the human! The Master El Morya once told me, "You can't help it if a bird lands on your head, but you don't need to let him build a nest in your hair!"

It's quite simple but it's also very apropos. All people at one time or another become victims of mass thoughts. The thoughts of the people, any people, you see, flood into their consciousness—unwanted thoughts, undesirable thoughts, aggressive suggestions that distort reality and get you to start thinking nasty things about people that have no relation to Reality. And if you let this keep up and you don't challenge the demons of the mind, you're going to start thinking your best friend is your worst enemy. And people are going to tell you you've got bats in your belfry.

And that's what I mean about the attic debris. It's a combination of old memories and twisted thoughts that accumulate dust and mildew up there. And you've got to clean out the old filing cabinets and records by disciplining your thought and feeling patterns as you give the violet flame daily (and fast and pray if you want to) until you experience a new clarity of the mind and memory of God and you start functioning as God intended you to—as your Real Self.

So when you're tempted to say to yourself, "What a terrible thing that I thought this," don't be alarmed, the bird is landing on your head. You don't want him, so you shoo him out. You tell him to fly away, to go about his business, because your thoughts are going to be orderly thoughts—of brotherhood, of decency, and of the mastery of yourself.

This is the difference between a master and a slave consciousness. The world is full of slaves, and they all think they're masters because they master their egos, you understand—and the ego manipulation of others. They try to impress people with their own importance, but in reality the greatest gift that any man can have is the gift of simple honesty, directness, love. That's the example that a little child needs. And Christ said, "If you don't receive the kingdom of God as a little child, you shall in *no way* enter in."³⁵

You think about that. Because from that point you approach the altar of the violet flame and you put the THINGS of your human creation—the human accumulations of its miscreations, you see—that you've been collecting as flea market collectibles for aeons in your attic and basically in your basement of base elements (I'm teasing you now with a little word play) into the flame! And if you didn't follow that, all I really said was: Put the miscreations of your miscreant into the 'boiling' violet flame, which simply boils down to: Put it into the flame!

Yes, smart people that I know not only put *it* into the violet flame, they put themselves into the violet flame and pretty soon they're so one with the violet flame that all you see is two eyes peeping through, dancing in de-light of the violet flame. And first thing you know, they begin to look like violet flame salamanders.* And then that Eastern guru comes over all amazed and he says to you, "Where did you get all that violet light in your aura?" And you say, "I got it from my Master Jesus and my brother Saint Germain—the same place you can get it too!"

We Can All Use the Violet Flame—Transmutation

We can all use the violet flame. We can all use change. We can all use transmutation. If we can't use it, then we're really stultified, we're stuck in the mud. We're down in the mud and the mire and we can't move. But if we can use it, then, you see, God has the power to free us. And when he frees us, we go up—we are no longer confined to the sense of limitation.

First, it has to be freedom in the mind, freedom in the soul, freedom in the heart, freedom in the being of man. Eventually it manifests in everything he does and after a while he's literally soaring because he understands who and what he really is.

So when, juxtaposed between the forces of Light and Darkness assembling for Armageddon, you decide to use the violet transmuting flame as all who have ever ascended to God have done as part of the ascension process, I want you to

---
*elementals of the fire element

understand that it has what has been described as a vigorous bubbling or 'boiling' action as it blazes through the four lower bodies with an intense alchemical heat.

As you invoke the power of the Holy Spirit through your violet flame decrees, I want you to recite them from the very depths of an inner dynamism of the spirit and a joyous heart—in anticipation of being a participant in the greatest freedom the world has ever known.

So we're going to use a violet flame decree right now. Number 70.17, "Violet-Purple-Pink."

Now, when you give this decree, in order to attune with the Ascended Masters it is desirable that you concentrate upon the color violet surrounding the lower figure in the Chart of Your Divine Self. It's a vibrant, moving color of violet/purple/pink flames leaping up and all around you. (The third, fourth, and fifth color bands of the causal body illustrate the spectrum of the flame from the pink to the violet to the purple, ranging from pure pink to a deep rose violet to a deep blue purple.)

Concentrate on the colors of the flames enveloping the lower figure, and think of those colors alive in the background of your mind all the time you're saying the decree. And then intensify the power of your thought and feeling of the violet flame pulsating up through your world.

This does not necessarily mean that you are stepping up the volume. Let the volume step itself up because it's automatic from within. Don't try to force it. Volume alone without the Holy Spirit may become coarse if it is not accompanied by the mastery of the angelic hosts. Angels do exist and they do amplify the power of your decrees. And when they do, the volume naturally picks up without your having to force it.

And so, wherever you are, I invite you to use this violet transmuting flame with me now. We will give the verses and refrain which follow the preamble quite a while as a chant—like an Indian mantra:

In the name of the beloved mighty victorious Presence of God, I AM in me, my very own beloved Holy Christ Self, my beloved Jesus and all the servant-Sons of God in heaven and on earth, Ascended Masters of the Seventh Ray, beloved Melchizedek, King of Salem and Priest of the Most High God, all saints, alchemists and initiates of the sacred fire serving with him in the Temple Beautiful in heaven, beloved Maha Chohan and the beloved Seven Chohans of the Rays, Legions of Violet Flame Angels from the Heart of God, heavenly hosts and beings of the elements serving on the Seventh Ray: beloved Elohim Mighty Arcturus and Victoria, Archangel Zadkiel and Holy Amethyst, beloved Saint Germain and Portia, beloved Omri-Tas, Ruler of the

Violet Planet, beloved Kuan Yin and the
entire Spirit of the Great White Brotherhood
and the World Mother, elemental life—fire,
air, water, and earth! I decree:

1. Violet Flame, pass up through me
   With pink center keep me free.
   Love like a flower unfolds each hour,
   Wisdom in action releases God's Power!

Refrain: Violet, purple, pink,
          Flash through that I may think:
          God's in me—I AM Free
          Now and for eternity!

          Violet, purple, pink,
          Help me now to drink
          Electric hue, flashing through
          Into all I think and say and do!

2. Violet Flame, rise up and heal,
   With pink center my being seal.
   Love is flowing, increasing knowing,
   Wisdom in action God is bestowing!

3. Violet Flame, take control today,
   With pink center flash forth thy ray.
   Love's power sealing, the Real revealing,
   Wisdom in action is God I AM feeling!

You see, you can feel the flow of the flame in
the sounding of the Word, which resounds again in
your being. How many of you are experiencing the
joy of the flames of the Holy Spirit passing through

you? I mean, the flames enjoy passing through you!

The flame is the action of the Mind of God and as such it is endowed with certain qualities of that Mind—like bubbling joy, effervescent, luminescent, phosphorescent spiritual fire.

Now, we're going to use the power of the violet flame without the book and everybody can look to their Presence, this Chart just being a symbol of it. You can see the human self—the violet flame surrounding the human monad in the lower figure—the Holy Christ Self in the mother-of-pearl clouds of resurrection's fires, and the Great God Presence enveloped in the great causal-body rainbow rays with its concentric spheres embodying your cosmic consciousness of the seven rays.

So as we look to the Presence for help, we understand that the Presence says, "Draw nigh unto me and I will draw nigh unto you."[36] This is a promise of God. It is the promise of the Creator. It is the promise on which we have relied. It is the promise which has raised the dead. It has assisted people to actually experience a miraculous change in their consciousness and tremendous happiness that will not go away. That's because the medium whereby you do meet your God Presence—and one day *you will* meet your God Presence in the air as from etheric levels your soul ascends to God—is *the violet transmuting flame!*

Yes, you draw nigh to God by raising your vibrational frequency to his through the alchemy of violet flame decrees! The science of the spoken

Word is the highest alchemy that can be experienced in the full flaming Presence of the Holy Spirit by the true adept in the Aquarian age![37] Believe me, you'd better try it, or you are going to miss out on the greatest dispensation that has been given to mankind during the last four thousand years.

I'm saying, "that has been given to mankind." Jesus had it, Saint Germain had it. Mother Mary had it, Moses and Elijah had it—but now anyone can have it before they attain full God-mastery on the Seventh Ray, which was the requirement of the Law in the old dispensation. Now, thanks to the sponsorship of Saint Germain and the dispensation granted him by the Karmic Board, anyone can have it, anyone can experiment with it. It's the miracle and the miracle worker of the age!

So we'll give this violet flame decree in the fervor of our hearts' devotion to all the heavenly hosts who amplify the violet flame we call forth for the blessing of all life.

> I AM a being of violet fire
> I AM the purity God desires   (33x)

Now I'm going to play bobsled with you. I don't want anybody dragging their feet even if you don't know this decree. I want everybody in this room to give the decree. Do you know why? I have a reason for asking it of you.

If you give it, if you enter into it, even if it's for the first time in your life, you will have the opportunity of experiencing to some degree an assistance to your soul that you would never get if someone else gave it for you. So, because we are all individual self-starters and all inheritors of divine grace, because we want to wake everyone up to know that, we're going to give it together. We won't drag our feet.

And we'll start slow and then we'll speed up, because it's like a merry-go-round or a centrifuge. You're riding on one of those painted wooden horses. If the merry-go-round gets going fast enough—it doesn't matter if you're a little boy or a man—you're going to go right off of one of those horses into space!

So, this is how you get rid of negative patterns in yourself. It's the same principle—you just fling them off into the violet singing flame that sings as it transmutes, just like the calliope that plays as you and your atoms go round and round the merry-go-round. You can think of the action of the violet flame as it intensifies as being like the big cyclotrons and the atomic energy machines they use. The faster you go toward the end, the more the debris, the astral accumulation, and the negative energies will fly off from the centrifuge of your being.

The violet flame works scientifically, transmuting as it flings out, so that when it comes out it's just like a trailing light aura. And you get rid of the debris out of the inner patterns of your atoms and electrons by this fiery baptism, melting the elements of your human creation "with a fervent heat," as Peter saw it.[38]

If you start the whirling action clockwise with a strong visualization and a fervent call to God, you'll be surprised at how much can be done for you. So we'll say it together.

Beloved Saint Germain, we ask you and beloved Jesus to release a tremendous radiance of the violet flame through our decrees which we now offer to you for our healing and transmutation.

I AM a being of violet fire
I AM the purity God desires   (21x)

We got kind of fast. But this is what will help you to throw off all negativity. It's just what the doctor ordered. You can actually change your vibration in one night—but I don't expect that people who do it for the very first time are going to have the results of someone who does it time on time on time again.

Do you think I'm making a false claim? Well, go to the LORD. He said it through that Z-Ray prophet, Zechariah: "I will remove the iniquity of that land in one day." Furthermore, "In that day, saith the LORD of hosts, shall ye call every man his neighbour under the vine and under the fig tree."³⁹

That means in one cycle of your cosmic clock, one turning of the Great Wheel of your causal body during which you fast and pray with the violet flame and surrender your iniquities into the flame, you can be delivered of the karma of a certain cycle of your human creation.

And the LORD will take from you all that the Great Law will allow in that cycle. And you will enter a new cycle of freedom and rebirth in your own God Identity. And in that day you will sit under your Holy Christ Self and Mighty I AM Presence and you will know the LORD Sanat Kumara, called YAHWEH SABAOTH,[40] as you have not known him in all the ages of your descent from the Great Central Sun.

Why, if some of you disciples of El Morya who just love the blue ray of God's will and who look just like blue-flocked Christmas trees all decked up with blue lights and balls would just get so smart and dedicate your next 5-day, 10-day, or 2-week vacation to your physical/spiritual rejuvenation with true fasting and prayer with the violet flame and the grape of the vine—both drinking the juice and eating the fruit of the LORD's Holy Communion—out in the sunshine and fresh air and up in the mountains of God, far from the cities, shouting for joy and singing for freedom your violet flame decrees and songs to Saint Germain into the day and the night as your joyful noise unto the LORD: if you really knew and would carry out an alchemical, violet flame re-creation in body, mind and soul beginning with the ritual of forgiveness to all the world, beginning with yourself and everyone who has ever wronged you or whom you have ever wronged, and pressing on through the rings and layers of the electronic belt of your subconscious and clearing your whole house chakra by chakra—

I tell you what would happen to you blue-ray chelas of Morya's fame: you would unlock so much locked-up blue flame/white fire/power within your being that pretty soon old Hercules himself would raise an eye and an eyebrow at you with a beckon and a grin (no longer a chagrin), and he just might invite you to his retreat at Half Dome in Yosemite, there to give you the first steps of chelaship under the Elohim of the First Ray!

Now, how would you like that for a reward for fasting from the world and all that's in it for a fortnight? What's more, the violet flame will move right in in answer to your call to transmute all those vices and devices you have set up as blocks to the balance of your threefold flame.

So those of you chelas who love the will of God and its wisdom so much, the violet flame will just consume and consume and consume every vestige of your human creation that has caused your pink and yellow plumes to be shorter than your blue. And it will establish balance in your four lower bodies too.

Now, you know you must not fast inadvisedly without a doctor's careful monitoring. And it's alright to take your vitamins, minerals, and protein tablets if you need them. Because this is a spiritual fast and so you need to keep yourself in your body, clearheaded. So don't go off the deep end and get fanatical about this but do follow the latest scientific methods for safe fasting—and don't go out in nature without a buddy when you're fasting. And be sure you know your survival skills and have your survival kit along. Because this can be the greatest thing that ever happened to you if you do it right and don't overdo. Take it easy.

You can work up to this grape fast by starting with one day this week, then two the next, then three and so on. And always come off your violet flame fasts nice 'n' easy, gradually introducing varied fruits, then some finely grated carrots and cabbage and sprouts, then soaked sunflower seeds and soaked almonds (peeled) until you can take some cooked leafy greens and other vegetables, rice and cooked grains.

And I'm not even going to tell you the benefits or make any claims whatsoever for this spiritual fast because the fruit of the vine and the Lord's song in your heart will say it all!

Yes, prayer and fasting with the violet flame is the way we accelerate the Seventh Ray ritual of throwing off the dark wedges of substance between the atoms. We send the violet fire into the atomic structure of our being—into our cells where particles that are the size of a virus (and of the DNA or RNA of a virus) and even smaller are discharged. They are ejected from the four lower bodies, not just the physical, because the violet flame demagnetizes the debris of misqualified substance from all planes of matter. Fasting, praying, exercising your chakras and your four lower bodies, and taking in the sunlight, pure mountain air and prana increases the benefit of your violet flame decrees many times over.

Change Your Environment

As a would-be adept in the Aquarian age, you need to start experimenting with the laws governing the change of forcefields. You need to know that you have the ability to change your inner and outer environment at will. So that when, if ever, you are suddenly faced with a crisis of severe illness or pollution, you have a momentum on expelling toxins—whether they are caused by stress and fatigue, an emotional crisis, or chemicals or karma spilling over from the astral body.

You see, if you can't change your environment because you haven't practiced the technique, then when your environment starts closing in on you, you may be trapped.

Now, what I'm telling you is true. Have you ever gotten on a bus, a train, an airplane, or gone into a room in someone's home and felt a strange feeling of depression, where you are unhappy, and it stuck with you after you left—or you handled an object like a ring or a watch and somehow or other, although you didn't realize it was happening at the time, afterwards you felt very depressed and unhappy?

This is because these conditions can be brought about through charges. Negative charges will cling to objects and people, and even the leather of seats sometimes retains negative vibrations for a long period of time. Therefore, you see, we have to learn how to control our environment.

We have to learn how to make our own bed and then lie in it, and not let someone else make it for us. Or else we'll wind up like Goldilocks, who cried, "Who's been sleeping in *my* bed?"

In other words, we have to develop a sense of comfortability, we have to be comfortable in ourselves. How can a person make any progress if they're uncomfortable? We may not be comfortable in somebody else's human creation but we may not be comfortable in ours either!

Well, the violet transmuting flame works. It really works, and it will get rid of those negative vibes you've picked up here and around, and you're going to start feeling comfortable with yourself. And you're going to find yourself changing your environment if it's not comfortable, or else you'll either be removed from it by events or your own decisive action or the Holy Spirit will pick you up and put you where It wants you to be. And you won't have anything to say about it.

And then you'll realize that a greater hand than your own is guiding your destiny. And you'll be comforted in that. And then you can give the rest of your worries to the Holy Spirit's capable angels, and you're going to get more comfortable and less haggard every day. (Like Hagar, you know, she was twice haggard on the desert until the LORD's angel interceded for her and her son. And she was comforted.[1])

If I was ever skeptical about the violet flame, I wasn't after using it for six months—I'll tell you that. From the first occasion that I ever heard of the violet flame, within six months I knew. And the feeling of delight that comes with the discovery of the violet flame has been communicated to many young men and women as well as older people in this place of worship. Many of them had tried everything from chewing gum to something harder and they found out that the violet transmuting flame was the greatest happiness of their life because it gave them the freedom to enjoy God.

Well, of course they knew he was here all the time but they just didn't see him. Everybody wanted to see God and they didn't think they could, and because they didn't think they could, they didn't—and all at once they saw God in themselves. They saw their Mighty I AM Presence! This is the miracle of the violet flame.

Seeing God in Yourself

It reminds me of the Eastern saint who had a beautiful garland of flowers that he was going to throw around the neck of a statue of Lord Buddha. And just as he was getting ready to throw it, he said, "Suddenly I thought of myself and that God was also in me, and I threw the flowers around my own neck and immediately went into samadhi." He went into a deep experience of spiritual bliss, because he understood that the God of the universe was also within himself.

Similarly, Ramakrishna, recognizing himself

as having no separate existence from the Divine Mother, "would take flowers and sandalwood and decorate his own body, instead of her image."[42]

That's what I want you to do with the visualization of the violet flame! Create in your mind a garland of purple flame-flowers—orchids—and throw them around your neck to adore the Christ who abides in your temple. Then throw another garland around your soul and celebrate the alchemical (Seventh Ray) marriage of your soul to Christ, Krishna, Buddha, the Universal Self!

The violet flame is the key to integration with God—raja yoga. It is the yoga of fire—agni. The violet flame helps you achieve the goal of every yogic path and master: God Self-realization. Assimilation unto The Word.

But do you know the most amazing conception of all? The Eastern saint, nearly perfected, is often assigned a final incarnation in the West—to pour out his bliss to a people greatly beloved yet not fully awakened to Jesus' Eastern journey.

One by one the yogis come. You can see them as pilgrims coming from the cremation pyre, from the Ganges, from the Himalayas to be born in America. Here to lay upon the altar of Mother Liberty the song of their soul's liberation, the fiery coil of her white-fire freedom on behalf of her children—adepts to be.

And why do they come? They come to the altar of transmutation: to the burning gat—now

ablaze with violet flame. They come to the Royal
Teton Retreat to be initiated by the Ascended
Masters and to gain full mastery of the Seventh Ray
and its violet flame. Thus did Ramakrishna reincar-
nate in the twentieth century in the United States.
Perfecting his soul in the purple fiery heart of Saint
Germain, he made his ascension on the Seventh
Ray. And you can call to him—Eastern saint,
Western adept—and claim his mantle in the name
of the entire Spirit of the Great White Brotherhood
and the unascended Masters and devotees of India,
whose religion of the Divine Mother they brought
from the Motherland.

This knowledge should inspire new-age parents to use the violet flame fast every six months as
they pray for and prepare to give birth to souls of
Light being sent to the West to perfect their attainment in the seventh cycle of their causal body.

You know, it's so easy to find fault with someone else. You show me a man and I will show you
how you can find fault with him. That's the easiest
thing—it's gravitational. Everybody has faults in
this world except the very few arhats, and most of
us do not compare ourselves with the arhats. We
think of ourselves as being just ordinary people.
But after all, God has given us all the same goal,
and to that end El Morya has instituted his chelaship training which he calls "goal-fitting" because
he wants to be sure we are "goal-fitted."

So why should we be so different? We're all
pursuers and Saint Germain has given us the

shortest legitimate short-cut to the goal that you'll
find anywhere on planet earth. It's the violet flame
and it's kosher. So let's do it.

Now, when we say, "I AM," we're going to
feel that WE ARE! And why are we? Because the
Spirit of God IS. If for some reason the people in
the world got off, God would still be here. The
wind would still blow through the trees, life would
still go on in the world of Nature, even though
mankind had left. Because the Spirit is what IS.

So what is it that endures forever, that is
unmoved like the giant redwoods of California or
the cedars of Lebanon? What is it? It is the Spirit
of God that remains, presiding over all Nature.
And we in our spirits would also remain thus, for
we are a spirit as God is. And through the purification of our souls and the development of the Christ
consciousness, we come into the similitude of God
once again; and this is man's natural God-estate.

Picture Yourself in Violet Fire

So we will chant this "I AM." And feel, when
you say, "I AM," that you are—and that *God is*
where *you are*. Not that you're here today in 1972
or 1986 or 1998, but that you've been here as far
back as the year 1000, the year 4000, 5000 B.C.—
it doesn't matter. Go back a million years, you've
always been here. That's what's chanting—not this
temporal personality, but the living Truth that IS.

So wherever you are, as we do this together
please separate your hands and feet. (There's a

purpose behind this.) And you may hold your hands palms up, resting lightly in your lap, thumb and index finger lightly touching.

Now I'm going to play choo choo train with you. As we begin, it's like a railroad train. When it first starts out, sometimes it's so slow getting off the pad that it has to drop sand and it goes "shoop, shoop," and the wheels will spin around. "Shoop"—and they don't go anyplace.

And then it gets a little momentum, a little sand gets caught—"shoop, shoop, shoop, shoop, shoop, shoop, shoop, shoop, shoop, shoop, shoop, shoop, shoop, shoop, shoop..." and down the track it goes. So, remember that this acceleration is an important thing.

Let's take a mental picture of ourselves surrounded with violet fire from way down under our feet to clear up over our heads. You cannot create what you cannot visualize, just as an artist cannot paint a picture that he cannot see. Therefore, you must perfect yourself in visualizing and that's why we have the aid of the Chart.

We tried to set the 'angstrom units' of the colors of the Chart as close as possible to the vibratory action that is the true violet flame. You should have an actual sense of the motion of spiritual flames, just like physical flames, licking up around you. Now, remember this is the sacred fire and it's not going to hurt you at all; in fact, it'll do you a lot of good, if you let it.

So hold a strong vision of violet fire and feel it melting out of you the astral debris of centuries, patterns of discord in the emotions and the records of inner conflict that bind you to sin, disease, and death. So, visualize this violet flame around yourself and remember my demonstration of the train as we decree together:

> I AM a being of violet fire
> I AM the purity God desires   (33x)

I want you to take notice again of the increase of the vibrational frequency and how it has the tendency to act as a centrifuge, to throw off the emotional whirl of human despair and to replace it by a vibrational aspect similar to negatively charged ions that can be recognized after a rainstorm. You will observe how it gives a feeling of élan, of vibrancy, of buoyancy, of vitality, of awareness of God.

This is always important in the meditational experience. Without it, individual man may feel very limited—cast in the mode of his outer intellect and the either successful or unsuccessful exploitation of the egos of others.

The I AM Presence Is Your Authority to Create

We must recognize, then, that the authority for each lifestream, for each individual, is his own Beloved Mighty I AM Presence. We must recognize that it is the God in individual man who is able to unfold in him his identity and the latent powers that are inherent within him.

We read from time to time of people with extrasensory perception. We read of individuals who are able to look at someone and at a glance tell that one exactly what is acting in his world. Oh yes, there're a lot of people like that who have developed various psychic abilities. These latent powers in man are exactly that—powers; but their possession does not necessarily indicate God-mastery—your mastery of God's flame within you.

You may have the ability to play the piano and your playing of the piano may be recognized by the whole world, but your repertoire may be limited to the inspiration of others. If so, you are a mere mechanical genius. You have the power to reproduce but not the power to create.

It is the desire of the Ascended Masters of the Great White Brotherhood to engender in man that awareness, that God-mastery of consciousness which will enable him to create at will. If you cannot create at will, if you are always dependent on others to meet your every need, you are not fulfilling the ancient prophecy of the Guru/chela relationship given by the LORD to Isaiah:

> Though the Lord give you the bread of adversity, and the water of affliction, yet shall not thy teachers be removed into a corner any more, but thine eyes shall see thy teachers:

And thine ears shall hear a word behind thee, saying, This is the way, walk ye in it, when ye turn to the right hand, and when ye turn to the left.[43]

And who are your true Teachers who are no longer removed? They are the graduates. Only those who have ascended out of this octave are free from the taint of relativity. You can trust the Ascended Masters because they are no longer of this world. Having been through its courses and "clean escaped"[44] its pitfalls, they are thoroughly familiar with what you and I have to deal with on a day-to-day basis. They often console their chelas with the assurance that no matter what the problem, they've been through it too.

The Ascended Masters have earned their tenure in heaven through the mastery of life on earth (its cycles of time and space), balanced their karma, loved God to the uttermost and ascended to the heart of the Mighty I AM Presence by grace.

To consciously interact with them, for they are "thy Teachers," to know them face to face (even on the inner planes), is to enter into a co-creative relationship with the real Teachers of mankind. This you can do. If you will it so and if you love, truly love, the Teacher will appear.

The promise of the Guru is given even though the LORD, through the law of karma, will give you "the bread of adversity and the water of affliction." This is a great dispensation. Right while we're balancing our karma and bowed down with temptations and troubles, it says the people shall dwell in Zion and weep no more. The LORD Sanat Kumara will be "very gracious unto thee at the voice of thy cry; when he shall hear it, he will answer thee."[45]

The message of the Ancient of Days given to us through Isaiah in 700 B.C. is for today. His grace and graciousness to us is his gift of the violet flame. When the LORD the I AM THAT I AM hears the voice of the cry of the people, in other words their dynamic decrees—their calls to him, their mantras and fiats and affirmations of the Word—*"when he shall hear it, he shall answer thee."*

This is God's promise to us which he keeps through the I AM Presence of himself which he has placed with us. Yes! your violet flame decrees are answered by your Mighty I AM Presence, who is both with you and in the heart of the Great Central Sun simultaneously—for our God is one LORD.

God's promise to answer our decrees is a binding contract. It is a covenant between him and us. Only we can break it. For God keeps his commitments. And he has supreme respect for the honor of his Word once it is given. And so should we.

It is time you knew all the laws of God—or at least the ones most vital to your spiritual/physical survival—so you can confirm your participation in his promises. Because if you fulfill your end of the bargain—and believe me it's a bargain!—then God will always fulfill his. But if you don't know the Law, you can't put it to work for yourself and your planet. So, call upon the LORD and he will answer. Has he not said of the obedient, loving servant-Son:

> Because he hath set his love upon me, therefore will I deliver him: I will set him on high, because he hath known my name I AM THAT I AM.
>
> *He shall call upon me, and I will answer him:* I will be with him in trouble; I will deliver him and honour him.
>
> With long life will I satisfy him, and shew him my salvation.[46]

All you have to do to get these promises is to love God. Having so determined, the tests will begin. For to defend your love of God in your members on all counts of the Law of Love is the supreme testing and the supreme bliss of the Seventh Ray initiates of the Great White Brotherhood.

God in his promise to the I AM Race through Isaiah has guaranteed the divine encounter. Saint Paul had it, Saint John the Revelator had it, and many saints have had it—so why shouldn't you?

Jeremiah says that when this happens men will no longer say to one another, "Know the LORD, for they shall all know me, from the least of them unto the greatest of them."[47] They won't have to tell each other about God and his servant-Sons and cohorts of Light because each one will experience the divine encounter. "And every man will sit under his own vine and under his own fig tree."[48]

This means that as a part of the destiny of man, each individual will have achieved his own God-realization.

Now, chanting the violet flame as we do as part of the process of our God Self-realization, we create a decree pattern that is similar to the mantra. There is a very valuable lesson to be learned from the Eastern mantra in the sense that it is a magnetic approach to God. It creates the similitude of the vibration which has been chanted for thousands and thousands of years by God's seekers.

These God-seekers, having used a particular mantra, have also charged the mantra with the constructive momentums of their own life which then become a part of the cumulative momentum and vibration of the mantra as it—the Word—gathers unto itself the devotion of the saints who have used the formula in the ritual of drawing down the Light/Energy/Consciousness of the Word.

The mantra, then, is a thing in itself which exists independently of the giver of the mantra. And whoever thinks he is giving the mantra comes to realize that the mantra is giving itself, and it keeps on after the outer voice has become silent and the soul is the listener to the soundless Sound in the inner Mind. And the devotee experiences himself, in all of his chakras, to be the extension of the Universal Mind. And the Mind passes through her and she knows that she is also that Mind and the mantra sings on, chanting the lullaby of the Homing—Nearer, my God, to thee.

Man's use of the mantra—even the Hail Mary, as we say, the Hail MA-RAY, or the Our Father—then, is a means of attracting to himself, magnetically, those ecstatic experiences which are stable and which, in the world community and in the individual's mind, will enable him to attune with the frequencies of those special souls who have attained God consciousness in the past through the identical sound and word formula.

There is something very wonderful in the mastery of the earth, the air, the fire, and the water, because in the four lower bodies of man we find these elements predominating. The physical body equates with the earth. The body of air equates with the mind. The body of feeling, or emotions, equates with the water. And the power of man's memory, by which he integrates the whole, equates with the fire. And the fifth, ether, envelops and seals the four, integrating and harmonizing them in the Law of the One.

Have you ever stopped to think of the role of memory? Memory, mind you. Memory as the deciding, unifying factor of your whole life. What would you be if you did not have a memory of your identity? A memory of your fellowmen, their countenance, their expressions, their life? In fact, a memory of language and language skills, a memory of science, a memory of even the stars—if you are an astronomer?

Memory is very important to the integration of the whole. There is an automatic memory in the physical body which we call the subconscious, and there is the collective subconscious of the world. All men today feed into and out of the subconscious river of their unconscious drives and momentums, the lowest common denominator of which amounts to the sewer of their thoughts and feelings.

But don't forget, while they're down here, sinking in the human level, their God Self is also hallowing space by pouring into space those lofty thoughts and feelings which will draw them upward. This plane of constructivism, then, may be considered the collective Higher Consciousness of the race.

Who is the man who frees the world if he is not the one who can say "Our Father" rather than "My Father"? For in the lofty sentiment of "our," we eradicate the mere concept of "me, mine"— which, notwithstanding, is quite vital because in the unity of the soul of one man with God is the unity of the soul of all men with God. Christ was born two thousand years ago in a manger, but today Christ is still unborn in many hearts.

It is not enough to submit oneself to some form of religion: one must of necessity open the gates of the heart unto God. And although no one may know that we do it, we may do it—and he will know and he will answer and he will commune with that child mind which is not too simple to receive him in the temple of manifestation, knowing that when the babe of Christ appears in the consciousness, that babe will grow up, that babe will become the child-man. And then, the thirty-three years (symbolical of the Christ) will also manifest, as man by the power of the three-times-three fulfills all his requirements for becoming one with the Divine Triad, the cosmic triangle, which may be spelled t-r-y, *try-angle.*

The Dark Night of the Spirit, the Trial by Fire

We are all in the midst of trial—self-trial, the trials of the Ascended Masters, the tests of the world, and the tests that, in the final analysis, will determine whether or not we are worthy to be the ongoing Son of God and therefore to pass through the initiation of the crucifixion, and whether, when we are left to stand alone in the final test (the dark night of the Spirit), our soul can in fact keep its commitment to stand, face, and conquer every last vestige of human selfishness.

The individual undergoing the initiation of the dark night of the Spirit, as depicted by Saint John of the Cross,[49] can speak forth, "My God, my God, why hast thou forsaken me?"[50] because that individual will understand and feel that tremendous passion when God seems to flee the temple and be there no more.

For all of man's lifetimes, throughout all of his life, he has always had God there, the comforting presence of the Father/Mother God. Now, in the crucifixion, in which one perforce undergoes the dark night of the Spirit, the Lord suddenly flees the temple; and the child-man, grown up hopefully into the spiritual attainment of his spiritual mastery, will be able to take dominion as Christ did at that moment and stand against the whole world and all the challenges of the universe and say, "Lo, I AM!"—because he will BE.

You see, the test we face, when fastened to the cross of world karma as Jesus was, is to be able to sustain the threefold flame and the Christ consciousness (which, up to this moment, the I AM Presence has sustained for us by the crystal cord)— and to sustain it sufficiently to hold the balance of Light for the karma of the entire earth and its evolutionary chain.

Hence, it is called the dark night of the Spirit because the Light of the Holy Ghost is withdrawn—for the Son of man within us has (or it would not be given the initiation) become the Trinity incarnate. He is the Avatar—the God-manifestation.

Though expected and prepared for, the suddenness of the withdrawal of the sustaining Presence evokes the cry "My God, my God, why hast thou forsaken me?" To this Goal aspire, O Son of the Most High. And may God be with you all the Way to that moment of the birth of thy Godhood.

The initiation of the dark night of the Spirit is the spiritual cutting of the umbilical cord; henceforth the Son of man is called the Son of God because his God Self-awareness is become the sufficiency of the Presence to sustain the Light of the heart. He has become a blazing sun (the sun born of the parent Sun); in this final test, he must prove it. This is his solo flight. And he may be solo for days, weeks, months, or years.

When he has passed the test, the causal body descends upon him as a mantle of God. He is no longer tied to God by the crystal cord; he is One with God, he *is* God—all seven spheres in manifestation. Heretofore he has affirmed, "I and my Father are one." Now he is become that One.

Because he has attained God consciousness, the one who has passed this initiation receives the appellation "God" before the new name of his sainthood (in this case Godhood). It is the God consciousness of his I AM Presence to which he has attained, the Presence who is the LORD. And his whole house is filled with the appellation, the LORD he is God.

Thus the God and Goddess Meru, Manus of the sixth root race who preside at the retreat of the feminine ray at Lake Titicaca, embody the God consciousness of their twin flames and twin causal bodies on behalf of billions of souls. They are the embodiment of the Father/Mother God perceived as one with God. Their titles have naught to do with any pagan, polytheistic or pantheistic cosmoconception but are rather the affirmation of the Being of God as One. Their title is a reminder of the God-goal of all twin flames: that the full flowering of each one's divinity reveal Godhood where I AM.

In the case of Archangel Michael, who has attained to the God consciousness of the First Ray of the will of God, his name (meaning "who is as God") reflects his mission and his momentum in the internalization of the God flame.

It is one thing to perceive the Flame out of the burning bush and the bush is not consumed,[51] but it is another thing, as Saint Paul says, to pass through the trial by fire when man's works are tested and he himself is tested as to whether or not he can sustain the Christ consciousness, "yet so as by fire."[52] (The trial by fire is not the equivalent of the dark night of the Spirit but a preparatory initiation on the Way.)

So we must always bear in mind that we build not for one moment but we build eternally, and this is the great quandary of man today. How shall he build on earth, yet build for eternity temples made without hands? Clearly we see temples of the mind, temples of the heart and the flocking of the birds to feed from the immortal Light Body we have created. And we, too, are sustained by the eternal flame.

We can live forever, but the ego must pass away. Or, put another way, we can live forever as Christed ones, but not until the ego passes away. But this does not mean the end of man. For the violet flame achieves both the dissolution of the not-self and the resolution of the soul in the Real Self—simultaneously. Isn't that wonderful! Why, the violet flame is just full of wonders and full of marvels! So neither process need be abrupt, but a daily ritual in the Seventh Ray alchemical joy of your LORD.

"Thou Wilt Not Leave My Soul..."

Many years ago in my meditations, there came to me a thought, and it was the same thought that Christ thought; and, as the shepherd boy, David, he also had the same thought: "Thou wilt not leave my soul in hell, neither wilt thou suffer thine Holy One to see corruption."[53]

In my moment of meditation I was thinking and I said to myself, "What man has done man can do." What any one member of the I AM Race has accomplished, any member can accomplish if he tap the same creative power.

Look at all these things that man has accomplished—these automobiles, aeroplanes, television sets, computers, and the tremendous advances we see in the field of medicine. One in particular that comes to mind is in cataract surgery. Whereas they used to operate to cut out cataracts from the eyes of the aged, now they merely insert into the eye what amounts to a tiny steel drinking straw and they suck up the damaged lens and replace it with a lens implant, and the person is able to see within a relatively short time.

I thought of all these advances that mankind has made in the field of science, and then I began to think of the simply amazing functioning of our whole neurological system, of our physiological system, of our mental system, and our spiritual system, and on and on. And then I said to myself, but the most amazing function of all is that we can echo the sentiments of the Christ!

Surely God did not create anyone—I said, *anyone*—in order that that person should be interred and be no more. God created man to have a matrix of perfection, but man individually has failed to perceive it. And because he has failed to perceive it, he has failed to manifest it; for without the power of vision, the people perish.[54] The people fall into the image that perishes because they don't perceive the image that lives.

And I saw that the secret of Life is really very, very simple, but that only a child can discover it. And it was in part my faith in God and in his great advancement of the Spirit in me that discovered it—not my human intelligence—because I perceived behind the screen of mere intelligence the eternal values and motivations of God.

These motivations are one with all that lives immortally. As Krishna says in the *Bhagavad-gita*:

> Never the Spirit was born,
>   the Spirit shall cease to be never;
> Never was time it was not,
>   End and Beginning are dreams!
> Birthless and deathless and changeless
>   remaineth the Spirit for ever;
> Death hath not touched it at all,
>   dead though the house of it seems!

But in and through and beyond all our musings, awareness must come to us of the meaning and definition of Life. For through our creation and re-creation of the divine matrices in thought and feeling, we are able once again to be one with God. And through unity with God, nothing is impossible unto us.

If we seek to do anything by human strivings, we will always find that human strivings may carry us a certain distance, but that distance will be a distance of limitation because man has limitation. But if we tether ourselves to a star—and I'm not speaking of an astronomical star, but a spiritual one—then as the star rises in hope, so we will also rise. That is the difference.

Build Up an Ocean of Violet Fire

And so we are going to use the power of our dynamic decrees to effect world change. We're going to build up an ocean of violet fire about a hundred feet high around the whole world, and it can start as a vortex of pure violet fire from wherever you are at this moment.

And it will fill all the house where you are praying and then the neighborhood and you can visualize this ocean of violet fire moving in waves to saturate and purify your state and section, and then your country, continent, and hemisphere until you just see and feel the planetary action of world transmutation taking place.

We're going to send it around the world, from

the East to the West. As the lightning cometh out
of the East and shineth even unto the West, so let
the coming of the Light, the violet Light of God,
the radiance of the Seventh Ray "Sun of man"
(Sun of *man*ifestation) be.[55] Let the Universal Christ
of the Seventh Ray and seventh age come out of the
white-fire ovoid—from East to West—and be the
wholeness of the whirling T'ai Chi.

Let the Universal Christ who said, "I AM
Alpha and Omega," be the culmination of the
Truth of all world religions, East and West, from
the beginning unto the ending of cycles in the age
of Aquarius, truly the Universal Age. Because this
is how we realize the Christ consciousness of the
seven rays and seven rings of our causal body.

Let's give this decree for "More Violet Fire,"
which was dictated to me by Saint Paul, whom we
know as the Ascended Master Hilarion. Let's give it
with all of our love and with the powerful visualization of an ocean of violet fire saturating earth
and her evolutions with Christ's forgiveness, mercy,
grace, freedom and alchemical transformation:

> Lovely God Presence, I AM in me,
> Hear me now I do decree:
> Bring to pass each blessing for which I call
> Upon the Holy Christ Self of each and all.
>
> Let Violet Fire of Freedom roll
> Round the world to make all whole;
> Saturate the earth and its people, too,
> With increasing Christ-radiance shining
>   through.

I AM this action from God above,
Sustained by the hand of heaven's Love,
Transmuting the causes of discord here,
Removing the cores so that none do fear.

I AM, I AM, I AM
The full power of Freedom's Love
Raising all earth to heaven above.
Violet Fire now blazing bright,
In living beauty is God's own Light

Which right now and forever
Sets the world, myself, and all life
Eternally free in Ascended Master
    Perfection.
Almighty I AM, Almighty I AM,
    Almighty I AM!   (5x)

The rhythm and the power of that decree, put
on by you as a forcefield of Light through the
science of the mantra, will magnetize to you the
mantle of the apostle Paul. You who would be
ambassadors for Christ, effective as he was to
transmit the flame of Jesus to a world of non-
believers, so-called pagans and the sin-sick and
helpless, you can enter the fiery coil of his attainment in Christ through the spiral staircase
(a geometrical chain not unlike the DNA) of his
spiritual patterns. You can magnetize by the magnet of your threefold flame the spiritual qualities
of his genes and genius.

And this Saint Paul will help you to do the
Work for Christ in Aquarius even as he did the Work

for Christ in Pisces. You can bring the Everlasting Gospel to the world as an apostle of the Universal Christ—of that One who has become the God Self identified, and uniquely identifiable, in every Ascended Master of the Great White Brotherhood.

Everybody in the world needs the violet flame. And the violet flame angels need you to bring the Everlasting Gospel of the Seventh Ray to those who are stuck in the mud and can't get out because only the violet flame will do. Only the violet flame can get them out of their karmic ruts. Who will tell them? You will, once you've tried it and proven it for yourself. Then you'll be just like me—you'll want to tell everybody about the violet flame and show them how to use it, how to decree "I AM a being of violet fire, I AM the purity God desires" and how to do the violet flame spiritual fast.

All around the world people are facing the same things—many wedges of darkened human substance, vibrations of negativity, of fear, of doubt, of distrust, of greed—all types of negative emotions that are tiny, splinterlike, silvery black wedges of misqualified energy that have gotten lodged between the atoms of man's physical body. These are the actual causes of disease; and we can take the word *disease* and interpret it as "dis-ease," or an "absence of ease and comfort."

And the violet flame will transmute all of it. Because through the violet flame you center in the heart and in the heart of God's love for freedom, and you reestablish your equilibrium and your harmony and that's when you begin to understand what is wholeness. And then the healing process begins. And you start communicating that love of freedom to all your cells and systems and organs and molecules. And as you decree they all start spinning faster and faster. And you get real peppy and you start singing waltzes and cleaning your house. And life feels new and so do you.

And you experience direct contact with the violet flame angels, and their violet light and love floods your being and you feel flood tides of gratitude responding from your being to them and you swim with the undines in a violet flame sea of light on the etheric plane, and your whole body is full of light and you begin to feel a great clockwise spin begin to turn your entire aura until you are revolving like a violet flame sun and all darkness flees and you are healing and being healed right now!

And once you've experienced all this, the Maha Chohan is going to pick you right up and send you on a mission to tell the whole world about the violet flame. And you'll be transmuting all the way, until one day an angel of the Karmic Board taps you on the shoulder and tells you you've balanced 51 percent of your karma! And that'll be the day! That'll be the day you vow not to stop going until you've balanced all 100 percent.[56]

And then, instead of electing to take your ascension as is your prerogative, you will ask God to let you stay and break the Bread of your Life and give to the incomplete ones the momentum of

your violet flame spin to consume world sin. And if
they grant your request, you'll be on your way to
becoming a world saviour. And then you'll know
just why the brothers of the shadow worked so hard
to get you off the violet flame merry-go-round.
Because it only takes one to light the whole world!
And lo, you have become that One.

Eradicating Negative Energies in Time and Space

So now I'll tell you what you have to know to
help people understand the violet flame and become a Christ on the Seventh Ray: We all recognize that between the Earth and Mars and Venus
and all the planets, there's a great deal of space.
Similarly, there is space within the molecular and
cellular structure of your physical, astral, and
mental bodies. And this is a very important point
that the Masters have always desired their students
to understand, because when they understand it,
they can understand a little more about how the
violet flame works in their bodies to free them from
their karma, which accumulates layer upon layer
in those vessels of life.

Now, under ordinary conditions human
thought and feeling that is misqualified does not
penetrate the nucleus—the sun-center of the atom.
The white fire core of the atom does not readily
permit the penetration of misqualified energy, but
the wide open spaces between the electrons of
both atoms and molecules and in the cellular
structure of the body do. Thus, the dense vibrations

of misqualified energy collect and clog the very pores of life with that tarlike substance, or debris. Nevertheless, in the case of Absolute Evil, the entrenched Darkness of the fallen ones, the core of self and atom is not only penetrated but permeated with blackness, and the sun-center of cell and soul are now become devouring vortices as black holes in space.

What is the real reason that humanity today are not able to let the Divine Tao or the Divine Energy or the Divine Flame or the Holy Spirit pass through their consciousness?

Why is it that people fail to accept the Law and the true science of Being?

What is it that keeps them from accepting the power of the angels and the control of the elements and the mastery of themselves?

It is nothing else at all except human density. Human density. It is brought about because our furnaces are clogged with clinkers.

Do you know what that means? We didn't have a clean burning flame. The flame is sooted with human doubts and fears—all these negativities— and eventually the sooting, as we keep burning the flame of Life, creates the clinkers through which the draft of the Holy Spirit cannot pass. And therefore we have a system that is literally clogged with negative energy.

Actually, the mind would never become senile as it does in some people if it were not for the burdens of the body itself that becomes clogged with the substance of misqualified energy which the individual has either misqualified himself or absorbed from other people who have misqualified it.

This is a very important point in your study and mastery of the Great Law because you don't have to have this condition existing at all. The violet flame will remove the cause and core of this condition. You can absolutely cook this misqualified energy right out of you and evaporate it with violet flame. It gets so 'hot' that it actually melts the impure substance out of your being.

When you first start doing it, if you could see clairvoyantly, you would see hunks of black tarry substance popping right out of your being and crackling in the flame. And you'd see them tumbling and bouncing in there and then you'd see them melt and then disappear in a puff of smoke.

Most of the people who come to our services can't see this, but some of our students can. And it's a wonderful thing to see, because all through our physical body is this disease-causing accumulation of black tarry substance which is the precipitate of negative energy we've put in there through many embodiments. It's astral but it's definitely physical.

The Masters have used the illustration of someone taking a pail of tar that's been melted and pouring it over a barrel full of marbles. Now, all of you recognize that there's space between the marbles. Because they're round they can't possibly fit together with each other. So the tar runs down those spaces in between the marbles, and the first thing you know, the whole mass is all wedded together and welded together with this sticky, tarry substance.

And that's exactly why people die. That's what happens to them physically. It's the hardening of the arteries of their light, in one sense of the word. By their hardness of heart they've dammed the flow, in more ways than one, because the flow is God, and people from time to time do resent God—so they damn him. Misqualified energy settles down in, through, and around the parts of the body. It has to go somewhere, and your body is the universe where you see precipitated out the products of your conceptions and creations. If it didn't happen that way, you'd have no way of knowing how you're doing in your apprenticeship to become a co-creator with God.

So when you see manifestations of disease, decay, debilitation, decrepitude, senility and insanity, you're supposed to say, "Something's wrong. I've got to change the method and the madness of my experiments in the laboratory of matter. I've got to find out what law it is that I'm breaking and then get on the right side of it and be sure it's on the right side of me. Because my left side over here is giving me trouble."

Well, people don't do this, do they? They curse God instead; they deny karma and their karmic accountability for what they are, and they go to their graves not once but many times over denying the part they have played in their own mortality—when, during the same amount of time they could have become the Wonderman of Europe! Or at least an adept in the Aquarian age. In the same time it took them to become a nobody a dozen times over!

In this world, time and space and energy are all we've got to get us where we want to go. One of these days they'll run out, and if you're not ready for the ascension, you'll be starting all over with that oatmeal on your chin. And I for one am not about to start that story all over again.

And so people come back and they still seek to explain their woes by the three-score-and-ten methodology. They just accept old age as though it were preordained by the omnipotent God. You know, they say, "Oh well, this is what has happened." They're victims of their false doctrines, their diets, and their human density, and they don't fight any of the three d's that are damming up the flow of light in their systems, even as they themselves are damning their entire existence!

Speaking from a human standpoint, let's examine it for a moment. Mankind starts out at a very early age with a completely beautiful arterial and cardiovascular system. The blood vessels of the body are all nice and open, like the great culverts when you install a new sewage system—our pipelines are all open.

And so everything works very well when we are children. We see the sun shining in a blue sky, we watch the wind ambling merrily through the trees, and we are spirits blithe and gay. Life does not present serious problems to us. We do not know about the economic and social difficulties our parents are facing for us. We're not aware of the implications of dogma and the encrustations of endless human questionings and records of death.

You don't think of that. The baby's in the lap of its mother and the baby feels immortal life flowing through it and it has no awareness that it will ever die. So it's completely happy, OK? Now what comes along? They tell us that at the age of nine and seventeen atherosclerosis has already set in in man's physical body, and this is because of the intake of food.

Today there is little or no regard in the marketplaces for human beings by human beings. Human beings hardly regard one another at all. They sell you, for example, french-fried potatoes that are saturated with saturated fatty acids. Not unsaturated fatty acids, but saturated fatty acids. These are heated to 350 degrees Fahrenheit.

When we eat them, what happens to our body? The enzymes and the action of the digestive juices all begin to work and churn in the stomach, creating the chyme which goes into our intestines. There, of course, they are assimilated through the circulatory network by the proximity of that network to the lining of the digestive tract as peristalsis is taking place.

And so, what is happening all the time to

these saturated fatty acids? Shall I tell you? Well, they are being deposited in your arterial system. And so the aging process that is going on all the time in people is accelerated because of the saturated fatty acids. And we hear more and more of people in their thirties dying of heart attacks.

And the Bible speaks of it. Jesus says that the hearts of men will fail them for fear.[57] And why is it? Because the solar plexus in man, that superb network of light which is located right over the navel, is impinged upon by vibrations of fear and doubt and man's inhumanity to man.

When we were recently in the Hawaiian Islands, we were able to perceive spiritually the records of the ancient Hawaiian chiefs and some of their tortures. Did you realize that they submitted their own people to hideous forms of torture?[58] And I'm sorry to say that this has also happened in Africa and on the American continent. In fact, I know of no place where man's inhumanity to man has not been apparent.

Violet Flame Footprints on the Sands of Time

These records, remaining, then, as old momentums of negativity, must be destroyed. They are best destroyed by those who created them or by those who recognize that they have been created and that they are a negative concentration of energy—a negative snowball or an avalanche going down the human mountain of despair. And these negative energies both personal and planetary must be eradicated, and no other method is as effective as the giving of these violet flame decrees.

This is the most marvelous system which Christ certainly brought forth in his recognition of the chalice of the grape, saying, "I will not drink henceforth of this fruit of the vine, until that day when I drink it new with you in my Father's kingdom."[59] And we are doing that today, because it is not just a matter of assimilating the physical body and blood of Christ in a Eucharistic sense, for the true Eucharist is the absorption of the principles of Christ Reality—starting with the Teaching "they" left out.

When we are able to recognize this, we will void all man's inhumanity to man and people will understand that everything that they do is done to themselves. Do you see what I mean? This is a very important point.

If no one does anything, creates no harms at all to anyone else, then no one will suffer harms. Does that make sense? It seems to make great sense to me, and yet all over the world we are perceiving more and more of man's inhumanity to man cloaked in what we may call a soft glove. A mailed fist is always apparent in the world, but now we cover the mailed fist with a soft glove—the veneer of society that still practices great cruelty upon its members, depriving mankind of opportunity for economic equality in the world.

And yet we must, of course, be extremely careful of this because there is a law of karma involved, and the law of karma clearly states that man shall receive whatever he sends out. If we send out to our neighbor darkness and despair, darkness and despair will return to us. But if we send out the labor of love and light and beauty and instruction, then this will return to us also. And as we amplify in our society those constructive Christ elements that will strengthen the bonds of mankind, we will usher in the kingdom of heaven.

Now we legislate our laws. Then they will come from the heart. Now we make rules and enforce them by police action, of necessity. Then they will be self-administered because we will love one another enough not to violate those sacred principles which make our lives worthwhile.

As Longfellow said, "Lives of great men all remind us we can make our lives sublime, and, departing, leave behind us footprints on the sands of time." Do you understand? We can do it. We can leave violet flame footprints on the sands of time. "Footprints, that perhaps another, sailing o'er life's solemn main, a forlorn and shipwrecked brother, seeing, shall take heart again." And this is also God's will. We can be our brother's keeper by sowing the violet flame everywhere we go.

So, "Let us be up and doing with a heart for any fate, still achieving, still pursuing—learn to labor and to wait."[60] In that spirit of achieving and pursuing our God-realization day by day, with the violet flame angels our constant companions, we're going to take the "Six Mighty Cosmic Light Calls."

I will ask you to stand for this, because this is offered unto Saint Germain, who works with Jesus Christ, Gautama Buddha, Lord Lanto and Confucius and many of the Masters of the Great White Brotherhood in the behind-the-scenes action of developing a new body of God upon earth, a greater awareness, a reawakening.

Let's say this together:

1. Unfailing Light of God, I AM calling your Perfection into action in me now!   (3x)

   Unfailing Light of God, I AM calling your Perfection into action in this organization now!   (3x)

   Unfailing Light of God, I AM calling your Perfection into action on the earth now!   (3x)

2. The blazing Light of God in the fullness of its Power is victorious now!   (3x)

3. Mighty Arcturus, thou Elohim of God, descend with that Light of a thousand suns to transmute all human selfishness and discord on the earth now!   (3x)

4. *The Light of God never fails! (3x) and the beloved Mighty I AM Presence is that Light!   (3x)*

5. We speak to all misqualified energy: You have no power! Your day is done! In God's name, I AM, be thou dissolved and transmuted into Light, Illumination, and Love forever!   (3x)

6. The unlimited hosts of Light now move with lightning speed around the whole world and all human shadows melt away before God's Love! (3x)

Now, while you're still on your feet, those "pillars of Pisces," let's take the "Decree for Freedom's Holy Light":

Mighty Cosmic Light!
My own I AM Presence bright,
    Proclaim Freedom everywhere—
In Order and by God Control
I AM making all things whole!

Mighty Cosmic Light!
Stop the lawless hordes of night,
    Proclaim Freedom everywhere—
In Justice and in Service true
I AM coming, God, to you!

Mighty Cosmic Light!
I AM Law's prevailing might,
    Proclaim Freedom everywhere—
In magnifying all goodwill
I AM Freedom living still!

Mighty Cosmic Light!
Now make all things right,
    Proclaim Freedom everywhere—
In Love's Victory all shall go,
I AM the Wisdom all shall know!

I AM Freedom's holy Light
Nevermore despairing!
I AM Freedom's holy Light
Evermore I'm sharing!
Freedom, Freedom, Freedom!
Expand, expand, expand!
I AM, I AM, I AM
Forevermore I AM Freedom!   (3x)

Isn't that beautiful? You are experiencing the momentum of the decree of the heavenly hosts releasing to all mankind, through your exercise of the science of the spoken Word, God's very own violet flame—this time as Freedom's holy Light.

It is not as though *we* owned it; we all own it together. It is not our exclusive right, except through our togetherness and the world's togetherness—not in mere physical union but in a spiritual unity of hearts. Yes, the violet flame, the science of dynamic decrees and self-knowledge through the I AM THAT I AM belongs to everyone on earth. And we shall stump the nations until all people have heard the message of the Everlasting Gospel and are enjoying its fruits.

We are seeking to develop in you a greater awareness of the violet fire and its use in the decree patterns given to us by the Ascended Masters. So now we'll sing to the violet flame to the tune of "Santa Lucia." Let us give the preamble to "I AM the Violet Flame." This is the call we give for the violet flame sea to cover the earth. "Santa Lucia" is an Italian song and one sees the Bay of Naples, the blue water. And you can visualize that beautiful bay as the violet fire sea.

Let's give the preamble together:

> In the name of the beloved mighty victorious Presence of God, I AM in me, and my very own beloved Holy Christ Self, I call to beloved Alpha and Omega in the heart of God in our Great Central Sun, beloved Saint Germain, beloved Portia, beloved Archangel Zadkiel, beloved Holy Amethyst, beloved Mighty Arcturus and Victoria, beloved Kuan Yin, Goddess of Mercy, beloved Oromasis and Diana, beloved Mother Mary, beloved Jesus, beloved Omri-Tas, ruler of the violet planet, beloved great Karmic Board, beloved Lanello, the entire Spirit of the Great White Brotherhood and the World Mother, elemental life—fire, air, water, and earth!

> To expand the violet flame within my heart, purify my four lower bodies, transmute all misqualified energy I have ever imposed upon life, and blaze mercy's healing ray throughout the earth, the elementals, and all mankind and answer this my call infinitely, presently, and forever:

> > I AM the Violet Flame
> > In action in me now
> > I AM the Violet Flame

> To Light alone I bow
> I AM the Violet Flame
> In mighty Cosmic Power
> I AM the Light of God
> Shining every hour
> I AM the Violet Flame
> Blazing like a sun
> I AM God's sacred power
> Freeing every one

Let us conclude our session in the violet flame consciousness for the achievement of God-realization by fully entering our mantra once again:

> I AM a being of violet fire
> I AM the purity God desires

And as you give this decree, visualize your family, all the people you know in your state and nation and hemisphere and world. Visualize the millions of people in the Americas, in Europe, the Middle East, all of Africa, Russia, China, India, throughout Asia, the islands and Australia. By the authority of the Word which God placed within us through the divine spark, we're going to saturate the whole world with violet flame.

When you say, "I AM a being of violet fire," you are saying, "*God in me* is a being of violet fire." So wherever God is I AM—you are—the violet flame—by your consciously directed decree. You see, it is the prerogative of the divinity within you to decree: It's your divine right, because you are divine. You have to know the difference between human rights and divine rights, and champion them both!

When you say, "I AM the purity God desires," you are saying, "The I AM Presence in me is the embodiment of God's purity as he is desiring it for me now." So we see this action through the insight, the inner sight, of the third-eye and we decree it through the power released in the throat center multiplied millions of times for all the beautiful faces of God's dear children on earth.

Together:

> I AM a being of violet fire
> I AM the purity God desires   (33x)

In conclusion, having given to you all that the law of the Seventh Ray and its hierarchs allow for this chapter of our meeting together, we bring you from the violet flame Master himself, Saint Germain, excerpts of his message as well as his more recent comments (dictated especially for this volume) on the violet flame for world transmutation and for America's fulfillment of her destiny in the Universal Age. His Teaching is the culmination of our climb with you up the highest mountain of your divinity made known through the Lost Teachings of Jesus Christ. He delivered this dictation through Elizabeth in our nation's capital and anchored there his flame and that of beloved Portia for the protection of the flame of freedom and God-government in America and every nation.

For we are still working together, as they say, "as Above so below," for the freeing of this planet. Saint Germain's plan was and is that our twin flames—the "other two, the one on this side of the bank of the river, and the other on that side of the bank of the river"—verily as the Two Witnesses,[61] should keep the flame of Christ's universal Teaching on earth until the Ancient of Days, Sanat Kumara, "shall have accomplished to scatter the power of the holy people," as Daniel was told.[62] In Jesus' words, "And this Gospel of the Kingdom shall be preached in all the world for a witness unto all nations and then shall the end come."[63]

So may you read and run with the words of the Hierarch of the Aquarian Age, servant of Christ—Saint Germain, our friend and yours:

"The Harvest" by Saint Germain

'Tis the season of the harvest. Observe: Leaves are falling from the trees. The ripe fruit of the apple is gathered and kept for a year's worth of eating. Thus, every tree brings forth fruit in its time.

Is it possible to roll back the harvest, to change the poisonous fruit into the golden pear of divine consciousness? This is indeed the question that ignorant mankind must face. Yet they will not face it. Therefore, let the sons and daughters of God face it.

Let them understand, beloved hearts, that in this hour, truly there is a harvest of two hundred years and more of this nation's history. Taking into account from the point of my discovery unto this moment, it is evident that nigh five hundred years have passed.[64]

I come, therefore, to explain that it is a period of harvest of right and wrong decision—a harvest of souls and a harvest of hearts. Thus, beloved, no longer a wilderness land where the prophet might ensconce himself, but a land teeming with lifestreams, the crossroads of a planet—yea, a planet and a solar system and beyond. One nation under one God with multifaceted lifestreams that ought to blend into the seven rays and then into the white light.

But, alas, some of the harvest are colorless and have no fruit. Therefore, where shall the barren fig tree appear?

Christ has already cursed—which means judged—the barren and the unfruitful consciousness,[65] that the disciples might understand that in order to retain the right to Life in cosmos, one must bear fruit, and quality fruit—not the white page we *might have* written upon, beloved hearts.

This presents a taxing equation for the Ascended Masters and their chelas: to intricately withdraw the threads of evil from the fabric of the nation, from the body politic. How can one take the crochet hook of the Mother and remove these threads—some of them not entirely black but woven as gray and subtle gradations? *(gray-dations)*

Where does one define Light and Darkness?

Where does one draw the line and, in drawing the line, cut off the arm or the leg as opportunity to improve, to change?

Many times we have recommended far less karma upon the individual, for should he receive what is due as the penalty of the Law, it would wipe out his very opportunity to accept grace in another day and to move forward. Thus, it is not quite the moment to obey the injunction "If thy right arm offend thee, cut it off,"[66] for tomorrow the right arm may not be the offense but the blessing to life.

Now, understand why the violet flame is so necessary. It is because it is the age of opportunity—the opportunity of the Mother that is with us. Understand, then, that in sorting out human history and the history of the lifewaves who have migrated to this soil, one must perceive the causes and name them and call for their binding by the violet flame, and then the effects will disappear as easily as one erases a chalkboard.

Let us become more astute. Thus, I acknowledge that you are already astute. This astuteness that I call forth is the outsmarting of the tendency to forget to call daily to the violet flame on the issues that are fundamental.

There are fundamental neutrons and protons in the nucleus of this nation that must be changed if the atom of self is to swing with the necessary electrons of the freewill sons and daughters of God (freewheeling in the sense that the ritual of their courses—orbital paths around the central sun of

Being—is apparently beyond the understanding of the observers).

Thus is the Holy Spirit. Thus is every atomic particle—not fashioned after a preordained destiny but fashioned to include the element of free will! Thus, let everyone who is of God receive the Holy Spirit of the seventh age and therefore move with that Spirit, unconfined by the mechanisms of worldly thought, its entrapments, its compartments.

Now, if it were not so, it would be impossible to do anything with the law of karma or the effects of causes set in motion. It would be impossible to change history and therefore to change the present. But as you have been told, if you discover the key of the cause, the key and the nucleus of any happening or series of events of history, the undoing of this and its transmutation by the violet flame will collapse the entire spiral unto the present.

I speak of the powers of control. I speak of age-old conspiracies at inner levels and on the astral plane so that, try as they may, men and women of goodwill have not been able to bring in an age of peace and freedom and enlightenment for all.

God knows, so many have tried, so many have prayed for it, so many have determined and have given their lives. God knows, these men and women of goodwill are far in excess numerically of those evildoers who have stopped the course of the onward movement, the spiraling of the Central Sun, from physically manifesting.

The Hour of Change

The hour of change is come, even as the hour of the harvest is come. Change is the order of the day, for the experiencing internally of that fire of the violet flame sun, beloved hearts.

I AM come. I AM your beloved (I trust) Saint Germain. You are my beloved (I do know) Keepers of the Flame and of the Spirit of the God most holy.

Let us look, then, to causes—causes of war. These concern me. For civilization may hold together imperfectly for many centuries, but world war and world holocaust can set back the planetary body, cutting off the right arm, the right leg, destroying genes and so forth, so that the morrow does not bring the new dawn of opportunity.

Let us examine, then, causes of war most recent in this hemisphere in Central America, in Afghanistan, war that parades across the planet—causes of war in Vietnam, in Korea, in World War II, World War I.

Beloved Children of the Sun, these causes go back to the same forces—those exterrestrials[67] in the earth who desire to keep the control of the population by arraying brother against brother, aligning them in causes and polarities not their own but foisted upon them by serpentine minds who have known how to work them up to a fever pitch of emotion—mutual suspicion and hatred—by their indoctrination and propaganda and contrived shortages of food, hunger, disease, and manipulation of the basic commodities of the oil and the wheat.[68]

Blessed ones, the gold that is in thy hand from the God of Gold—this, too, they have tried to manipulate. Let us concentrate, then, not on surface events, but let us pull the black threads from the fabric of world consciousness. And then let us go to the hands that have woven these, and behind the hands to the controlling consciousness, and behind the controlling consciousness to the core of Evil in the Matter cosmos.

Let Children of the Sun be less disturbed by day-to-day events. Let Children of the Sun, which ye are—the Great Central Sun where Alpha and Omega, thy Father and thy Mother, attend thy Homecoming—understand the meaning of life and interpret effects by prior causes and go after those causes which are often hidden behind closed doors in smoke-filled rooms.

Treacherous are the ways of the fallen ones. But the Word—the Word of the Holy of Holies—is the power. It is the very power of the pulling of the threads ere the threads know they have been pulled. It is the stripping of the anti-power amassed by the enemies of humanity before they realize that it has been taken from them.

I, Saint Germain, need your call. As was said by Kuthumi,[69] I need, as never before, the call of the faithful in dynamic violet flame decrees to avert and turn back conspiracies working against humanity in this hour—against this nation and every nation.

I ask for protection for America and its government. I ask you to make daily calls to Archangel Michael for the protection of all governments of all free nations and the protection of the true sons and daughters of God who are the real representatives of the people wherever tyrants have raised their heads in the name of this or that particular political persuasion.

Beloved ones, the holy purpose of the Great White Brotherhood requires your support. Thus, the ramparts of freedom at Camelot and the Royal Teton Ranch must be reinforced, not merely by timbers but by timbers of heart and flesh—of those individuals who recognize in this hour the predawn hour of the victory of this divine plan.

It takes more than funds, though funds are indeed needed. It takes more than goodwill, though goodwill we cherish. It does take your physical presence, for it is an age of physical initiation. The threat of nuclear war is physical initiation. The threat of world pollution and annihilation of elemental life [animal and plant life] is a physical initiation.

This the sons and daughters of God, suns of blazing violet flame, must face, and face squarely, on behalf of the Children of the Sun.

The Violet Flame Is a Physical Flame

The violet flame is a physical flame! And what do I mean when I say this? I say the violet flame is closest in vibratory action of all of the rays to this earth substance, to these chemical elements and compounds, to all that you see in Matter. And therefore, the violet flame can combine with any molecule or molecular structure, any particle of matter known or unknown, and any wave of light, electrons, or electricity.

Thus, the violet flame is the supreme antidote for food poisoning, chemical waste, toxins, pollution of drugs in the body. The violet flame is an elixir that you drink and imbibe like water, like the purest juice of the fruit of the harvest of the elementals' consciousness.

The violet flame is the supreme antidote for physical problems. Wherever chelas gather to give the violet flame, there you notice immediately an improvement in *physical* conditions! And thus, you see, the tares sown among the wheat[70] have contrived to bring Armageddon to a physical level, even in your own households and in your own relationships with people.

Yours is the supreme test of raising that alabaster pyramid in the physical octave, the test of building the temple of man in the face of any and all obstruction that comes your way through self-degradation and the degeneration, the very crumbling of physical matter. Whether organic or inorganic matter, there is a disintegration spiral that works in the buildings, in the land, in the sea, and in the bodies which can best be counteracted by the violet flame.

The violet flame turns around the spin of electron and atom. It turns around the downward spiral of the chakras and the energy. It is forever the power of conversion—and conversion means "to turn around"! The violet flame is the buoyant joy of the Holy Ghost that turns around spirits and minds and souls and emotions!

Freedom has this power. It has had this power in every age and century. Let the flame of freedom descend anywhere, and all rejoice and leap for the power of their own divinity—else they leap to misuse that freedom if they operate on the dark side of life. But freedom itself is a power that moves, and it moves for change. And when it is misused, that change does not become constructive but destructive.

An Acceleration of Light and Darkness —Drugs and Rock Music

Beloved ones, even in the six months that have passed since we came last to the Heart of the Inner Retreat, while you have seen an acceleration of Light, there has been a corresponding and unseen acceleration of Darkness. And this is as it has been through past ages when cataclysms in the economy or in the land have been nigh.

Therefore I tell you, it is necessary to counteract this Darkness with increasing violet flame, increasing the call for the reversing of the tide of the downward spiral of civilization, and then binding, by the astuteness of the mind, the cause and core of that deceleration, which, as you know, has its manifestation in drugs of all kind sweeping the land

and in the polarity of drugs, which is rock music—
the off-beat expression of the core-rebellion of the
recently reembodied Atlanteans.

No matter how much you like rock music or
how much you are addicted to it, or how much
your livelihood or life-style depends on it, I, Saint
Germain, sound the warning: rock music is self-
destructive—yea, more than self-destructive, it is
self-annihilating. Rock music is the tool of the
sinister force which was used by black magicians
on Atlantis to collapse nations and continents
and governments and bodies and souls and self-
esteem—and to lower the Kundalini to the base
chakra.

The international drug craze is the sign of the
last days of Atlantis come again. It is also the sign
which precedes the period of the Great Tribulation.
This sign is called by Jesus "the abomination
of desolation," spoken of by Daniel the prophet,
"standing in the holy place where it ought not."[71]
The holy place, or places, are the chakras in the
temple of Man.

The sound, vibration, and energy of rock music
vibrating in the chakras is unto the death of the soul,
of the mind and consciousness, and the cells of the
body. The Light that flows from your I AM Presence
over the crystal cord to your four lower bodies is
received by every atom in a clockwise spin, charging
it with Light from the Central Sun.

Rock music, by its syncopated 4/4 time, channels energy through your aura and chakras in a

counterclockwise spin, thus turning around Life and the Life-force to the Death spiral of the forces of Darkness. Rock music now saturating not only the media and advertising but also the houses of worship (for the false pastors desperately desire to be popular with the people) is the spearhead of the false hierarchy of Antichrist to decimate and destroy the ranks of the youth and children of the world. It is the sound of Hell paving the way by Abaddon's angels for the Four Horsemen[72] to devour the land and the people.

Let all who read my words and study my message know that you are accountable before God, having been told the Truth, for your participation in or promotion of rock music. To stand idly by while others are self-devoured in the trance of the rock beat—with all of its visuals of horror, death and sex, every one a perversion of the Mother flame (the pure white Goddess Kundalini of the base-of-the-spine [Skt. *mūlādhāra*] chakra)—is to suffer the same fate of the damned who are bringing civilization down upon their own heads and households.

Thus, drugs and rock music become the antithesis of you and your twin flame. You and your twin flame, as the representatives of Alpha and Omega, beloved ones, represent the Light of God Wisdom and God Love. Thus, we find the absolute perversion of Wisdom in rock music and the absolute perversion of Love in drugs.

Oh, 'tis a "sweet death" that causes the imbibing of the death drug (marijuana) in the name of

Love, in the name of an experience, in the name of a sensation. It is hard to believe or to conceive that any one individual could accept drugs into the system in the name of reality or even in the name of pleasure.

Beloved hearts, thirty years ago you could not have imagined such an eventuality as we have today. Yet, it does nothing but multiply. And thus, the astute ones know that it is spawned out of Death and Hell and from the minds of those fallen angels who are bound and yet have not been brought to the Judgment—whose minds yet have influence over the young. Therefore, go after the causes and see how swiftly the lines can be drawn and the bodies and temples of the Lightbearers be preserved to serve another day—when you give your decrees to the violet flame.

Our Flame for the Protection of This Government

I come, then, into the nation's capital this day, through the body of the Messenger and your own blessed temples, to release my flame and the flame of Portia for the protection of this government and right decision, and to stand and hold back conspiracies unknown.

And therefore, you may name "conspiracies unknown" as an insert in your violet flame decrees for world transmutation of the cause behind every negative condition. And then you may call to the Elohim Cyclopea, God's All-Seeing Eye, to reveal that which is hidden which ought to be revealed—

those things done in secret against the very integrity and flame that is the flame of freedom in America and every nation.

Beloved ones, someone once said that history is made by the little people and not by the important people. Well, it is so when the little people discover on that mighty day of their soul liberation that a William Tell[73] or a David[74] or a single voice or a single one holding the finger in the dike can make the difference.

The little people do not shape history unless some among them get the idea that the power of God is in *their* hands, that the ball is in *their* court, and that if they act, truly, nations and continents can be preserved for another day of grace, another day of freedom.

Understand the Times and the Seasons

There is a time for sowing, a time to water, a time to watch the summer breezes and sun, a time for harvest, a time for going into the seed within itself.

Understand the times and the seasons:

There is a time for the coming of the Ascended Masters and the Avatar and the Divine Mother with us.

There is a time that is an interval of space where a civilization and a people must take that flame and demonstrate it.

There is a time when the dark ones move across the land and all are bowed down, and the trees also are moved by strong winds of dark desire and many of them are broken.

And there is a time for the coming of the Helper and the Comforter and the One who enlightens.[75]

Take heed, then, that you understand that that which occurs on a planet and in spiritual cycles is a sine wave. Thus, it is written that there is a tide in the affairs of men. When this tide is taken at its crest, so it leads on to fortune,[76] and that fortune is a divine fortune.

Thus, there is a tide in the cycles, the sine wave of being, and you must mark those points of the peaks and the lows. You must understand there are economic cycles, though they are denied. There are waves that are predictable in all areas of existence because they line up with the cycles of karma which have been observed and plotted on graphs by those who were inspired by us to warn humanity of the hundred-year cycles and more.[77]

Therefore, you are experiencing cycles. Do not count, then, on another day as an opportunity. When you have the maximum attunement and light, it is time to capitalize on it. It is a good investment that will bear fruit from your causal body. At the moment that you have the greatest Light to invest yourself in the greatest Word and Work for God, it is like being on a giant roller coaster.

When you have the momentum behind you and the wind in your sails, I say, make the most of it. For the hour comes when you will harvest that which you sow and you will be on the receiving end and it will be extremely difficult, if not impossible, to undo the consequences of the course you have set, or not set, in motion. Thus, if you do not sow, you do not reap, and then you are hungry in the winter.

The Heyday of Opportunity for America

Thus, the heyday of light, the heyday of opportunity for America is now—and it is for you also. Much can be accomplished in the next four years if watchmen of the night will watch with me through this period, if you who become more astute will then go to the very heart of the problem and capitalize on the opportunity.

Let us not count on anything that we have today being sustained tomorrow unless we invest ourselves in that momentum. Let us not think that we have ten years or twenty, or ten days or five to enter into the mighty caravan of Light. Let us realize that all of us who have lived in past centuries have lived one day and seen peace and when we have awakened in the morning, war has been in progress, destruction has been wrought, Pompeii has been destroyed.

Thus, one must know that in the given cycle one has given one's all to meet the mathematical equation descending from the I AM Presence. Each day a gift descends. Not all days are the same. Wise is the individual who says:

Ah, thou mighty Light of my causal
body, I catch thee now. I run with thee!
I will maximize this potential of God. I will
break the bread of Life. I will contact those
I have been waiting to contact!

"Now Is the Time to Act"

Sometimes you receive an inspiration and an
idea. And it grows in consciousness and it builds.
And one day the holy angels come, they tap thee
on the shoulder, and they say, "Now is the time to
act. *Act! Move! Now!*" And sometimes you do not
respond. You do not sense that there is such a thing
as the urgency of the moment.

Not all ideas are like a juggler's balls that will
go up and down and up and down. There are ideas
that must manifest or else they die. Like the great
spawning power of the fishes of the sea, there is a
moment when the seeds must be sown—and if they
are not sown, they die. And there is a survival of
the fittest, and the strongest seed ideas become
manifestation.

The Fruit of My Harvest

Some gestations require a year, three, or ten.
In a given lifetime, how many gracious fruits of
Maitreya can you bring to fruition? It is time to
consider and plan. Although you are immortal
now, you must plan on a lifespan and what you will
accomplish. You must know what is the single fruit
that you will bring at the conclusion of this life to
Lord Maitreya and say:

O blessed LORD, this is my harvest. By thy love I have kept the flame. I have tended the Tree of Knowledge and the Tree of Life. This is the fruit I render unto thee as the victory of the fruit thou gavest me when I came forth in this life.

So, beloved, let us realize that in the course of a nation, there are only so many cycles and moments when the tide can be turned or new pinnacles of freedom and blessedness won for a people. We are in this hour. Dire predictions have been sounded for 1984, yet many victories have come forth. Many of those prognosticators have not understood the subtle nature of the negative influences of the year. Thus, some of our students have failed to observe that which I have spoken of as a certain acceleration of negativity.

Let us capitalize on the thrust of Light!

The Goddess of Liberty over the Capitol

Thus, I have come and I have called. Now I give you the vision of the Lords of Karma—in the center, the Goddess of Liberty. This Goddess of Liberty has placed herself in a large form, congruent not only with the Goddess of Freedom over the Capitol building but extending to the very basement of that building as a mighty, mighty focus of the ancient feminine ray sponsored by Amazonia and Hercules.

Thus, the Goddess of Liberty comes—the one who embodies the Mind of God, the Mind of the Mother. Truly, she is Sarasvati, Lakshmi,

Durga, Kali. Truly, she is the fourfold action of feminine being and the infinite capacity of Omega to yet steer this nation aright. I ask for sons and daughters of Liberty to contribute nothing less than their lives for this victory.

Your Messenger has spoken my own words, "A patch of earth is needed." I have designated the Inner Retreat at the Royal Teton Ranch as that patch for the Great White Brotherhood, and America as that proving ground for the world of Lightbearers. Let both be defended as sacred. And let this defense, when the cup is full, be extended as the defense of freedom in every nation.

Let our devotees who hear me in Sweden and Norway, in Finland and Denmark, let them understand that I am with you and I commend you for your effort. Increase, then, the mighty threefold flame and call for the union of Scandinavia. And let that union produce, through hearts of Light who are that union, a bulwark of freedom that can move south and encompass Europe, the Isles, and then move east.

Betrayers of Polish Patriots Shall Be Judged

Blessed ones, the betrayers in the Roman Church of the true patriots of Poland must hang their heads in shame before the Lords of Karma this day.[78] The compromisers in the Protestant movement must also know that they receive the judgment of the Lord Christ. Let all those who—by neglect, fear, sympathy, or their own evil hearts—

protect and give place to the murderous ones sent by the Soviets know that they shall not pass, that the Law is just, that God is just, and that Jesus does act in this hour to protect his little ones from the wolves in sheep's clothing.

I assure you as I, Saint Germain, live, these oppressors of the faithful shall not pass! And they shall retain upon their hands the blood of the holy innocents whom they have slain. And it shall be required of them this day and in the day of judgment to come. And not one jot or tittle of the misuse of the sacred fire by these fallen angels in embodiment shall pass. As they have withheld mercy, so mercy shall be withheld from them. And I speak it in the physical octave. And the violet flame does make it physical this day.

Mother Mary's Circle of Light for Afghanistan

Therefore, let my chelas make it physical. And let the Circle of Light of Mother Mary[79] be repeated for Afghanistan, for every nation on earth where dark ones lurk to destroy by any cause or murderous intent. Let the agents of Light, let the agents of the Holy Spirit go in their finer bodies as they visualize in the Circle of Light the ring of fire. It is indeed true—we can reinforce and intensify the release of Light in every circle you form because of the protection and the multiplication factor and the action of the Law of the One.

Thus, pray in the circle and know that Christ is always in the center—"There am I in the midst thereof."[80] And this "I" is the Universal Christ of every Ascended Master and cosmic being. Understand the Law of the One of the Great White Brotherhood. Being is one; manifestation is perceived as the many. But the one Christ of us all is the entire Spirit (or consciousness) of the Great White Brotherhood in the center of your circle.

Endure to the End and Thou Shalt Be Saved

Blessed are ye who have tarried and waited for my message to you. How hard it is to tarry until the coming of the Lord. How hard it is to refrain from giving in to the agitations of the world. He that endures to the end of his karma shall be saved;[81] and I shall be the one to impart that salvation, for it is my role in this Aquarian age and with the violet flame.

Endure to the end and it is my hand that shall pull thee up. I ask only one, one virtue: It is endurance. To have endurance requires trust and faith in the one who asks it of thee. Endure in the service of Freedom and thou shalt be saved.

My Place in Your Heart

Beloved ones, it is good to be with you. And because it is so, with your permission, I shall take up my place in your heart for a season. Thus, my place in your heart denotes a tide in your affairs. Take it, for my self [my person] includes my causal body and my mantle.

I have pressed the limit of dispensations optioned in my direction. And in that limit, I find myself nestled in the heart of the freedom-fighters of Saint Germain.

I pay tribute to the striving ones. Thus, if you do not count yourself a striving one, you may become so within twenty-four hours and also receive my tribute. Thus, all may have my grace while it is God's good season to give me the opportunity to extend it. And there is good reason for my message. Let the word to the wise be heeded, and let those who are becoming the wise trust the Word until they have the comprehension of it.

By faith, by faith ye are made whole.

In Honor of the Striving One

I stand in honor of the Striving One. Let us salute him, the Ascended Master El Morya. Thus, as we pay tribute to the sponsor of God-government in this city and nation, let us pour out our hearts' love. Let us implement his will and purpose, which is God's, for each and every chela. And let us know that this day and every day we have fought that good fight and won.

I address you as winners. I bless you as winners. And I send you out as the scattering of the good seed. May you find the good ground[82] and grow there and become mighty trees, known on the planet forever and forever.[83]

Chapter Fourteen

YOU WILL BECOME
ONE WITH GOD!

You Will Become One with God!

adies and gentlemen, it gives me great pleasure
to be able to come to you here in Santa Barbara
quite unexpectedly. I find that very shortly I will be
leaving California. We've been here almost all
week, and we'll be leaving tomorrow and heading
on back to headquarters in Colorado Springs. Then,
of course, I plan on going to the East Coast, and
then we'll be coming back and getting ready for the
Easter conference, which will be held in Colorado
Springs this year.

Caught in the Jar of Mystery

And I specifically want to invite you, all who
are able, to attend that conference. I can promise
you that this year there will be a large number of
surprises that some of you may have anticipated
and some of you may not have anticipated. It
promises to be a very great conference, one that
I hope you will not miss.

But I know that if you knew all that was to
take place, none of you would miss it—that is, I'm
quite sure most of you would make every effort to

get there. But on the other hand, I can't make premature announcements because I'm sort of caught in the jar of mystery where I have certain things that are restricted at this time and we are not announcing because we're getting ready to announce it, and we can't blow the whistle on ourselves.

And I think that to see as many of you turn out for an unexpected occasion as have done so today makes me feel a very warm feeling in my heart toward the people of California. And quite naturally this is so because we had this in our heart when we first dedicated this center here as a place where young people, together with people of all ages, could come and not only worship, but also make contact with the higher level of thought that is represented by those who have gone on before us as a pillar of fire by night.

"I Ascend unto My Father..."

I would like to speak to you of the Ascended Masters—those who have followed in the footsteps of the eternal Christ, appearing in every age and enabling people to make those contacts with God which are so essential to our souls.

I think in many of us the figure of God is often anthropomorphic—that is to say, we have a God made in our image. And it is sometimes difficult for us to envision the living God in the great spiritual tides of reality that are involved with the Godhead.

However, one of the essential elements of the path to the Godhead is captured in Jesus' famous statements which he made on more than one occasion: "I go unto my Father...I go to prepare a place for you that where I am, there ye may be also. I ascend unto my Father, and your Father, and to my God, and your God."[1]

In this he would draw to our attention the absorption into the Godhead of the being and consciousness of the Christ, that from henceforth the very being of God himself would be richer because it would have absorbed into itself all the magnificent Christ qualities that were externalized in the life of the man Jesus.

The divine intent has not been to create beings that are solely subservient and dependent upon others but rather to create beings that rise to their own native God-estate—and in so rising are able to contribute something of worth from their own being to the Godhead.

Thus, the universe is enriched by each soul who returns unto God crowned with the Christ consciousness. And through the law of rebirth, one is able to be reborn toward that more perfect day which will one day dawn when all sons and daughters of the Most High will at last express the perfection of their God—their individualized I AM Presence—in their life.

This is the Christ-perfection that is "the chief cornerstone"[2] of the temple of man, already placed firmly upon its foundation by the LORD God in the beginning. And therefore, the temple of the individual can rise—an edifice of reality here upon the plains of the world's thought—to become the pattern for the universal temple of man. And we find that man can become one with God as Christ also did.

Pulling Both Strings of the Parrot

Now, in the midst of all this I would like to tell you a little story. It seems that it was the occasion of a man and his wife's wedding anniversary. And so, he decided that he would go downtown and buy her something that would please her. And as he was going by a pet store, he decided upon a parrot.

So, he brought the parrot home. And it had two strings, one on each leg as it stood on its perch. He said to his wife, "Now, you pull the left-hand string." So she pulled the left-hand string and the parrot said, "Happy anniversary, darling!" And so, he was quite delighted with this. And he said to her, "Now pull the other string." So she pulled the right string and the parrot said, "Good morning. It's a nice day."

So about that time, the wife turned to him and she said, "Why don't you pull both strings?"

And the parrot looked up at both of them and turned to the man and said, "You idiot! If you pull both strings, I'll fall off my perch!"

So today I suspect that many people would like to pull both my strings so I'd fall off my perch right now, you see—telling a story like that after such a sublime statement that preceded it!

Nevertheless, I think that sometimes we need

to relax because the world is far too tense. We find a great deal of tension as a result of man's concerns, and we find that these concerns have a certain validity.

We're concerned about the raising of our taxes. We're concerned about the high cost of living. We're concerned about the high cost of housing. We're concerned about what our president is going to do next. We're concerned about "Will the Communists take over this country?" We're concerned about "Will our souls be saved?" In other words, "What's going to happen to us individually?"

We have all manner of concerns that come to us. And these concerns, in return, create tensions in our being that do not give us the feeling of happiness that we ought to have in this beautiful universe. Because in reality—if you will stop and think of it—the replica, the divine replica, or the image of God in which man was made, brought forth a perfectly beautiful and magnificent body temple with a magnificent soul consciousness, and having a magnificent Spirit.

In other words, man was created Godlike and he was endowed with Godlike power.

A Dearth of Spiritual Reality

Something intervened. Something occurred in the exercise of the spiritual office that man had originally been endowed with. Now, we find that history has already proclaimed to us that there is a great deal of suffering in the world. And if you go back in history, you will find that in past ages the suffering was in some ways even more acute than it is today, because today we are able to find the answers to many of our material questions.

We punch a button and dial a number on our telephones and, lo and behold, we are connected with another party in another part of the world and we hold a conversation. We're able to get on a jet airplane and in two or three to four hours we can be almost anywhere in America. We are able to put a man on the moon in a matter of a few days, and that man can communicate across interstellar space with this world.

We are able to put new arteries in hearts that are damaged. And many people who were hopelessly ill a hundred years ago, today have hope. They can go to the hospital and have surgery or they can have medical treatment. Any of a number of different things can be done and these people's lives can be saved. We do brain operations, we do all kinds of things that were never heard of in the past.

And so, the quality of life on earth today is better in a material sense than it has ever been in history. Yet, all manner of conflicts are still raging in many of the underprivileged areas of the world and many people are still suffering.

We have existing side by side great wealth and great poverty. And we also have great wealth of a spiritual nature existing in some individuals, and yet all over the world we have people who are greatly impoverished in a spiritual sense—both in the churches and outside of the churches.

People are asking all kinds of questions and they're not satisfied with the answers they're getting. Isn't it a strange paradox, then, that at a time when we have advanced to such a high level of material attainment we should have such a dearth of spiritual reality in the world? Should it be this way? We don't think so.

Life Is Not Self-Elevating without Free Will

Now, some time ago, Mrs. Prophet and I began the writing of Book I of *Climb the Highest Mountain*, which some of you, of course, have read and some of you have not. In that book we set forth the synthetic image.[3] We tried to explain that man is really a giant computer of very great ability and that the subconscious being of man is able to receive sight and sound impressions which constitute the workings of the personality. These sight and sound impressions inscribed as they are upon the inner tape, or the inner memory disk, call it what you will—an ordinary blackboard of consciousness—thus create a synthetic individual.

But the individual whom God made—who has been endowed with the power of the heartbeat and the perfect control of the automatic functions of being—is, of course, different than the synthetic individual that is compounded of mere sensory impressions.

What are our first impressions? We often laughingly say that some of the earliest impressions are drawn from that big spoon that looks like a steam shovel coming at us with a whole load of oatmeal and sugar and God only knows what on that spoon! As a babe, we have no choice except to accept it. And if we try not to accept it, it probably lands on our face or runs down our chin or all over our bib.

So, you see, our early impressions are in some ways almost ludicrous. Then as we grow up, we're able to sort out these impressions and develop our own personalities and begin to understand after our own fashion what the world is all about.

Then we change. But we do not necessarily develop a spiritual consciousness at all, because these impressions do not cause us to develop spirituality. We develop a limited ability to cope. We have the ability of response. We find that we can become feisty or we can become so placid that we just sit there and more or less accept whatever is foisted upon us.

You know this really happens. There are people today who are truly Caspar Milquetoasts.[4] They just sit back and whatever happens—if the government decides to do a certain thing—they accept it. They say, "We're going to raise the price of stamps now to twelve cents, to fifteen cents, to twenty-two cents a stamp!" People say, "Well, stamps have gone up. Did you know that?" "Sure." They accept it.

Then you have others who are not placid at

all. These people get up on a soapbox and they say, "We've got to do something!"—you know, the old Boston Tea Party bit—"We've got to do something about it and improve the world!"

Now, if everybody in the world were like Caspar Milquetoast and the politicians were like they are today, what would happen to our world? What do you think would happen to it? Hmm? It would be an awful situation, wouldn't it? On the other hand, if we all became radicals and we began to find fault with everything and we could never appreciate the value of anything, it wouldn't be good either.

So we have to recognize extremism as undesirable, and yet we cannot be the kind of people who just sit back and do nothing about our lives. And it doesn't matter if you're a Caspar Milquetoast or if you're the other type. If you're the other type, you'd probably better temper the wind a little bit to the shorn lamb of people, because we can't always deal with situations on the basis of radicalism. At the same time, we've got to handle things by determinate and consistent effort.

And as long as you're going to do this in an outer way, concerning your little material life (which comes to an end in three score and ten in most cases), then certainly you ought to be concerned enough about your spiritual life to apply it there, too.

You know your inner awareness comes from the iceberg of the distant past into the moment where you see the tip of the iceberg and you know there's a lot more to it, and you know that eternity is going to face you. And you know that eternity is not necessarily a hostile environment but it is an environment of hope and promise.

Now listen to this. Hope and promise. But not hope and promise where we do nothing about it. It is not automated like our heartbeat. The heartbeat of the future is not automated. If we do nothing about it spiritually, if we do not accept our birth-right, if we do not accept the great tides of spiritual reality that are already running in our lives and do not open up the floodgates of reality within ourselves by application to the Ascended Master consciousness, to the Christ consciousness—if we do not make some effort or some attempt, we will become stultified.

We will become root-bound. We will stand right where we are and we will make no forward progress whatsoever. In fact, we may find ourselves even going a little bit backward, simply because we have not recognized our solemn responsibility to do something to bring ourselves into attunement.

You cannot listen to a television program anywhere in the world without turning the dial. Of course, if you leave the set pretuned, that's fine. But then you have to punch the button to turn it on again when you're ready to listen to a program. And so you must make the effort of turning the dial, of tuning in to the station.

Likewise, the magnificent station of Ascended Master consciousness must be turned on and tuned in to; it will not manifest automatically like our heartbeat and those elements of control in our bodies that are preprogrammed by nature and our Holy Christ Self.

I want all of you to stop for a moment and understand what I'm talking about. Supposing you could just lie there in an unconscious state and sleep indefinitely. Supposing you could take a sleeping pill that would make you sleep for, let's say, three or four days and your body would keep right on functioning. You wouldn't die. You could sleep for three or four days, presumably. The vital functions would carry on.

But what then?—would consciousness be propelled? Is life self-elevating? Not without free will. Not without motivation and decisive action.

Spiritually speaking—just because we are a vegetable, just because we eat, just because we sleep, just because we function, just because we have concourse with our neighbors—just because we do *something* does not mean that *anything* is going to happen to us spiritually. It will not happen automatedly. It will only happen because we desire it to and because we do something about it.

Well, people may say, "But God wants it to happen." Yes, he does. He wants the most wonderful things in the world to happen to you and to happen to me. He wants us to have the Christ experience. He wants us to pass through what is called the cycle of regeneration—not just generation, not just being born physically, not just growing up and going to school and learning the three R's.

You know what God wants? He wants us to

begin the process of communication between the divine and the human levels of consciousness. And the divine level of consciousness is not the ordinary level of our awareness.

Precognition and Christ in You

We hear about phenomenal things like: someone receives a letter in the mail and he touches the letter and he immediately knows who it's from before he reads the return address or recognizes the handwriting. Even if it's a typewritten letter, he still knows who it's from. And this is known as precognition.

The telephone rings and we say to ourselves, "Oh, that's Aunt Minnie." We know and it turns out, yes, it's Aunt Minnie. So we were right. And sometimes it's someone we haven't heard from for months or years, and we'll still get who it is.

We think that phenomenal manifestations indicate that we have achieved something of spiritual growth. Yet, all we have experienced is a psychic manifestation that denotes that we are starting to tune in with these powers of precognition which exist in the universe—they exist for everyone's use. This does not necessarily guarantee to us a condition of spiritual growth, but that we are beginning to develop a psychic quality—a quality of increasing soul sensitivity, drawing upon one's subconscious faculties—that is often confused with spirituality.

Now, I'm not running down psychic abilities or phenomena. I'm merely saying that to possess them does not guarantee that we possess spiritual gifts. And when I speak of spiritual gifts, I will take you back to that great theologian who was taught "at the feet of Gamaliel"—Paul the apostle.[5]

And what did Paul have to say about spirituality? He said, ". . . until Christ be formed in you,"[6] denoting, then, that the emanation of the Godhead through the Christ consciousness of Jesus the Christ and through the Christ that was even before, from the foundation of the world—"Before Abraham was, I AM"[7]—was intended to be formed in us, which consciousness he knew had a sense of unity with the Father.

That is the great news of the gospel of Christ: that through the *formation*, or the gradual *assimilation*, of Christ as your Real Self, you can attain to that oneness of soul with the Person of the divine Sonship, which is unity with the Father, with all that that unity with the Father implies.

The divinely inspired apostle taught us that we have a spiritual creativity within ourselves. It is dynamic and flowing. And when we start the release of the magnetism of God in our lives, there are transcendent changes that occur that can be transmitted physically as well as spiritually to other human beings.

And these changes will be a catalyst in their lives—to work change magnetically and spiritually in response to the vibratory chords of the Holy Spirit. And this change that we experience is something entirely different from the world phenomena.

And you begin to know: ". . . until Christ be formed in you."

We see in the drama of the woman at Jacob's well (and we have drunk from that well) that Jesus sat there next to the woman, and he looked at her and he said, "Thou hast had five husbands, and he whom thou now hast is not thy husband." And she said, "Sir, I perceive that thou art a prophet."[8]

You see, there is a tendency for everyone to equate the quality of prophecy with precognition, or the ability to read what is in the human aura of an individual—that magnetic emanation that comes out and up the spinal column to the medulla oblongata and emanates through the atmosphere just around the head.

We look at this and some of us are able to read the very lives of those upon whom we gaze. But this in itself does not denote that we possess spiritual qualities. Because spiritual qualities are not to be equated with soothsaying, fortune-telling, or even reading the human aura—which is perfectly alright, understand, and valid, but it does not guarantee spirituality, that being guaranteed by the statement ". . . until Christ be formed in you."

When Christ is formed in our life, what does take place in our life? We cannot just get into the outer imitation of the personality of Jesus Christ or of what we think that personality was or is, but we have to be able to get into those inner qualities of the character of Christ which he exhibited in his life when he stood upon the mount of temptation and said, "Get thee behind me, Satan. For it is written, thou shalt worship the Lord thy God, and him only shalt thou serve."[9]

Things of This World, Things of God

We must be able, then, to make a distinction between the things of the world and the things of God. Well, you may say, "But God owns everything. God made everything." Quite true. But his real estate seems to have passed into other hands. And title to it is now held in the temporal domain. And so the real estate of this world is always being conveyed from someone to someone. In reality, it came from God, but it has become the "things of the world."

Objects—they become the objects of our possession.

This is not our life. Remember what Jesus taught us. He said: Beware of covetousness, for a man's life does not consist of the abundance of the things which he possesses. But we have a tendency as human beings to have and to form certain attachments to those things that we possess—whether it's clothing, automobiles, houses, lands or fields or whatever. We say, "This is mine. That is mine."

And so, after a while, we come to feel that what we have is the all-important factor of our life, like the rich fool who laid up his treasure so he could retire in ease, but whose soul was required of him by God—"this night." Then it was quite clear that it didn't matter to whom his things should belong, but it mattered very much that he had not been "rich toward God."[10]

In reality, what we have doesn't mean a thing, but what we do with what we have to bless life is what counts because "the life is more than meat and the body is more than raiment."[11]

If you ever stand before a physician and he says to you, "You have a month to live"—you're going to say to yourself, "This life is the most precious thing that I own. The ability to live is my greatest possession." But now you'll be talking about your physical life. You'll say to yourself, "Well, physically, I'll be able to live for one month."

But what guarantee do we really have of our physical life? None whatsoever except the mercy and grace of God. The dictates of our karma, whatever we've sent out into the world as the meditations of our heart and mind and the gifts of self we've given to help others along the way—these are the things that determine how long we are going to live.

Each of us is given an allotment—"the very hairs of your head are all numbered."[12] But then I have seen example after example of individuals whose life span has been extended by their good karma. An individual who was intended to die December 13, 1962, for example, is still with us. And you say, "Well, how is that?" Yes, his karma in the akashic records clearly stated he would die December 13, 1962, but he's still here.

Well, the mercy of God endureth forever. And something in his life changed. He didn't bargain with God, but heaven took note that certain improvements were being instituted in his life. The Karmic Board noted it, and so he was given a life extension. I've seen this done for many, many people.

But, after all, is this physical life extension a meaningful thing? Yes, it is. It's meaningful to the person at the time because it gives him an extension to understand what the purpose of his life was in the first place.

Reincarnation So That We Can Be Perfected

The purpose of life in the first place, on the physical plane, is so that the elements of perfection from the higher planes may be brought into our life and builded upon the chief cornerstone of the temple, which is Christ—the consciousness of the universal God, the sense of oneness that identifies us with God, the link between selfhood and divinity. And selfhood and divinity are an ongoing process.

Now, I realize that many people in this world have an idea of God as an old man resembling Father Time or Father Christmas, and they think, "Yes, this is God." And yet we learn from Jesus, who knew the Father intimately, that "God is a Spirit: and they that worship him must worship him in spirit and in truth."[13]

And so, we see that men's concepts of God are very warped. They're very warped because people have so many different ideas about God. It doesn't quite work the way people think it does. God, in reality, is all of us and a great deal more than all of us. We have a universe here that is so large that I don't know of anyone who could ever fathom the dimensions of the objective physical universe.

And they tell me that the physical universe hangs beneath the etheric universe—somewhat the way a little breadbasket would hang below a dirigible. So you have a great blimp of an etheric universe up here, and down below it you have a physical universe. And all of this is actually suspended within a cosmic egg—and that's much larger still.

And so, we have this universe and we know that with all the sosophoric rounds and all the stretching out of time and space, we have these measurements—the bounds of our habitation.[14] And these seem to be appointed unto us according to a certain length or order. And this is order in our universe.

The Dragon of Chaos Is Devouring Time

And yet, in contradistinction to all of this order that exists in our universe, we have the great dragon Tiamat, the symbol of chaos. And we have the chaos that seeks to devour the *kala* of time.

In other words, what they're trying to do with you and me is (and if you don't believe it, listen to some of your television commercials) waste our time! That's the whole thing.

They know very well that you've got just so

many years to live. Everyone has so many years to live. And so they very successfully manage to fix it so that most of us don't have any time. Yet we have just as much time as everybody else does. But they make us feel that we don't have any time.

They sit there and the commercial is cute, so we listen to the commercial. And then the program is entertaining, so we become entertained—and we've whiled away another hour.

And then we say, "Well, now I'll procrastinate. I will not read this spiritual teaching. I will not engage in this spiritual exercise. I'm not going to do my decrees tonight because I'm into this program." Or, "I've got a neighbor coming over." Or, "Aunt Minnie's dropping in." Or, "Something else is happening." Or, "I don't feel too well. I think I'll lie down and rest."

And so, most people find (and we know this to be true) that their time is devoured in little pieces. The old Tiamat is just chewing up *kala*, the time, and the first thing you know *kala* is gone. There isn't any more time. There they stand, face to face with eternity.

"Well," they say, "that won't matter too much because in eternity 'a thousand years is as one day and one day is as a thousand years.'"[15] And so they look at eternity and they say, "Well, that doesn't mean too much because when I'm dead I won't know too much about time."

Well, physically speaking, no, you won't. This is true. But there is a statement in Revelation that

I want to quote to you. What does it say? It says,
"He that is unjust, let him be unjust still: and he
which is filthy, let him be filthy still: and he that is
righteous, let him be righteous still: and he that
is holy, let him be holy still."[16]

And what does it mean? What it really means
is that you're not going to get any better on the day
of your death than you were the day before. If you
think you're going to go to the other side of life
and suddenly improve your posture and become
perfected, you are wrong.

Because the whole raison d'être, the reason for
having a physical incarnation, is so we can be
perfected in this incarnation to draw down the
great perfection of God from higher realms and
manifest it in our dimensions. So, whatever we
attain of righteousness and holiness in life—that is
where we are and there isn't anymore.

That's your rating on the divine stock market.
That's exactly where you are in the divine stock
market. It's in the paper—you can read it there. It
says, "Stock: 78½." And that's exactly what it is,
you see. Your stock is at a certain rate on the
market, on the divine market. That's your stock. It
isn't anybody else's and it can't be anybody else's.

So you write your own ticket. It's you, individually, who determines whether or not you're
going to attain the mastery of your soul.

And what do the people do who fall off their
perch because somebody pulls both strings? You
know what happens when they pull both strings?

They go to India looking for a guru. They go looking for a spiritual teacher. They're looking for some great man who's going to tell them all the wonderful things that're going to happen to them. The guru.

Oh yes, the guru will look at them and he'll say, "Now, what you've got to do is you've got to become a vegetarian." Or, "You've got to give up this..." or "You've got to give up that..." or "You've got to sit and meditate so many hours a day and then you'll be safe."

Your Salvation Is in the Christ Consciousness

Well, I'm here to tell you that the salvation of your life is in the Christ consciousness and that you can have it as easily as you can reach out and pick an apple—a beautiful, golden, ripe apple—off a tree. You can pick it and take it into your hand and you can eat it.

And this is what you can do. You can take in the Body of the Christ consciousness, the Sacred Eucharist. You can take it into your being, you can improve—you can take the seed of God and absorb that into your consciousness.

Christ can be formed in you and it will change your character. It will change your life. If you were dishonest before, you'll be honest. If you were a creator of viciousness before, you will create beauty and love. I mean, whatever is in your world, Christ will make it better. You may have been using energy before but now you'll use energy in greater power and you'll create blessings in greater measure. And your creation will be a creation of God, because Christ is formed in you and you cannot create after the flesh anymore.

In the Bible it says, "Henceforth know we no man after the flesh"[17]—not even Christ! And why is this true? It goes back to the synthetic image. We know people after the synthetic image. And what happens to the synthetic image? Well, if you know them when they're thirty, they're different than when they were twelve or when they were twenty. People keep changing.

Well, "if any man be in Christ, he is a new creature: old things are passed away. Behold, all things are become new."[18]

When we read about the Christ consciousness, it says, "Jesus Christ, the same yesterday and today and forever."[19] Well, is this the sameness of boredom? Of course not. It's not the sameness of boredom. It's the sameness of perfection.

And is perfection uncomfortable? Why, of course it's not uncomfortable! What a ridiculous idea it would be if we would think that divine perfection, the state of God, would be uncomfortable or undesirable. It is not undesirable!

The perfection of God is a magnificent state which we know in part and we gather in part, but when that which is perfect is come, then that which is in part is done away with[20]—simply because it is absorbed into the wholeness of God, you see.

So, it's all very wonderful. And you can have it and I can have it and we all can have it—and that's what the Ascended Master consciousness is all about!

Every Man Shall Bear His Own Burden

You know, people get hung up on the idea of wanting a World Saviour. And the one thing that Jesus Christ was the most frightened about—people look at me and they say, "What do you mean? Jesus was never frightened!" Why, of course, he wasn't frightened. "But you said he was frightened." Yes, I did. But I wasn't talking about the kind of fright that you think.

Jesus was only concerned—and I should have used the word *concerned*. And he was so concerned that he *cried* when he said, "He that believeth on me, believeth not on me, but on him that sent me. And he that seeth me seeth him that sent me."[21]

What he was concerned about was that people would be satisfied with the idea of having someone pick them up and then carry them all the way to heaven like one of these ski lifts that you get on, you know—you trade in your money and get your ticket and get on the ski lift, and you get to the top of the hill.

Very easy, it just runs. You don't have to do anything—just sit on it. And that's what people are looking for. They want something they can just sit on, and then Jesus will carry them all the way up to heaven, to the very summit of life! Well, it is not going to work that way because if it did work that way, they would never really enjoy the fact that they got there.

Unto every man the burden of that man will come and, like it or not, *every man shall bear his own burden*[22]—the burden of his words and his works and the burden of his salvation. There's nothing wrong in that.

But Jesus was actually saying, "See, it's not me, it's the One that sent me"—he is the Saviour, even the Word. And this Word is the I AM THAT I AM. Here is the Master's Lost Teaching on Christ the Light of the world.

The Son of man, Jesus, was the Incarnation of the Word who is with us—the I AM Presence. He is not only One with the Father, he is the embodiment of the Father's Presence. Therefore he said to Philip:

"He that hath seen me hath seen the Father.

"Believest thou not that I am in the Father, and the Father in me? the words that I speak unto you I speak not of myself: but the Father that dwelleth in me, he doeth the works."[23]

"You who believe on me, the man Jesus, believe not on me but on him—the I AM Presence—that sent me, that is with me and in me.

"For lo, I AM that Christ incarnate because I have first believed on him. Even so, believe ye!

"I AM come a Light into the world[24] that whosoever believeth on me—on the Christ Truth that

I AM and that I bear—should not abide in darkness. Because he can apply the same Truth to dispel error, and the same Light shall he bear. And he shall become the vessel for the same Beloved Father, the I AM Presence—the One who also sent me.[25]

"Therefore the I AM in me is the Light of the world—so long as the I AM of me is incarnate in the world.[26] And when I AM ascended to my God and your God, then ye are the Light of the world. Therefore, let your Light—the Christ of you—so shine before men that they may see your good works and glorify your Father which is in heaven."[27]

Your assignment is clear. When Christ is taken up from you and you see him ascend in clouds of glory, you will remember his words to you: "And I, if I be lifted up from the earth, will draw all men unto me."[28]

Then you will take up your Master's work by raising up the Light of the Mother on your spinal altar and in your chakras. You will let your Christ Light shine and you will let the Light of Jesus' Lost Teachings light up the whole world and you won't let anything, I said *anything*, stop you until you have delivered the Everlasting Gospel to every soul whom the Father has sent you "in my name."

Why, if it had been intended any other way, if there'd been only one Son to wipe away all sin, including sins our souls had not yet sinned, I can tell you one thing—from the moment Christ hung on the cross there would never have been any more death, any more sin, any more sorrow. There wouldn't have been a single trace of wickedness left in the world when he said, "It is finished."[29] But now you know it wasn't intended that way. Now you know you were sent to bear witness to the same Father, the same Light, the same Word I AM THAT I AM who sent Jesus.

You see, when he said, "It is finished," he referred to the fact that his own mission was finished. His mission was finished, but not yours. In fact, at that moment, wherever you were on earth in that life your mission was about to begin whether you had met the man Jesus or not!

You think about that and then you think about what you might've been doing these last two thousand years since his victory; and if you haven't spent the last twenty centuries getting ready to be Christ's vessel and messenger today, well you can start right now by studying and putting into practice the Teachings of the Ascended Masters.

Jesus told his disciples, "You shall follow me in the regeneration. You shall indeed drink of the cup that I drink of."[30] And that means that in your words *and* in your works you must drink in his life and his mission if you want to get where he is. And you who have followed me in the regeneration when the Son of man shall sit in the throne of his glory (with the Father in the heart of the I AM THAT I AM), ye shall sit upon twelve thrones judging the twelve tribes of Israel.[31]

Thus Jesus proclaims the Everlasting Gospel as the gospel of the Judgment that binds the seed of the Wicked One and blesses the Lightbearers until in the Second Coming, Christ should fully dwell in their hearts.

Christ's Doctrine vs. Church Doctrine

That is the thing. The cup is the ageless Holy Grail that comes to our lips—each one. Are we worthy to receive it? It is not based upon human worth. It's based upon divine idealism—the ideals of God for man.

What did God envision for man? When God made you, he thought just as much about you as he did about Jesus. Because, you see, in reality there's only one beloved Son. One Christ. Just one. And that Christ is he by whom all things were made. In other words, he was and is the perfect image. And he was and is "the Lamb slain from the foundation of the world."[32]

You see how different this is, how people have warped and twisted it? The Councils of Nicaea and Trent have altered the true intent of the scriptures.[33] And the churches of the world have inherited a doctrine that was neither Christ's nor Paul's. Because we are born late in time without a knowledge of Hebrew, Aramaic, Greek and Latin, we don't suddenly spout divine theology. We have to relearn, and for the same reason our theologians relearn. And sometimes they relearn according to a dropped sight. People have dropped their sights.

A major turning point was when the philosophy of Origen of Alexandria was overthrown. Origen, who was a Church Father in the truest sense of the word, though never so named, was anathematized around A.D. 553, as we have pointed out.[34]

And so, the mysticism of the early Church was removed. And the mysteries of Christ which Jesus revealed to the pure soul of Origen have remained forbidden mysteries ever since—forbidden by whom? By strangers to his Love who sit on his throne on earth, and in his Church anathematize his Doctrine and deny his glorious mission to the East during the so-called lost years prior to his Palestinian mission.

Seeds of Horror Sown by a False Theology

All of this precious Teaching and the true accounting of his life from which we could have learned so much and done so much for the world that, God knows, needs it more than we—all of this went down. And in its place we have had a substitution of the Divine Image with the spectre of a very severe Father and the creation of a place called h-e-l-l, which we already know about because we see it all around us.

And so what happens? Men have actually stood right in front of me and looked me in the face and said, "That man over there had a baby born a week ago and his baby died. And that baby is going to h-e-l-l. And that baby will burn forever and ever and ever and ever because he was not baptized."

O God, pity us as a nation, as a world, that we do not understand the mercies of God that endure forever. How can we believe God worthy of things that we ourselves would not, in our worst moments, be worthy of? And yet we find it in the world. We find that we impute qualities unto one another that are not there.

And horror is in the world. And why is horror in the world? Because the forces of darkness and destruction, the dark powers of the world, desire to create the illusion that darkness is greater than Light. And it is not!

The only thing of any worth, the only thing of enduring worth that's in you is the Light that's in you. And Christ said, "If the Light that is in thee be darkness, how great is that darkness!"[35] And so we should learn to repudiate and to burn our darkness and decide instead to dwell in Light, in sanity, in reason, in Christ's consciousness.

And what does *reason* mean? It means "re-sun"— r-e-s-u-n. Go ahead and get the sunlight of God through your mind! Aerate your mind and your heart. Begin to understand how you can till the soil of consciousness until the rose of Sharon is blooming within your heart, until the flowers that spring up in your minds are flowers of hope and reason, not the density of the world's horror and confusion.

I heard of two girls whose decapitated bodies were found in the mountains near Santa Cruz. Who perpetuates such darkness as this? Let the hound of heaven find them out, and let them receive that which they have sent forth, according to divine justice![36]

We should not live in a world where darkness and horror can dwell. We should let the heaven of consciousness within ourselves be free from those things. We should see that everyone has the opportunity to improve the state of his mind reinforced by love so as not to go down into darkness and despair.

There is no strength or power in witchcraft. There is no strength in devil worship. These things are on the side of the pit, and they will be brought down to where they belong. And they will never produce the fruit of divine reason and beauty in the world.

Practical Aspects of "Feed My Sheep"

The things of Christ were from the beginning. They were the creation of God through the Only Begotten of the Father, full of grace and truth.[37] And we should learn to understand what this means to our lives. We can make this beauty of the eternal Son come alive.

And if we sit and say an Indian mantra and we say it thousands of times every day, but we say to our brethren, "Depart in peace, be ye warmed and filled," and we do not give them, as James says, "those things which are needful to the body," what doth it profit?[38]

What is going to happen to the world if this is how we put our religion into nonpractice? We have a world of impracticality dwelling side by side with an unseen yet very, very practical spiritual world.

We of the Great White Brotherhood are of

the order of the Essenes. We understand the meaning of the hospitalers. We understand the meaning of service, "I am my brother's keeper," of going forth in the name of Christ to give the cup of cold water. We understand the practical aspects of "Feed my sheep."[39]

We must feed the sheep of Christ. We must recognize all men as his brethren. But we must also understand how to divide the fruit of that which is Good from the fruit of that which is Evil. That which is Evil must not continue. That which is Good must be multiplied—and abundantly multiplied in the world order and in ourselves.

We are guardians of our own domain. We must guard ourselves—we must guard the vineyard of our heart. If we don't guard it, someone else isn't going to guard it for us.

"Do You Believe in Yourself?"

Now, I will agree that the Masters will do many wonderful things for us. And this is the problem. You know, every once in a while I run into this problem where someone comes along and says, "Well, I love Jesus only and I don't believe in any other Master but Jesus."

A few years ago I used to say to them, "If you only knew the Masters! Why, they're all brothers of Jesus—and they came later in time and some before. Enoch was before. But the point is, all these Masters have their functions, their part to play in the role of Christ."

But now I don't say that anymore. I say to them, "What about you?"

And they say, "Well, what do you mean 'What about me?' I'm not very good."

I say, "No, I know you're probably not very good. Because even Jesus backed off from being called good. You know, it was when a man came to him and said, 'Good Master. . .' The Master looked at him and said, 'Why do you call me good? There's only one good and that's God.'"[40]

And so, the God in Christ is the God in you. So you're just as good as Christ—deep, deep, deep down inside—from the standpoint of the image creation.

In other words, God made you in his own image. You can't get any better than that. That's a twenty-four-carat-gold stamp. When you've got that, you've got the pure gold. And everybody's got it. The only problem is that people don't realize that they have it. So they don't live according to it. They live according to the synthetic stamp—you have a little synthetic standard inside of you, too. And too often that's what you go by.

So, I turn back to them, and I say, "You don't want to believe in the Masters? Well, do you believe in yourself? Because someday you're going to be a Master."

They say, "Not me." They get embarrassed, you know, and they laugh a little bit. And they say, "Oh no, not me. I mean you've got this wrong, brother. That's just not right, you know. Why, you know, I used to drink a little, and I did a few things, you know—I did a few things I shouldn't have done."

And I say, "Well, God can never wash out that stain, can he? He can never wash it out. It's dyed too deep." Then you get them to think a minute. "Why, of course. That's what's meant by the cleansing of the blood."

Renewal of Consciousness through Reincarnation

You know that the churches have it wrong. They don't understand. Most of the churches don't understand what is really meant by the ability of the life of God to flow through and eradicate the things that are not Godlike. It's not an impossible task at all. But that's exactly what happens when you reembody.

The records are cleared from your conscious memory bank, even though they're still there in the unconscious. Because if they weren't you'd lose your identity and the momentums of your achievements of the past and all you ever did would have been for naught.

You see, identity—God-identity is cumulative. And we take every bit of it with us when we go. Up, that is. When we ascend and shuffle off this mortal coil we take with us forever all the God-Good we have ever consciously become by free will. Isn't that marvelous! You see, you can never lose yourself—your true self, that is, even when you reembody. You can always be who you want to be and if you're being something or somebody you don't want to be, well you can cease to be that anytime you so choose in this life or the next—in this world or beyond the stars.

You know, my mother used to be quite a believer in only one lifetime. She didn't believe in reembodiment. So she and I used to have some terrible arguments, but in friendship, you know. You should always be friends with your mother, as a rule.

So, dear sweet mother, she thought that there was never going to be another chance when she died—that was the end of it all, and life was over, and she'd have to stand and be judged on that forever and ever and ever. And there'd never be any chance of her being any better than she was when she died.

Well, we never did settle the matter. And so she died. And now she's living in Baltimore, reborn as the daughter of an insurance executive. I've never met her. I know she's there. I know the house she lives in—I know the description of the house. But I've never called on her. I don't intend to, because I'm going to leave her completely alone as I told her I'd do. I said, "You're just a wonderful mother and you've been a wonderful mother to me all my life. And I'll always love you." And now she's leading a new life.

So, you see, the scenario goes on a little bit. And people do not realize that we've all had these experiences. I remember many of my experiences from past embodiments and I'm sure many of you do, too. But the interesting thing is, you don't usually get these pieces of knowledge until you've reached a certain development in your life.

It would be kind of terrible, wouldn't it, if like that little girl in India, Shanti Devi, you were born with the memory of your husband and sons who lived in another town and you recalled the house you had lived in?[41] For some reason, some fluke of the cosmos, she came into life with a memory of all this. Well, that was pretty hard on her. You can understand that—you who are mothers and fathers and have children.

Well, if you died and were reborn and then you remembered your former family and you were living in another place and you knew how to get there but you didn't have the bus fare and weren't able to get there and you couldn't convince your new family that you should—well, that'd be quite a problem, now wouldn't it?

You'd be a little uncomfortable, wouldn't you? It'd really pull on your heartstrings to have a family one place and then have another family somewhere else. Nevertheless, that's the way it is with life, but we don't know it. Actually it happens to all of us, but life shields us from the knowledge and memory of it.

At the moment of birth the veil of forgetfulness descends, by Mercy's hand, and it remains until, for a purpose, God lifts the veil (or you puncture it by psychic probing) because God wants you to have a clean white page to write on and he wants you to enjoy this life with all of the newness of springtime and first love.

Structuring Our Lives to Fit Heavenly Patterns

And so, there are many different experiences that could happen to us. But quite frankly, I think it's better that we don't get too carried away in consciousness unless we're very solid spiritually—twenty-four-karat gold. In other words, we'd better be solid spiritually so we don't get caught up in the phenomena of events without understanding the importance of structuring our lives according to inner patterns—heavenly patterns. And as Paul says, the longsuffering of Christ himself is a pattern to them that believe on him to everlasting life.[42]

Now, a lot of people don't think it's important how they treat their fellowmen. They say, "Well, what is really important is how I feel." That's not important at all! It's what you do and what you be that counts.

Nevertheless, one of the greatest feelings I ever had was the time I was down on my hands and knees scrubbing the floor before one of our conferences. I put on a pair of overalls and I was scrubbing the floor with a colored lady from New York. She was a millionaire—and she got down and she was scrubbing the floor with me. And we were down there scrubbing the floor together. I felt more of Christ in that gesture of humility and in realizing that I'm not all that important and I'm not all that unimportant.

It doesn't make any difference. God is down here on the floor and he's up here on the pulpit, or he's anywhere in the world. He's the banker—the butcher, the baker, and the candlestick maker. Wherever we are, it doesn't make any difference, if we can only understand that God is doing it and not ourselves.

Yet we enter into it by the lever of the will. And if we don't enjoin ourselves to the Lord's Work, we may be a bump on a log for a long time. It's all up to us—what we make of ourselves in this life.

People like to have all these wonderful experiences of spiritual ecstasy. Well, I can produce all these things, too—by God's grace. You know I can produce these ecstasies. I can sit there in the samadhic state and other states of consciousness. But, you see, in the final analysis, you have to get down to the reason for creation in the first place.

The reason for creation in the first place was so that man could become a god of his own universe, so that consciousness could expand according to what we call the pattern of the Eucharist.

Now, many people don't understand too much about the Eucharist. But the Eucharist is like a beehive. I mean, it's made up of little cells. And when you break it, these multiply because they're seeds of Light. And they go out all over the universe—because God is the most abundant, the most expansive, the most radioactive, the most magnificent of all creation because he's the Creator.

And so, into the Eucharist he put all these beautiful patterns—the patterns of the honeycomb, in effect, you see. He honeycombed the Eucharist with all this consciousness of Light, a seed of Light. It glows. There's a fire to it.

And that is why real spiritual people sometimes have beings like Archangel Michael appear to them and put the host right on their tongue. And people say, "Well, what does that mean?" It means that all of us are children of the Light, children of God! And it means that we are drinking in the sunlight of God's love, we're drinking in love and we're drinking in universality. We're drinking in the qualities of the universe, we're becoming Godlike.

Why, for heaven's sake! Didn't Jesus teach us that unless we're willing to sacrifice something of ourselves we could not multiply the Christ consciousness? Unless a corn of wheat falls into the ground and dies, it abides alone. But if it falls into the ground and dies, it brings forth much fruit.[43] "First the blade, then the ear, after that the full corn in the ear."[44] The law of your life is abundance— multiplication. Both here and hereafter your spirit fructifies.

You, Too, Will Be Multiplied for the Many

You've got to understand the miracle of the loaves and the fishes.[45] It was the breaking of the bread. It's the bread of Christ, the bread of your life.

It's *you*. Your heart must make contact with his—by fire—and then you, too, will be 'broken'—that is, multiplied—for the many.

"Did not our hearts burn within us as he talked with us on the way to Emmaus?"[46]

Don't you see what it really means? It means the breaking of the bread of consciousness. It means that *you will become one with God*—that you'll have your own universe. And there's plenty of lebensraum in cosmos for you to function in, so that in all things you can show yourself as a pattern—a Christic pattern—of good works.[47]

People think in terms of, "Well, I'm such a little guy, I live in Los Angeles," or "I live in Chicago" or "I live here in Santa Barbara" or "I live in Darjeeling, I'm a schoolboy playing a violin." (We saw a number of schoolchildren with little violins walking along the road in Darjeeling, India.)

People have an idea that they are a certain kind of a person. Well, Jesus was a shepherd boy, too. Did you know that? David was a shepherd boy. Blessed be thou, son of David. But the point is he became the Son of God. He realized his Sonship. He laid down his life for the many but he took it again.

He said, "Therefore doth my Father love me, because I lay down my life, that I might take it again. No man taketh it from me, but I lay it down of myself. I have power to lay it down, and I have power to take it again. This commandment have I received of my Father."[48]

So accept the promise that God will work his Work in you so that you can be in control of your life and live it for others. This is true bliss.

We Are in the State of Becoming

We have to understand that whatever we are is not that which we shall be. Because we are now in the state of becoming—we're becoming more than what we are. As John, so close to Jesus, said, "It doth not yet appear what we shall be: but when he, Christ, shall appear, we shall be like him, for we shall see him as he is."[49]

To see him, in fact, is to become like him and then to be one with him. And every day sees the dawn of new opportunity for creation after the inner Christ image ". . . until Christ be formed in you" and in me!

We must catch this vision. Otherwise, stultification sets in and then comes rigor mortis. And I don't like that guy. Do you like rigor mortis? And his first name is Rigor, you know, and the last name is Mortis. I mean, he sets in and then we get stiff, you know. But we're already stiff. That's why we get stiff.

You see what I mean? I mean we're stiff in our lives. We don't relax. We don't allow the Light to flow through. We don't allow ourselves to be part of the universe. We don't allow ourselves to generate and regenerate.

We generate, but we don't *regenerate*. That's the trouble with people. They just sit there and generate. What are they generating? It's a funny brew sometimes, isn't it?—what's going on in the world.

So the whole concept is the Christ concept of ongoingness and the multiplication of the loaves and the fishes in consciousness. Be able to generate and regenerate. Be able to expand your consciousness until you can accept the fact that you're going someplace.

Stop this business of feeling that you're Joe Blow sitting there in a little house somewhere and you have a deed to that house and you have a 1972 car and you decide your bank account is you. Don't identify with any of this! Forget it! Get rid of it all!

I don't mean you should give it away. You don't have to give it to me or to anyone else. You can do whatever you want to with it. It doesn't mean that much and it shouldn't mean that much to you or to me! You can do whatever you want to with what you have. If you don't have something, you can get something. You can get abundance of all kinds. You can get material things.

Why Be Satisfied with Material Things?

But why be satisfied with material things? Let's get spiritual things. We are spirits, you know, "the spirits of just men made perfect"...by Love.[50] We've got to have the sense of divine justice in ourselves.

The biggest problem in the world today as I see it is people who think that God is unjust. God is not unjust—we're unjust! People are unjust. And there's so much injustice in the world. But we can't correct it all. Can we now, really? Can we correct it all? The best way to correct it is to go right straight to the Father and become one with him.

You know, Abraham—all he did was to become a "friend of God."[51] If we'd only develop friendship with God and not place so much importance on developing friendship with the world, we would have all of the answers.

And so, the Ascended Master consciousness is grand and glorious and beautiful and blessed. And we are most fortunate to be able to have contact with the Masters and to have the testimony of Jesus. No, I'm not going to hang my shingle out here and say, "This is the place where only God is."

It's true. Only God is here, but he manifests as Jesus Christ and as other Ascended Masters, too—and as you and me. In other words, we all have a place in the sun.

Now then, this is a little different than some people think. They think, "Holy, holy, holy, Lord God Almighty. Only thou art holy," and they imagine God sitting on his throne with the seraphim fanning him. And they have this idea that all the angels are up there fanning God with big fans.

They have a vision of God as a great pharaoh, when in reality "the Lord of Love," as Henry Van Dyke said, "came down from above, to live with the men who work."[52] And that's the concept we have to understand—that God is practical and that he sent his Son for the reason that all might live abundantly by his grace. And his Son said, "My Father worketh hitherto, and I work."[53] That means my Father and I are working together for the same goal: that Christ should manifest himself in me and in you.

And who is the Son? He is the Only Begotten of the Father, full of grace and truth. The Lamb of God slain from the foundation of the world. This means he was there quite a while before the incarnation of Jesus, doesn't it? "Slain from the foundation of the world."

He knew that! Well, you start to know that. You start to know that you were really a creation of God in the Universal Christ from the beginning. And start to get yourselves back on the firing line of Truth. And watch how all of those atoms inside of you start exploding! You'll wonder what's going on inside of you. You'll find regeneration is working.

Caught Up in the Work of the Brotherhood

And when regeneration works, the first thing you know, you're going to find yourself right in the midst of the work of the Brotherhood. You'll get caught up with the Brotherhood. Caught up "to meet your Lord in the air."[54] Yes, right here and now. It'll happen right while you're on earth.

That doesn't mean you're not going to get caught up in some way afterward in the resurrection, but before you pass from the screen of life, you're going to get caught up in the arms of the

Beloved—your beloved Christ Self—and you're going to see the Light. And *you will* have a genuine Saint Paul experience. *You will have the Christ experience.*

You'll get out of the prison that Paul was in, you know—when there was a great earthquake and the prison doors opened wide and the jailer came running.[55] You're going to get out of all the jails of human creation. You're going to be free at last. And you'll say, "Thank God that I was able to understand the Everlasting Day!"

I'm going to say it again: "Thank God that I was able to understand the Everlasting Day!"

You know, the sun stood still.[56] And in reality, the Son of God and the timelessness of the Christ will stand still for you wherever you are. And you will be caught up in the caravan of those who are moving forward in the vanguard of this age.

We must produce the kingdom of God upon this earth. And it can be done. It is not a great fanfare. It was a little tiny thing that happened over in Bethlehem on the eve when Christ was born. Just a few people came, you know—a few angels and shepherds and whatnot. They came and the drama was very small. And then suddenly Christendom dawned.

But it has not yet produced what it is intended to produce. And it is up to us today to honor God by making it produce what God intended it to produce. And where better can you start than in your own life?

Thank you and God bless you.

Welcome to the Heart
of the Inner Retreat
where people of every nation
gather to study and apply
the Lost Teachings of Jesus
in a celebration of Life

*I must work
the works
of him that
sent me.*
        Jesus

Walk while ye have the light.
                    Jesus

Epilogue
"QUO VADIS?"

Mark L. Prophet began his spiritual path as a Bible-quoting fundamentalist Christian. Praying to Jesus hours a day, summer and winter before the little altar he set up in the attic of his Wisconsin home, he received the Holy Spirit and all nine gifts while yet a teenager.

The Lost Teachings of Jesus is the record of what that Spirit of Pentecost taught our twin flames. Written down in the presence of His holy angels, these are the Messengers' tracings of the Mind of God: A transcript left for those who expect the Comforter to come into their hearts. Scrolls of the Master found again for those who fear not the experience of the Lord's coming—suddenly into their temple—with joy and acclamation and the enlightenment of the Paraclete!

"You Will Become One with God!" was Mark's last public sermon, delivered at the Keepers of the Flame Motherhouse in Santa Barbara on Sunday, February 18, 1973. It contains all the keys to coming events short of the announcement itself. In this delivery Mark tore the mask from the face of mortality. And he confronted the Fourth Horseman with his indomitable: "I Shall Not Be Moved!"

For him, Death and Hell were swallowed up in Christ's victory *and* Wisdom's smile.

The last words of the Prophet to his own, it is as fine a mockery of the death mask as you'll ever come across—worthy of his Morya who, as Thomas Becket, met his four assailants with the Christic poise of a martyr at the altar of Canterbury Cathedral December 29, 1170—yes, worthy as was Thomas More in the Tower of London and at the block July 6, 1535.

Truly, Mark Prophet lived and died and ascended for his principles and his loves, which were God's.

And when the angel of the LORD came to take him, it was not the Death Angel but the Angel of the Resurrection. Death could never touch him. He was too much alive and continuously so, apart from a vehicle no longer useful (which, in any case, he was planning to trade in for a later model!).

Only the sacred fires of cremation could steal the remains and leave the rest and the best—the heart and message of America's twentieth-century Prophet and his mantle for any and all who would claim it.

This one who had determined to master his fate and did—for all of us—was heard to cry out as he entered the portals of eternity, "Behold, I AM everywhere in the consciousness of God!"

Before us he had shone, a star that could wait

for heaven no longer. Now we saw him from afar— the one for whom heaven itself could not wait.

On Monday morning, February 26, 1973, at Colorado Springs, he made the transition, and from inner levels his soul entered the fiery coil of the ascension unto the Presence, I AM THAT I AM.

Only days before, his parting words to his chelas were heard to resound in the rotunda of La Tourelle, the retreat in Broadmoor where we had lived and served together for seven years with our beloved staff and four children.

His voice echoing strong and loud, he said, *"Death comes unexpectedly!"*

To me from whom he kept the foreknowledge of the event to come—though I knew but could not say—he simply said, "Elizabeth, you'll miss me when I'm gone." To which there could be no reply but the soul's whisper, "Where are you going, Lord?...Can't you take me with you?"

And truer words the Prophet had not spoke. Not only his wife and ardent chela, and his little ones, but a student body of thousands around the world would miss him more than they could ever tell. And for a planet and her people the loss could not be calculated.

As in all cases when a giant such as he appears among men, those left behind must find consolation in internalizing the Word he spoke, the Love he bore, the Example he set. Thus we carry on— our night illumined by his torch.

Wherefore, we, yet the Messengers of our Lord, joyously present these four volumes of *The Lost Teachings* as a sequel to *The Lost Years* and an adjunct to the disciples' ongoing study of the Everlasting Gospel. This message, delivered by the angels of God through the empowerment of the Holy Ghost, we two of the surname Prophet have and are continuing to set forth in *Climb the Highest Mountain* and the weekly *Pearls of Wisdom* and dictations of the Ascended Masters.

This is our joint effort which neither Death's partings nor Hell's tauntings could take from us. For the veil between worlds is rent in twain by the Love of twin flames and the entire Spirit of the Great White Brotherhood—ascended and unascended.

Begun in Mark's sermons, fireside chats, his lectures and private sessions with me and continuing in Jesus' and his dictations delivered from beyond the veil, the Lost Teachings herein set forth have become the Bread of Life for tens of thousands whose search for God and Truth has culminated in the discovery of lifetimes through the thirty-three-year span of the ministry of our two witnesses.

The unity of the Lost Teachings of Jesus, their practicality for us in this troubled time, is a testimony to God's anointing of our Messengership and to the crystal chalice of our spirits which He has raised up in His service. Therefore, in our oneness—as Above, so below—we offer this work upon the heart's altar of the dear followers of the Lord and Saviour Jesus Christ.

At last the mystery of our Love is unveiled!

Elizabeth Clare Prophet

October 12, 1986
Camelot
Los Angeles

...And did Nostradamus
speak of Mark Prophet when he wrote:

The Divine Word will be struck from heaven,
Who is not able to proceed any further:
With the revelation, the secret is closed up
So that they will march over and ahead.

The penultimate of the surname of the Prophet
Will take Diana for his day and rest:
He will wander far because of a frenetic head
In delivering a great people from impositions.*

Only time will tell...

*Nostradamus (1503–1566), Century II, quatrains 27, 28. "Penultimate" means
the next to the last member of a series or the next to the last syllable of a word.
"Diana" (goddess of the moon, which rules the "day of the moon," *Lunae Dies*,
or "Monday") is taken to mean Monday.

. . . How long shall it be to the end of these wonders?

And I heard the man clothed in linen, which was upon the waters of the river, when he held up his right hand and his left hand unto heaven, and sware by him that liveth for ever that it shall be for a time, times, and an half; and when he shall have accomplished to scatter the power of the holy people, all these things shall be finished.

And I heard, but I understood not: then said I, O my Lord, what shall be the end of these things?

And he said, Go thy way, Daniel: for the words are closed up and sealed till the time of the end.

Many shall be purified, and made white, and tried; but the wicked shall do wickedly: and none of the wicked shall understand; but the wise shall understand.

Daniel

Notes

For an alphabetical listing of many of the philosophical and hierarchical terms used in *The Lost Teachings of Jesus*, see the comprehensive glossary, "The Alchemy of the Word: Stones for the Wise Masterbuilders," in *Saint Germain On Alchemy*.

Epigraph, page xiv Heb. 12:22–29, Jerusalem Bible.

Chapter Twelve THE RELATIONSHIP OF MAN AND GOD

1. "Never the spirit was born; the spirit shall cease to be never; / Never was time it was not; End and Beginning are dreams! / Birthless and deathless and changeless remaineth the Spirit for ever; / Death hath not touched it at all, dead though the house of it seems!" Sir Edwin Arnold, trans. *The Song Celestial or Bhagavad-Gita* (London: Routledge & Kegan Paul, 1964), p. 9.
2. II Tim. 1:5.*
3. **Experiments of Nephilim gods and birth goddesses:** Ancient Sumerian texts tell the story of the creation by the god Ea (Enki) and the mother goddess, Ninhursag, of a race of primitive workers designed to perform the work of the gods on earth. Based on his study of these texts, Zecharia Sitchin believes that they used genetic manipulation to accomplish this—extracting the eggs of female *Homo erectus* evolving on earth, fertilizing them with the "essence" or sperm of young Nephilim gods, and then reimplanting them in the wombs of birth goddesses.

*Bible references are to the King James Version unless otherwise noted.

Sumerian texts speak of deformed beings produced by Enki and Ninhursag in revelry or mischief; Sitchin speculates that these were the result of the trial-and-error creation process that took place before the procedure was perfected and that this could be the explanation for the half-man/half-animal creations depicted on ancient temples in the Near East. See Zecharia Sitchin, *The 12th Planet* (New York: Avon Books, 1976), pp. 336–61; and *The Stairway to Heaven* (New York: St. Martin's Press, 1980), p. 102.

4. Gen. 6:5, 7.

5. Edgar Evans Cayce, *Edgar Cayce on Atlantis*, ed. Hugh Lynn Cayce (New York: Warner Books, 1968), pp. 71–72.

6. Ibid., pp. 60, 69.

7. Brad Steiger, *Atlantis Rising* (New York: Dell Publishing Co., 1973), p. 63.

8. **Sons of Belial:** the seed of the fallen angel Belial who sought to supplant the seed of Christ at every hand. In the Old Testament, *belial* is usually interpreted as a common noun meaning worthlessness, ungodliness, or wickedness. In II Cor. 6:15, Belial is used as a proper name for a prince of demons. Some Jewish apocryphal works make Belial synonymous with Satan and he is described in Milton's *Paradise Lost* as one of the fallen angels.

9. **Antahkarana:** Sanskrit for internal sense organ, the seat of thought and feeling, the mind, the thinking faculty, the heart, the conscience, the soul. The web of Life. The net of light spanning Spirit and Matter connecting and sensitizing the whole of creation within itself and to the heart of God.

10. Dan. 12:1; Rev. 12:7–9.

11. Gen. 6:4. **Nuclear annihilation of Sodom and Gomorrah:** see p. 309 n. 65.

12. "The Thing," words and music by Charles R. Grean, 1950.

13. **Golem:** See *The Lost Teachings of Jesus*, Book Two, pp. 296–98 n. 25.

14. Acts 7:48; 17:24.

15. Rev. 11:19.

16. Job 3:25.

17. Deut. 17:14, 15; I Sam. 8.
18. Rev. 6:15–17.
19. Gen. 6:7.
20. Rev. 2:9; 3:9. Christ spake of them which say they are Jews and are not, but are of the synagogue of Satan. We use the term not in the context of the place of worship of the Jews, but of the assembly or gathering of the seed of Satan in their mockery of the Light and their murderous intent toward God's chosen.
21. John 13:11.
22. The desire for the **union of man and machine** was dramatized in the 1979 movie *Star Trek—The Motion Picture,* based on the popular science fiction television series *Star Trek* (1966–69). The film depicts the starship *Enterprise*'s confrontation with a powerful computer spaceship called V'Ger—a damaged NASA space probe (Voyager 6) that was restored and improved by highly advanced machines inhabiting a far-off planet. V'Ger is on its way to earth to find its creator, intent on learning what lies beyond the limits of its vast, mechanically gathered knowledge. When the *Enterprise* crew realizes that V'Ger intends to destroy earth unless it is allowed to evolve through union with its creator (man), Captain Decker of the *Enterprise* declares his desire to unite with V'Ger by merging with Ilia—the *Enterprise*'s female navigator who has been taken over and programmed by this "living machine." In the final sequence, Decker is united to the mechanical, computer consciousness of V'Ger in a dazzling special-effects display of light and animation that portrays Decker being electronically transfigured. As he becomes one with Ilia/V'Ger, the electronic forcefield surrounding the alien spaceship expands and accelerates and they disappear into what we are led to believe is another dimension. As one reviewer noted, the film dreams of "an evolutionary leap in the synthesis of human and machine, of love and logic" (*Newsweek,* 17 December 1979, p. 111).
23. **Supermice:** In November 1983, a team of scientists headed by Professor Richard D. Palmiter of the University

of Washington in Seattle reported successful injection of the human growth hormone gene into fertilized mouse eggs, producing mice which grew larger than normal and which manufactured the human hormone in several of their organs. See "Metallothionein-Human GH Fusion Genes Stimulate Growth of Mice," *Science*, 18 November 1983, pp. 809–14.

24. **People of the shem:** In the original Hebrew text of Gen. 6:4, the word *shem* is translated as "name," thus rendering the last phrase in the verse "the people [or men] who have a name" or "the people of renown." However, the etymology of the word *shem*, according to Zecharia Sitchin, can be traced back to the root *shamah* 'that which is highward', thus suggesting that *shem* should be translated as "sky vehicle" and the people of the shem as "the people of the rocket ships"—i.e., the Nephilim. See Zecharia Sitchin, *The 12th Planet* (New York: Avon Books, 1976), pp. 148, 171–72.

25. See Zecharia Sitchin, *The 12th Planet* (New York: Avon Books, 1976), pp. 397–400, and *The Stairway to Heaven* (New York: St. Martin's Press, 1980), pp. 106–7, 140.

26. Luke 12:32.

27. "Lethal Legacy," *Time*, 25 January 1971, pp. 56, 59.

28. Arthur J. Snider, "The Genetic Control of Man," *Science Digest*, April 1971, p. 56.

29. Luke 19:13.

30. Edward Bulwer Lord Lytton, *The Coming Race* (Santa Barbara: Woodbridge Press Publishing Co., 1979).

31. Matt. 13:24–30, 36–43.

32. Matt. 12:34; 23:33.

33. Matt. 16:3; 22:18; 23:13–15, 23, 25, 27, 29; Mark 7:6; Luke 11:44; 12:56.

34. John 8:44.

35. Eph. 6:12.

36. Luke 3:7, 9, 16, 17.

37. **"Watch With Me" Jesus' Vigil of the Hours** is a one-hour worldwide service of prayers, affirmations, and hymns released by Elizabeth Clare Prophet, which the Master

called Keepers of the Flame in 1964 to keep individually or in groups for the protection of the Christ consciousness in every son and daughter of God and in commemoration of the vigil Jesus kept alone in the Garden of Gethsemane when he said: "Could ye not watch with me one hour?" (Matt. 26:40) Jesus' desire is that every hour of the twenty-four be kept by at least one devotee somewhere on earth. A chart at The Summit Lighthouse headquarters noted who volunteered to keep this vigil of the hours, thereby assuring that all hours were filled, some by the many, some by a few in this unceasing watch for world peace. Available in 44-page booklet, $2.70 postpaid; on audiocassette B87096, $6.95 postpaid.

38. Matt. 7:15.
39. James 3:17.
40. Rev. 12:10.
41. John 8:32.
42. Matt. 7:29; Mark 1:22.
43. II Cor. 6:2.
44. John 14:18.
45. The Great Divine Director, "The Mechanization Concept," in *Pearls of Wisdom*, vol. 8, nos. 15, 16 (Livingston, Mont.: Summit University Press, 1965), pp. 79–81, 84–89.
46. Taken from a dictation by Jesus Christ, August 6, 1978, Camelot, California, "They Shall Not Pass!" Posture for giving this decree: Stand. Raise your right hand, using the *abhaya mudrā* (gesture of fearlessness, palm forward), and place your left hand to your heart—thumb and first two fingers touching chakra pointing inward. Give this call at least once in every 24-hour cycle.
47. Matt. 10:28.
48. Gen. 4:9–15.
49. Rev. 11:18.
50. Rev. 10:7.
51. II Chron. 20:7; Isa. 41:8; James 2:23.
52. See *Saint Germain On Alchemy: For the Adept in the Aquarian Age* (Livingston, Mont.: Summit University Press, 1985).

53. Rom. 7:15–25.
54. Rev. 3:8.
55. Mal. 4:2.
56. Exod. 28:36–38.
57. Zech. 14.
58. I Pet. 3:4.
59. Rom. 8.
60. *Nephilim*, in the passive voice, refers to "those who were made to fall" or "those who were cast down"—i.e., the fallen angels who were cast out into the earth because of their prideful rebellion (depicted in Rev. 12:7–9)—whereas *Nophelim*, in the active voice, refers to those who fell of their own accord through inordinate lust for the daughters of men (Gen. 6:4)—i.e., the Watchers described in the Book of Enoch. See *The Lost Teachings of Jesus*, Book Two, p. 303 n. 44; Elizabeth Clare Prophet, *Forbidden Mysteries of Enoch: The Untold Story of Men and Angels* (Livingston, Mont.: Summit University Press, 1983), pp. 63–67.
61. I Cor. 10:13.
62. Exod. 13:21, 22; 14:24; Num. 14:14; Neh. 9:12, 19.
63. Isa. 66:1.
64. Gen. 18:1, 2, 16–33; 19:1–28.
65. **Sodom and Gomorrah destroyed by atomic energy:** Confirming this statement made by Mark L. Prophet in 1971, Zecharia Sitchin writes in his book *The War of Gods and Men* that when Abraham "looked toward Sodom and Gomorrah, and toward all the land of the plain, and beheld, and, lo, the smoke of the country went up as the smoke of a furnace" (Gen. 19:28), he was witnessing "a 'Hiroshima' and a 'Nagasaki'—the destruction of a fertile and populated plain by atomic weapons." He bases his conclusions on accounts of the cataclysm in biblical, Babylonian, and Assyrian texts and also notes recent scientific research: "Leading archaeologists, such as W. F. Albright and P. Harland, discovered that settlements in the mountains around the region were abruptly abandoned in the twenty-first century B.C. and were not reoccupied for several centuries thereafter. And to this very day, the

water of springs surrounding the Dead Sea has been found to be contaminated with radioactivity, 'enough to induce sterility and allied afflictions in any animals and humans that absorbed it over a number of years' (I. M. Blake, "Joshua's Curse and Elisha's Miracle" in *The Palestine Exploration Quarterly*)." Zecharia Sitchin, *The War of Gods and Men* (New York: Avon Books, 1985), p. 315.

66. Gen. 15:5; 22:17; Heb. 11:12.
67. Matt. 26:26; Luke 22:19; I Cor. 11:24.
68. John 1: 3, 4.
69. Adrian Hope, "The Brain," *Life*, 1 October 1971, pp. 42–59.
70. Rev. 3:14–16.
71. Ps. 8:1, 3–6.
72. Rev. 1:7.
73. Matt. 24:6; Dan. 12:1.
74. Heb. 10:26, 27.
75. I Tim. 5:24.
76. Deut. 4:24; Heb. 12:29.
77. I Tim. 5:25.
78. The motion picture *The Song of Bernadette*, starring Jennifer Jones, was produced by William Perlberg in 1943 based on Franz Werfel's novel by the same title published in 1942.
79. Matt. 19:28. See Thomas à Kempis, *The Imitation of Christ*.
80. I Cor. 15:54, 55; Rev. 1:18.
81. Rev. 15:2; 17:8, 11.
82. Exod. 13:9.
83. Exod. 13:17–22; 14.
84. Jer. 31:33.
85. Job 1:21.
86. Phil. 2:6.
87. Num. 21:9.
88. Rev. 11:18.
89. Rom. 12:19.
90. John 8:32.
91. II Cor. 3:18.
92. Matt. 13:55; Luke 4:22.
93. Gen. 15:1.
94. Acts 10:34.

95. Matt. 5:15, 16.
96. Matt. 6:34.
97. John 13:10.
98. Gen. 22:1–14.
99. Rom. 3:25; I John 2:2; 4:10.
100. Rom. 12:1.
101. Matt. 11:29, 30.
102. Luke 2:49.
103. Matt. 10:7, 8.
104. Isa. 53:3.
105. Matt. 28:18.
106. Exod. 3:2, 14.
107. Heb. 6:6.
108. I Cor. 15:22.
109. II Cor. 5:17.
110. Ezek. 18:4, 20.
111. Ezek. 18:20.
112. Rev. 22:18, 19.
113. Rev. 22:11.
114. Eccles. 11:3 (see Jerusalem Bible translation).
115. *Manvantara:* one of the 14 intervals in Hinduism that constitute a *kalpa*, a period of time covering a cosmic cycle from the origination to the destruction of a world system. *Pralaya:* a period of dissolution and destruction of a manifested universe at the end of each kalpa and preceding the new creation.
116. Isa. 34:8; 61:2; 63:4.
117. Dan. 12:2, 3.
118. Rev. 22:12, 13.
119. James 1:21.
120. **Saturated solution:** a solution in which the dissolved substance, called the solute, is in its most concentrated state; i.e., the solvent has dissolved all of the solute it can under a given condition. **Supersaturated solution:** a solution in which a greater quantity of substance is dissolved than the solvent would normally hold; this can be achieved by mechanical means—usually heating a saturated solution, adding more of the solute, then cooling the solution.
121. Matt. 7:21–23.

122. Jer. 23:1.
123. Matt. 25:31–46.
124. John 6:53–58.
125. I John 3:2.
126. Gal. 6:5.
127. Phil. 2:12.
128. Luke 22:44.
129. II Thess. 2:3.
130. Matt. 12:36, 37.
131. Heb. 6:4–8.
132. Heb. 6:9–12.
133. Rev. 20:13, 14.
134. Isa. 29:13; Matt. 15:7–9; Mark 7:6, 7.
135. II Pet. 3:16.
136. Matt. 23:33–36.
137. Luke 17:23; 21:8.
138. John 11:20.
139. Luke 7:36–50.
140. Mark 10:25–27.
141. Ezek. 20:47.
142. Mark 10:29–31.
143. Jer. 31:34.
144. Rev. 19:1, 2.

Chapter Thirteen THE VIOLET FLAME
FOR GOD-REALIZATION

1. Matt. 3:11, 12 (see Jerusalem Bible translation).
2. Matt. 6:27.
3. Matt. 6:33.
4. Mal. 3:1–3.
5. Levites, the Levitical priesthood, and its corruption:
   See Gen. 46:11; Exod. 6:16–27; 32:26–29; Num. 1:47–
   53; 3; 4; 8:5–26; 18; 35:1–8; Deut. 10:8, 9; 12:18, 19;
   14:27, 29; 18:1–8; Josh. 14:3, 4; 21:1–42; I Kings 12:31;
   13:33; I Chron. 6; 15:1–27; 23–26; II Chron. 5:4, 5, 7,
   11–14; 11:13–15; 13:9–12; 17:8, 9; 19:8–11; 23:4–8; 29:4,
   5, 11–36; 30:15–17, 25–27; 31:2–19; 35:8–15, 18; Ezra
   3:8–13; 6:16–18, 20; Neh. 8:7–9, 11; 11:15–19; 12:22–30;

13:5, 10, 13, 29, 30; Jer. 33:22; Ezek. 44:10–31; 48:11–14; Mal. 1:6–14; 2:1–10; 3:3; and the Book of Leviticus (meaning "relating to the Levites"), which is principally a manual for Levitical priests.

6. Rev. 11:1.
7. I Cor. 3:13–15; I Pet. 4:12.
8. Luke 17:21.
9. Gen. 15:17.
10. Ps. 102:16; Isa. 60:2; Matt. 24:30.
11. Exod. 7:8–12.
12. Rev. 3:8.
13. John 10:1.
14. John 10:7, 9.
15. John 14:6.
16. Rom. 8:17.
17. Rom. 8:26, 27, 34.
18. Rom. 8:28–31.
19. **Emmanuel, or Immanuel:** Hebrew word meaning "God with us" or "God is with us." Used in Isa. 7:14; 8:8; Matt. 1:23; associated with the Messiah and Jesus Christ. The word carries the vibration of the Christ Presence with each child of God and may be a title, like Son of man, of one so anointed with the Light of the Holy Christ Self.
20. Matt. 18:19, 20.
21. Prov. 4:7.
22. Isa. 45:5–7, 11.
23. Prov. 26:11; II Pet. 2:22.
24. I Pet. 5:8.
25. Luke 22:53.
26. John 14:30.
27. Jude 4, 16–19.
28. Rev. 13:6, Jerusalem Bible.
29. Matt. 23:13, 15.
30. Jude 20–23.
31. Rev. 12:11.
32. See Jude 23, Jerusalem Bible.
33. Elizabeth Clare Prophet, *Archangel Michael's Rosary for Armageddon*, a rosary with invocations, hymns, and dynamic decrees, available in booklet and single cassette;

"The LORD's Ritual of Exorcism," in *Invocations to the Hierarchy of the Ruby Ray through the Messenger Elizabeth Clare Prophet*, looseleaf.

34. Rev. 12:12.

35. Mark 10:15; Luke 18:17.

36. James 4:8.

37. For further teaching from the Ascended Masters and Messengers on the science of the spoken Word, see Mark L. Prophet and Elizabeth Clare Prophet, *The Science of the Spoken Word*; Jesus and Kuthumi, *Prayer and Meditation*; Mark and Elizabeth Prophet, *The Science of the Spoken Word: Why and How to Decree Effectively*, 4-cassette album; Elizabeth Clare Prophet, *"I'm Stumping for the Coming Revolution in Higher Consciousness!"* 3-cassette album; *Prayers, Meditations, and Dynamic Decrees for the Coming Revolution in Higher Consciousness*, Sections I, II, and III, looseleaf.

38. II Pet. 3:10, 12.

39. Zech. 3:9, 10.

40. YAHWEH SABAOTH: from *Yahweh* (Heb. LORD) and *Sabaoth* (Gk. form of Heb. *tsebâôth* 'armies', 'hosts'), translated as "LORD of hosts" throughout the Old Testament; its equivalent in the New Testament is "the Lord of Sabaoth" (Rom. 9:29; James 5:4). The term Yahweh Sabaoth expresses God's great power and may have been used to refer to his role as commander of both the armies of Israel and of heaven.

41. Gen. 16:7–12; 21:14–19.

42. Christopher Isherwood, *Ramakrishna and His Disciples* (Hollywood, Calif.: Vedanta Press, 1965), p. 69.

43. Isa. 30:20, 21.

44. II Pet. 2:18.

45. Isa. 30:19.

46. Ps. 91:14–16.

47. Jer. 31:34.

48. Mic. 4:4.

49. See St. John of the Cross, *The Ascent of Mount Carmel* and *The Dark Night*, in *The Collected Works of St. John of*

the Cross, trans. Kieran Kavanaugh and Otilio Rodriguez (Washington, D.C.: ICS Publications, 1973), pp. 66–389; *Saint John of the Cross on the Living Flame of Love*, 8-cassette album, Summit University Lecture Series for Ministering Servants taught by Mark L. Prophet and Elizabeth Clare Prophet.

50. Matt. 27:46; Mark 15:34.
51. Exod. 3:2.
52. I Cor. 3:13–15.
53. Ps. 16:10.
54. Prov. 29:18.
55. Matt. 24:27.
56. **Balancing 51 percent of karma as a requirement for the ascension:** Under the dispensation of the Aquarian age granted by the Lords of Karma in this century, when an individual balances 51 percent of his karma he is given the option of taking his ascension and balancing the remaining 49 percent from etheric octaves or of remaining in embodiment to balance a greater percentage and be an example to others on the Path. (Prior to this dispensation, balancing 100 percent of one's karma was the requirement for the ascension.) The Ascended Lady Master Portia has explained that the reason the Lords of Karma gave the dispensation for the ascension of souls after the balance of 51 percent is that the next 24 percent involves the descent into the astral plane. This is an even greater challenge than the balancing of the first 51 percent. You see, when they came to that level of transmutation many among mankind who were pursuing the Path fell back and lost even the 51 percent that they had gained, so treacherous is the walk in the labyrinth of the astral plane. Because an individual's karma ties him to the system of worlds where he made that karma, an Ascended Master who has taken his ascension before balancing 100 percent of his karma is still obligated to work with and through the evolutions of earth from inner levels to balance the remaining percentages of his karma.
57. Luke 21:26.

58. **Tortures of Hawaiian chiefs:** In ancient Hawaii, hundreds of taboos were enforced by kings, chiefs, or priests to control the people, who lived in fear of their rulers. Originally a taboo *(kapu* in Hawaiian) was applied to persons or objects to distinguish them as sacred—i.e., something restricted or forbidden. As the power of the rulers increased, the religious significance of the taboo was corrupted and taboos were assigned according to the whim of the leader to common situations. For example, a man could be punished for letting his shadow fall on the house of a chief, on the chief's back, or on any of his belongings, or for passing through the chief's private doorway. The people were required to prostrate themselves when the chief appeared in public or when his clothing, food, or bath water were carried by. Those who violated taboos such as these were condemned to die by being burned, strangled, stoned, clubbed, or in some cases subject to tortures that lasted for days before the final blow was given.
59. Matt. 26:29.
60. Henry Wadsworth Longfellow, "A Psalm of Life," stanzas 7–9.
61. Dan. 12:5; Rev. 11:3.
62. Dan. 12:7.
63. Matt. 24:14.
64. Saint Germain was embodied as Christopher Columbus (1451–1506), who discovered America October 12, 1492.
65. Matt. 21:18–20; Mark 11:12–14, 20, 21.
66. "And if thy right hand offend thee, cut it off and cast it from thee: for it is profitable for thee that one of thy members should perish, and not that thy whole body should be cast into hell" Matt. 5:30. See also Matt. 18:8; Mark 9:43.
67. **Exterrestrial:** variant of *extraterrestrial.*
68. Rev. 6:6.
69. See Kuthumi, "The Light of Winter Solstice," in *Pearls of Wisdom*, vol. 27 (1984), no. 58, pp. 518–19, 520, 523.
70. Matt. 13:24–30, 36–43.

71. Dan. 9:27; 11:31; 12:11; Matt. 24:15; Mark 13:14.
72. Rev. 6:1–8.
73. **William Tell** (c. 13th–14th centuries): legendary Swiss patriot and hero from the canton of Uri who defied tyrannical Austrian rule. Historically, the official founding of the Swiss Confederation occurred in 1291, when representatives of Uri, Schwyz and Unterwalden (later known as the forest cantons) banded together to form the Everlasting League—a defense alliance to protect against the encroachments of the powerful Hapsburgs. The story of their valiant struggle for independence is linked in Swiss tradition with the much-loved figure of William Tell. According to popular accounts, in 1307 the Austrian bailiff Gessler placed his hat on a stake in the main square of Altdorf and ordered that all who passed by bow before it in deference to Austrian sovereignty. When Tell, a peasant noted for his marksmanship, refused, Gessler forced Tell to shoot an arrow through an apple on his son's head. Tell successfully performed the feat but declared that, had he missed, he would have sent a second arrow through Gessler's heart. Tell was then arrested but later escaped and slew Gessler, setting off the uprising which led to Swiss independence.
74. **David** (c. 1043-c. 973 B.C.), one of the most beloved and revered figures in Hebrew history, was born the youngest son of Jesse of Bethlehem. I Samuel 17 records how, as a young shepherd boy, he single-handedly slew the Philistine giant Goliath. Anointed by the prophet Samuel as the successor of Saul, David rose to become king of all of Israel, reuniting the twelve tribes as one nation and greatly extending its borders. He established Jerusalem as the capital and there enshrined the Ark of the Covenant. David is honored as the "ideal king"—symbol of the bond between God and nation. Author of the psalms which anticipate his Sonship, his soul reembodied as the Lord Jesus Christ.
75. John 14:16, 26; 15:26; 16:7.
76. "There is a tide in the affairs of men which, taken at the

flood, leads on to fortune; omitted, all the voyage of their life is bound in shallows and in miseries." Brutus in Shakespeare, *Julius Caesar*, act 4, sc. 3, lines 215–18.

77. See Edward R. Dewey with Og Mandino, *Cycles: The Mysterious Forces That Trigger Events* (New York: Hawthorn Books, 1971); Nikolai Kondratieff, *The Long Wave Cycle*, trans. Guy Daniels (New York: Richardson & Snyder, 1984); R. E. McMaster, Jr., *Cycles of War: The Next Six Years* (n.p., 1978; distributed by War Cycles Institute).

78. **Betrayers of the true patriots of Poland:** The 1984 murder of Father Jerzy Popieluszko—the popular 37-year-old parish priest at St. Stanislaw Kostka Church in northern Warsaw and ardent supporter of the outlawed Solidarity trade union—not only touched off a political crisis in Poland but also sparked new criticism of the nation's Roman Catholic hierarchy for allegedly backing down to government pressure in incidents involving the young priest. Shortly after General Wojcieck Jaruzelski imposed martial law in December 1981, "Father Jerzy" began to conduct "Masses for the Homeland" on the last Sunday of every month to nurture Solidarity's dream of a free Poland. Cassettes and reprints of his sermons spread across the country, and people from all over Poland came to hear this simple priest who was unafraid to speak out against government repression. As a consequence, Father Jerzy was followed by secret police and was subject to constant harassment and anonymous death threats as well as increasing rebukes from Polish primate Josef Cardinal Glemp, who had publicly ordered Polish priests to stay out of politics.

On October 19, 1984, Popieluszko was abducted by Polish secret-police agents outside Torun, Poland, on his way home from conducting a rosary service, and was brutally beaten, strangled, and tossed into Wloclawek reservoir on the Vistula River, where his battered body was discovered 11 days later. In the face of the new surge of unrest following Popieluszko's death, a public trial—unprecedented in the Soviet bloc—was opened on December 27,

1984, to try four secret-police officers for the kidnap-murder. On February 7, 1985, the officers were convicted and sentenced to prison terms ranging from 14 to 25 years, though many Poles believed that the priest's death was plotted at higher levels of the government.

During the trial, a connection between the Catholic church hierarchy and the Polish government was revealed when Gen. Zenon Platek, a top official in the Interior Ministry, testified that government officials had persuaded church authorities to restrain its more radical priests. In addition, a Warsaw priest in whom Popieluszko had confided was quoted in news reports as saying that Glemp had asked Father Jerzy to prepare a written request to be transferred to Rome for study. A Polish Church spokesman denied the allegation, stating that the government had been pressuring the Church to transfer Popieluszko but the primate had no intention of giving in to the pressure. Earlier in 1984 Glemp had come under fire from fellow Catholics for transferring another pro-Solidarity priest from Warsaw to a rural parish, and hard-line church leaders have criticized the cardinal for attempting to act as a mediator between Solidarity and the state instead of taking a stronger stand against Poland's Marxist regime. See John Fox, "Murder of a Polish Priest," *Reader's Digest*, December 1985.

79. **Mother Mary's Circle of Light** is a ritual in which devotees join hands to form a ring of light and offer prayers, hymns, mantras, and meditations for the healing of specific problems plaguing America and the nations of the world.
80. Matt. 18:20.
81. Matt. 10:22; 24:13; Mark 13:13.
82. Matt. 13:3–9, 18–30, 36–43; Mark 4:3–20; Luke 8:5–15.
83. Isa. 61:3.

Chapter Fourteen YOU WILL BECOME ONE WITH GOD!

1. John 14:2, 3, 12, 28; 16:10; 20:17.
2. Eph. 2:20; I Pet. 2:6.
3. See Mark L. Prophet and Elizabeth Clare Prophet, "Your

Synthetic Image," in *Climb the Highest Mountain: The Path of the Higher Self, The Everlasting Gospel*, Book I (Livingston, Mont.: Summit University Press, 1972), Chapter 1.

4. **Caspar Milquetoast:** the extremely shy, meek-mannered cartoon character of H. T. Webster's daily cartoon panel *The Timid Soul* that first appeared in 1924 in the *New York World* and other newspapers subscribing to Webster's series. Milquetoast, with his oversized hat, long, drooping white mustache and slumped shoulders, typified the more cowardly, timorous traits of human nature and quickly became a favorite of comic strip readers. In Webster's own words, Milquetoast was the kind of man who "speaks softly and gets hit with a big stick." One of the most popular cartoons showed Milquetoast standing on a busy downtown street corner in the pouring rain without an umbrella, saying, "Well, I'll wait one more hour for him, and if he doesn't come then he can go and borrow that $100 from someone else." Another panel pictures him making a hole in one while playing golf alone but recording a score of three because "they'd even think I was lying if I put down a two." *The Timid Soul* was run daily in many American newspapers until several years after Webster's death in 1952.

5. Acts 22:3.
6. Gal. 4:19.
7. John 8:58.
8. John 4:18, 19.
9. Luke 4:8.
10. Luke 12:16–21.
11. Luke 12:23.
12. Matt. 10:30; Luke 12:7.
13. John 4:24.
14. Acts 17:26.
15. Ps. 90:4; II Pet. 3:8.
16. Rev. 22:11.
17. II Cor. 5:16.
18. II Cor. 5:17.
19. Heb. 13:8.
20. I Cor. 13:9, 10.

21. John 12:44, 45.
22. Gal. 6:5.
23. John 14:9, 10.
24. John 12:44–46.
25. John 5:36; 6:38, 39; 7:16–18, 28, 29; 17:21–23.
26. John 9:5.
27. Matt. 5:14–16.
28. John 12:32.
29. John 19:30.
30. Mark 10:39.
31. Matt. 19:28; Luke 22:30.
32. John 1:3; Rev. 13:8.
33. For a discussion on the decisions and import of **the Council of Nicaea** (A.D. 325), see *The Lost Teachings of Jesus*, Book Two, pp. 255–63. **The Council of Trent**, the nineteenth ecumenical council held during three different sessions (1545–47, 1551–52, 1562–63), was one of the most important councils in the history of the Roman Catholic Church. It was convoked to deal with the challenges of the Reformation at a time when the Church was suffering from moral corruption and many were leaving its ranks to become Protestant. The Council of Trent clarified the Catholic position on each point of dispute with the Protestants, condemned Protestant principles and doctrines, and ended any real chance of reconciliation between the Protestants and the Church of Rome, which many had hoped this council would effect. The council also attempted to rout out corruption within the Church by a reformation in discipline and administration.

 Among the doctrinal questions it addressed were the nature of original sin, purgatory, clerical marriage, the veneration of saints, and Luther's doctrine of justification by faith alone. Its numerous decisions included the reaffirmation of the Nicene Creed, issued at the Council of Nicaea, as the basis for Catholic faith, the setting of the traditions of the Church on equal authority with scripture, the fixing of Old and New Testament canon and the number of sacraments, reforms and regulations concerning the sale of indulgences, the education of the clergy and the celebration

of mass, and the enlargement of papal authority (all patri-
archs, primates, archbishops, and bishops were required to
vow complete obedience to the pontiff, who was declared to
be the vicar of God and Christ on earth). One of the most
important outcomes of the council was its declaration that
the Church had the sole right to interpret the Bible. In effect,
Catholicism claimed the infallibility of its dogmas at the
Council of Trent and left no room for private interpretation
of scripture. In 1564, Pope Pius IV ratified the decrees and
definitions of the synod in a bull (papal letter) that required
obedience from all Roman Catholics and forbade all un-
authorized interpretation under pain of excommunication.

34. **Origen anathematized:** See *The Lost Teachings of Jesus,*
Book Three, p. 289 n. 55.

35. Matt. 6:23.

36. **Murders near Santa Cruz:** On February 15, 1973, the
decapitated bodies of two University of California Santa
Cruz students, Alice Liu, 20, and Rosalind Thorpe, 22,
were found in the mountains in Alameda County, California, the victims of confessed murderer Edmund Emil
Kemper III, 24. Kemper, 6 feet 9 inches and 280 pounds,
was arrested April 24, 1973, at a Colorado phone booth
when he telephoned the police, confessed that he had killed
his mother and her friend, and said he was afraid he might
kill again. He subsequently confessed to murdering six coed
hitchhikers. In 1964, at age 15, Kemper had been committed
to the Atascadero State Hospital for the Criminally Insane for
killing his grandparents but was released five years later when
psychiatrists declared him cured of paranoid schizophrenia.
The Madera County district attorney disclosed three days
after Kemper's 1973 arrest that on September 18, 1972 (just
three days after he murdered one of the coeds) two court-
appointed psychiatrists had declared Kemper "no threat to
society," and at the request of his attorney his juvenile court
record had been sealed. On November 8, 1973, a Santa
Cruz jury, rejecting a plea of not guilty by reason of insanity,
convicted Kemper on eight counts of first-degree murder.
Kemper, who attempted suicide four times after he had

turned himself in, was ordered to serve eight concurrent life sentences and is being held at the Vacaville medical prison in California.

37. John 1:14.
38. James 2:16.
39. John 21:15–17.
40. Matt. 19:16, 17.
41. **Shanti Devi:** See *The Lost Teachings of Jesus*, Book One, pp. 42–43.
42. I Tim. 1:16.
43. John 12:24.
44. Mark 4:28.
45. Matt. 14:15–21; Mark 6:35–44; Luke 9:12–17; John 6:5–14.
46. Luke 24:32.
47. Titus 2:7.
48. John 10:17, 18.
49. I John 3:2.
50. Heb. 12:23.
51. II Chron. 20:7; Isa. 41:8; James 2:23.
52. Henry Van Dyke, *The Toiling of Felix*, "Envoy," stanza 9.
53. John 5:17.
54. I Thess. 4:17.
55. Acts 16:25–40.
56. Josh. 10:12, 13.

Index of Scripture

*References to the Book of Enoch are from the translation by Richard Laurence. This translation along with all the Enoch texts can be found in *Forbidden Mysteries of Enoch: The Untold Story of Men and Angels* by Elizabeth Clare Prophet (Livingston, Mont.: Summit University Press, 1983).

Index

THE LOST TEACHINGS OF JESUS
BOOK ONE *Contents*

THE LOST TEACHINGS OF JESUS
BOOK TWO *Contents*

THE LOST TEACHINGS OF JESUS
BOOK THREE *Contents*

Life Is the Ultimate Challenge

"Because it's there."

That said it all. Nature's challenge and one man's response. Feet upon the summit. Then the exhilaration. A world knew precisely how Sir Edmund Hillary felt when he made it to the top and what George Mallory meant when he told why he climbed Everest.

Yet there is a peak still higher. More arduous. More exalting to climb. It is the mountain of Being. Consciousness. Personal to each one. Satisfying as no other challenge in life can be. Compelling—because it's there.

Climb the Highest Mountain is the cornerstone of a century of metaphysical literature, *the* book about the Path of the Higher Self. In one volume the revelation of the lost code of Identity, Nature, Life itself. Page after page contains practical and scientific explanations on how to make contact and maintain a relationship with the Higher Self—and with those who have climbed the highest mountain before you.

The one essential guidebook, more precious than a Sherpa, no climber can be without. With a depth and heighth hitherto uncharted, Mark and Elizabeth Prophet systematically set forth the ancient wisdom of the Ascended Masters.

Ascending in the footsteps of Christ, the Ascended Masters are the true guides of those soaring spirits who *must* find new tools to course the untrammeled reaches of Higher Consciousness—who *must* discover, explore, conquer.

Why? Because it's there.

And so, the climb begins at the foot of the mount of attainment—inner space, level one. It does not end (and there is no turning back) until Infinity is summoned—and subdued. On the way the Adepts clarify the issues of Spirit and Matter, Good and Evil, and answer fundamental questions climbers are wont to ask on the way up—questions concerning the psychology and the destiny of the soul.

Yes, Why? Why climb, why ask? Because they're a breed who know there is a summit not seen, a riddle to be undone.

And simply *because it's there:*

Life—the Ultimate Challenge.

Climb the Highest Mountain: The book that is taking 20th-century climbers to the heights they've dreamed of. It's for those who want to see for themselves the Light upon the summit, and the Lord face-to-face.

8 full-color Nicholas Roerich art reproductions, 28 illustrations by Auriel Bessemer, charts, tables, comprehensive index. Softbound, 700 pp., #642, $16.95; hardbound, #100, $21.95.

SUMMIT UNIVERSITY ☙ PRESS®

Available wherever fine books are sold or directly from the publisher, Summit University Press, Dept. 764, Box A, Livingston, MT 59047-1390. Phone: (406) 222-8300. Please add $1.50 postage and handling for the first book, $.75 each additional book.

A Pearl of Wisdom *for You–* Every Week!

"The Pearls of Wisdom are the practical manifestation of the Great White Brotherhood's marvelous blueprint for man's deliverance in this day and age. They show the way out of the human dilemma."

—*Mark L. Prophet*

Since 1958 the Ascended Masters have released their teachings through the Messengers Mark and Elizabeth Prophet as Pearls of Wisdom. These weekly letters dictated for students of the sacred mysteries are delivered as a Holy Spirit prophecy from the immortal saints and spiritual revolutionaries East and West who comprise the hierarchy known as the Great White Brotherhood.

The Pearls of Wisdom contain both beginning and advanced instruction with a practical application of Cosmic Law to personal and planetary problems. Learn more about healing through the violet flame, the Lost Teachings of Jesus, Saint Germain's prophecy for the Aquarian age, twin flames and soul mates, karma and reincarnation, the science of the spoken Word and the path of initiation. And make contact, heart to heart, with the Teacher...

"He who has contact with us and retains it, he who learns the infinite lessons which we are able to teach, he who does not waver in his purpose to find his freedom from the psychic domination of others—from the nets of tradition, from the pit of ambition, and from the miasma of earthly existence—will come to our abode and find solace beyond his dreams. But our words must become nourishment for the soul; they must not be read carelessly or casually; they must be treasured as a bond with the Infinite and recognized for their intrinsic value....

"The Masters of the Great White Brotherhood and of the Darjeeling Council welcome you to the opportunity of reading Pearls of Wisdom week after week, and of silently weaving an attunement with the higher powers of the universe which will not fail to produce fruit in due season if you run and are not weary, if you faint not and use the torch that we send to

find your way out of the labyrinth of life into the sunlight of God's love—into the valley of Shangri-la, into the world where mastery becomes your own and service your free choice.

"In the interest of humanity, showered with all of the abundance cosmos extends as the fruit of purpose, we offer you our friendship. The choice is yours. No imposition will be made upon you, only the bond of our love, of our service, of our brotherhood which you may choose to make your own."
                                                              —El Morya

The Pearls of Wisdom are a lifeline from higher realms that will buoy you up amid the confusing tides of modern living. Subscribe today and receive weekly instruction and spiritual guidance on meeting your day-to-day challenges. You can also order bound volumes of Pearls of Wisdom published since 1958. They are a treasure-house of self-knowledge unprecedented in history.

Weekly Pearls of Wisdom $40 (1 year), $20 (6 months), $10 (3 months). Introductory 12-week series $5. Bound volumes available through our catalog. The most recent releases are the 1985 and 1986 two-volume sets: *The Ascended Masters on Soul Mates and Twin Flames* How to: Find your twin flame and discover your mission in life • Take advantage of the special opportunity and initiation the Ascended Masters are giving twin flames today • Gain freedom from karma and the rounds of rebirth. Includes 116 pages of full color. Books I and II, $19.95 ea. *The Handwriting on the Wall* Find out about America's mission, her returning karma, and exactly what her people can and must do to turn back that karma and fulfill their destiny. Books I and II, $19.95 ea. Make checks payable to and mail to The Summit Lighthouse, Dept. 764, Box A, Livingston, MT 59047-1390. Phone: (406) 222-8300. Please add $1.50 postage and handling for the first book, $.75 each additional book.

FOR MORE INFORMATION

For information about the Keepers of the Flame fraternity and monthly lessons; dictations of the Ascended Masters published weekly as Pearls of Wisdom; Summit University three-month and weekend retreats; two-week summer seminars and quarterly conferences which convene at the Royal Teton Ranch, a 33,000-acre self-sufficient spiritual community-in-the-making, as well as the Summit University Service/Study Program with apprenticeship in all phases of organic farming, ranching, macrobiotic cooking, construction, publishing and related community services; Montessori International private school for children of Keepers of the Flame, preschool through grade six; and the Ascended Masters' library and study center nearest you, call or write Summit University Press, Box A, Livingston, Montana 59047-1390. Telephone: (406) 222-8300.

Paperback books, audio- and videocassettes on the Lost Teachings of Jesus and those of the Ascended Masters dictated to their Messengers, Mark L. Prophet and Elizabeth Clare Prophet—including a video series of Ascended Master dictations on "Prophecy in the New Age," a Summit University Forum TV series with Mrs. Prophet interviewing outstanding experts in the field of health and Nature's alternatives to healing, and another on the defense of freedom—are available through Summit University Press. Write for free catalogue and information packet.

Upon your request we are also happy to send you particulars on this summer's international conference at the Royal Teton Ranch—survival seminars, wilderness treks, teachings of Saint Germain, dictations from the Ascended Masters, prophecy on political and social issues, initiation through the Messenger of the Great White Brotherhood, meditation, yoga, the science of the spoken Word, children's program, summer camping and RV accommodations, and homesteading at Glastonbury.

All at the ranch send you our hearts' love and a joyful welcome to the Inner Retreat!